D1267766

Innocent Bystander
The Scene from the 70's

Books by L. E. Sissman

DYING: AN INTRODUCTION (*verse*), 1968

SCATTERED RETURNS (*verse*), 1969

PURSUIT OF HONOR (*verse*), 1971

INNOCENT BYSTANDER: THE SCENE FROM THE 70'S (*essays*), 1975

Innocent Bystander

The Scene from the 70's

L. E. SISSMAN

with an introduction by
JOHN UPDIKE

THE VANGUARD PRESS, INC.   NEW YORK

LIBRARY OF CONGRESS CATALOGUE CARD NUMBER: 75–18426
ISBN: 0–8149–0769–5

DESIGNER: ELIZABETH WOLL

MANUFACTURED IN THE UNITED STATES OF AMERICA.

THANKS

to Louise des Saulniers, Garth Hite, Anne Bernays, Justin Kaplan, Will Davenport, and my wife for ideas and encouragement.

I would also like to thank the editors of the *Atlantic* magazine, in which all but one of the essays appeared; and Little, Brown and Co. for permission to use the following:

"In Bardbury." From *Pursuit of Honor* by L. E. Sissman. Copyright © 1971 by L. E. Sissman, by permission of Little, Brown and Co. in association with The Atlantic Monthly Press.

"Gare Du Midi." From *Scattered Returns* by L. E. Sissman. Copyright © 1968 by L. E. Sissman, by permission of Little, Brown and Co., in association with The Atlantic Monthly Press. This poem originally appeared in *The New Yorker*.

"The Tree Warden." From *Dying: An Introduction* by L. E. Sissman. Copyright © 1965 by L. E. Sissman, by permission of Little, Brown and Co. in association with The Atlantic Monthly Press.

"Dying: An Introduction." From *Dying: An Introduction* by L. E. Sissman. Copyright © 1967 by L. E. Sissman, by permission of Little, Brown and Co. in association with The Atlantic Monthly Press. This poem originally appeared in *The New Yorker*.

"Going Home, 1945." From *Dying: An Introduction* by L. E. Sissman. Copyright © 1967 by L. E. Sissman, by permission of Little, Brown and Co., in association with The Atlantic Monthly Press. This poem originally appeared in *The New Yorker*.

"Songs and Musical Pieces," sections XI, XIII, and XXI from *The Collected Poetry of W.H. Auden*. Copyright © 1945 by W.H. Auden. By permission of Random House, Inc.

For ROBERT MANNING,
editor, friend.

Contents

v. ASSIGNATIONS

Introduction

Ed Sissman was precocious enough to be a momentary Quiz Kid but he took his time becoming a poet and came even later to publish prose. At the age of forty, having for five years been enriching the pages of *The New Yorker* with his witty, elegaic, densely actual, airily effortless, often moving and usually blank verse, he began to write conspicuously even-tempered book appraisals for that magazine, and not long thereafter took to sharing his preternaturally keen observations and memories with readers of *The Atlantic Monthly*. This book is his selection—roughly two-thirds of the total—from a half-decade's worth of his monthly pieces. He calls his column "The Innocent Bystander," and indeed there is something upright, poised, and easily adaptable, like a stance, in his manner of speaking; no settled orotundities from an Easy Chair for him. His columns flit from complaints about restaurant service to homage to Auden and Wilson and Waugh, from detailed prescriptions for a better world or even a bigger Western movie to paeans upon the timeless cycle of seasons, from reminiscence that hurts us with its stab of loss to topical and political reactions that almost corroborate our bystander's alleged innocence. Not all good writers and bright minds are qualified to compose a monthly report on nothing in particular. Particularity, indeed, is one of the qualifications, and this Ed Sissman displays in abundance; first and in essence a poet, he was priorly and by profession an advertising man, and knows the names of products, can squint a fair distance

into the workings of American business, respects the noisy main
street of American life. A boyhood hobbyist, a quick study, a constant reader, he knows books and birds and cars and engines of
war, pops up with startling patches of expertise on architecture
and graphics, has travelled well in—of all countries—the United
States. When he evokes a city, it is Detroit or New York or Boston;
there is no confusing the tint of the pavements. When he recalls
a day from his life, though it comes from as far away as November
1944, it arrives not only with all its solid furniture but with its very
own weather—in this case, "thin, slate-colored clouds sometimes
letting through flat blades of sun." Sissman's painterly powers are,
of course, shown to best advantage in his poetry, where the metri-
cal form becomes a shimmering skin of wordplay, compression,
antic exactitude, sudden sweet directness, swoops and starts of
rhythm. Though possessing the declarative virtues of prose—hos-
pitable, even, to dialogue and narrative suspense—his poetry is
always poetic. His prose, correspondingly, but for its high quotient
of visual coloring and an occasional verbal exotic like "encar-
celled," "wodge," "umbel," "gormless," and "contrail," is surprisingly, and comfortingly, prosaic.

A sensible, decent man: that is the voice. His poetry is both
more tender and more cruel than his prose ever is; his audience,
we feel, has shifted in his mind, from the unshockable empyrean
audience, the single fierce inner attendant, to whom a poet ad-
dresses himself—has shifted to a congeries (another of his pet
words) of fallible, woundable, only slightly educable fellow mor-
tals. From Montaigne on, this is the voice of the essayist, this voice
inviting us onto the shared ground of a middling sensuality, a
middling understanding, a voice that, if it raves, raves never
against us, but against a perfidious other, some stronghold as
closed to our innocence as Mamma Leone's kitchen or Richard
Nixon's White House. To be sure, this particular bystander's
voice is raised rather often, as befits the good citizen of a democ-
racy, in protest; the contemplation of television's failure to seize
its "matchless opportunity for art, instruction, and edification" lifts
Sissman's prose close to melody: ". . . this outpouring of festering
garbage . . . the aforementioned All commercial, with its gaggle
of greasy-oil haters, the continuing series of Wisk 'ring around

the collar' commercials with their hackle-stirring nyah-nyah refrain . . . Detroit-car commercials that are still trying to sell us the
big old gas hogs (whose chassis engineering hasn't essentially been
changed or improved since 1936) on a platform of sex, showing
off, and spurious luxury . . . . it is instructive that our largest and,
presumably, most astute industry proved no more prescient about
the energy mess than the jowly clowns in Washington who guide
our destinies, God help us all." That largeness signifies astuteness,
that commercials are not intended to irritate and madden us, that
engineering will improve more than it needs to—these are the
presumptions of a believer in a perfectible world, which needs
only to be as energetic and decent as the writer himself, as willing
to find "a delicate balance, between the ideal and the real, between
the pragmatic and the impossible." And as brave, he is too modest
to say, as himself at facing the impossibilities that overwhelm us
as we live.

For these alert, sympathetic, manifoldly curious and basically
cheerful essays were written by a man who, for ten years, has been
suffering from a disease believed to be "routinely fatal." He has
arranged this collection so that not until near the end, in the two
remarkable "Night Music" pieces, is this fact about himself divulged. Nor to those of us fortunate enough to know Ed Sissman
in the flesh (he is six foot four, and holds his own in every sense)
is pain or anxiety ever divulged, or permitted to shadow his output
of amiable attentive intelligence. Only in a few of the poems, such
as the recent "October," does he betray a sense that he has been
dealt "bad cards." As he says in these pages, his reaction to the
diagnosis, in 1965, when he was thirty-seven, of Hodgkin's Disease,
was to sharpen his appreciation of life, step up his professional
activity, and quicken his muse, who had just begun to speak in
print. "Instead of a curtain falling, a curtain rose. And stayed up,
revealing a stage decked in defining light . . ." I do not believe,
strange to say, that the new urgency his life borrowed from darkness much changed the quality of his poetry, which from first appearance was nostalgic, lyrical, celebrative, reminiscent—lived
moments recaptured with great verbal gaiety. The quantity, both
of poems and of emotion, may have been heightened by the
challenge, but the tone has held steady; in an age when so many

of the healthy and lucky have been full of self-pity, he has shown none, and faced his talent outward toward a world that, like the month of May, is two-prongedly "merry, scary."

Searching for this last quote, I have just now reread this essay, with its punning cry for help ("M'aidez"), and have been struck, rereading, by how much I had missed or taken in dully—the Hopperesque evocation of early summer light, "turning white house sides to solid glare, falling into the cups of daffodils to recharge and redouble their goldenness;" the auditing of May sounds that even overhears "the tiny, quiet crackle as the old grass dries and curls still further," the miraculously precise paragraph on the emerging colors; all sweeping toward the sombre and gentle aphorism "We were not, either by temperament or experience, meant to live in paradise." Yet it is a function of art to show us the paradise that, disguised as the ordinary, surrounds us as we live; a lesser function is, as Sissman elsewhere suggests, to instruct us in "accommodation," the attuning of an imperfect environment to a perishing self. Both functions are well served in this book, a valuable binding-together of one man's monthly confessions, exhortations, celebrations.

JOHN UPDIKE

i
Aboard the 20th Century

Confessions of
an Ex-Quiz Kid:
A Vote for Children's Lib

Exterior: long shot: the Masonic Temple in Detroit on a damp
and chilling night in the fall of 1943. Decrepit Turret-Top Olds-
mobiles, Torpedo-Body Pontiacs, and pontoon-fendered Terra-
planes stop, squealing, to let shabby crowds of pedestrians cross
Cass Avenue to the almost windowless twelve-story Crusader-
Gothic monolith of the Temple. Interior: the Auditorium. The
coughing audience is seated, the house lights dim, the stage lights
rise. Out onto the platform, where a gleaming walnut conference-
room table waits unadorned except for microphones, troops a tiny
queue of undersized mock-scholars in black gowns and mortar-
boards, its rear brought up by an oversized mock-scholar, me. The
Quiz Kids take their seats, their quizmaster, Joe Kelly, bounds out
upon the stage, the red On The Air signs light up, an announcer
billboards the show, and, at eight o'clock straight up, the Blue
Network and its affiliates carry the program to a waiting nation,
coast to coast.

How did I, at fifteen, six-three, and a rather flabby 195, get
myself into this? You may well ask. Probably mostly because, for
a long time now, American children have been treated as extensions of their parents' and teachers' frustrated drives for power
and glory, as little guided missiles programmed to rise meteorically
and burst dazzlingly above the faces of the crowd. Probably partly,
too, because I, like many of these children—the child stars, the
infant tap dancers, the tiny, tail-coated piano prodigies—had dis-

covered that the way to an adult's heart, and the perquisites that flowed therefrom, was through the exercise of my trick intellect.

As an only child, I had been left largely to my own devices of self-entertainment, which netted out to a lot of miscellaneous (and undiscouraged) reading; when it became apparent to my parents and teachers that I was glibber than most in parroting things back, I was not quietly encouraged, as I might have been in Europe, to study deeply for a serious scholarly career—or a serious artistic one. Instead, being in America, I was loudly encouraged, not to say coerced, to become a competition winner. If I had been an athlete, I would have had my arm twisted to become an All-City or All-State (or even All-American) something or other; if I had been a pretty girl, which God forbade, I would have been tempted and goaded to become a Beauty, or, at least, a Homecoming Queen. Since, however, my bulge was in the brain, rather than the brawn or beauty department, I was early tagged as a contender in the various useless-information sweepstakes with which Americans beguiled themselves and bemused their children during the last years of the Depression and the first years of the war. (I hold my teachers, always eager to aggrandize my struggling private school, more responsible for this than my parents, who were perhaps too quick to endorse the teachers' schemes of glory.)

Anyway, my feet were set upon the yellow-brick road to wizardry as far back as 1938, when, at ten, I became the spelling-bee champion of my school and went on to lose the district competition. This was repeated in 1939 and 1940, years I chiefly remember as long, weary, eye-reddening sessions of dictionary-reading and spelling drills with my mother. By 1941, though, I was ready to make my move, and after winning the school spelling bee for the fourth time, I sailed through the district contest and found myself on the stage of WWJ, a local radio station, for the Metropolitan Finals, which, to my surprise, I also won. This sent me on to the, so help me, National Finals in Washington at the end of May, where, in the auditorium of the National Press Club, I bested some poor little girl from, I think, Kentucky on an easy word ("chrysanthemum," as I remember) and became the National Champion, the emoluments of which office included a $500 Defense Bond, a wooden plaque with two bronze owls on it, and an all-expense-paid trip to New York, where I was interviewed by, and received a column in, *Newsweek* before heading home to Detroit. Back home, as a nine days' wonder, I collected a gold watch and an unabridged dictionary from my grateful (and enrollment-conscious) school and a lot more publicity from the local papers. My main reaction to all this was to lose my lunch more frequently than usual, a long-standing symptom of my revulsion to performing in public, and to conceive a lifelong hatred for the exploitation of the young.

Admittedly, though, things were dull for all hands after the furor died down, and since I was disqualified from entering any more spelling bees, my mentors began to cast about for new worlds for me to conquer. Nothing showed up for two years or more, and I was left in peace to learn Latin, write several terrible, tear-jerking short stories about war heroes (mostly RAF fighter pilots), and design, with an air-minded friend of mine, model helicopters that actually flew. Then, in the summer of 1943, the fateful news burst upon us that the Quiz Kids radio show was planning a national tour in aid of the War Bond drive, and that they would include a local panelist on the program in each city they visited. There was nothing for it, of course, but for me to enter the various eliminations; and, memorizing the *Information Please Almanac* and the *World Almanac* flat out between rounds, I did.

This was an altogther slipperier proposition than a spelling bee, since one's showing was not based on absolute knowledge but on good luck in being asked a question in an area where one was more or less informed; the only answer was to know a little about everything, or, in the words of Oscar Levant, to possess a smattering of ignorance. With my wide but superficial reading, I was well equipped to start with, and the various almanacs helped. At any rate, I went up through the various eliminating contests much as I had for the spelling bee, and finally lucked out in the citywide contest, which automatically made me a temporary Quiz Kid. Thus I found myself an awed participant in a run-through with my tiny confreres (the questions were not rehearsed, of course, but I gathered that certain questions were directed at each panelist's areas of interest during the program) and, finally, in the grand finale, the show itself. I recall only that I was very glad indeed to sit down at the contestants' table, since I towered a clean foot over the next largest Kid; that I was not very brilliant, though I managed to clean up on one question about military weaponry named for birds and animals (Duck, Warhawk, Mosquito, Panther); and that I was damned relieved to have it over with, not even, this time, having lost my lunch.

Long after my brief appearance, I kept on getting breezy little newsletters full of the doings of the other Quiz Kids, all of which inspired gloomy thoughts of the grueling atrocity of that show-a-week life of being bright for money at home and on the road. Short-term, my spelling and quizzing experiences gave me an unwarranted confidence in my ability at handling myself in public; this got a comic comeuppance late in the war, when, in the course of an extemporaneous speech before the school on our armies in the Pacific, I got so patriotically wheed up that I ended by calling for three cheers for General Douglas MacArthur and getting, of course, dead silence. Longer term, my small ordeals soured me for life on the veracity of teachers and the validity of their desires for me, a sourness which led to my getting kicked out of Harvard for a couple of years after the war. In the longest term, as I've already suggested, my exploits on stage and radio fostered an unalterable belief in the sanctity of the child and his own wishes for himself, and I think that one of the things we're seeing now is a sweeping and national revolt by the young against their elders' plans for them. While I hope the kids will form real goals for themselves and not settle for such cop-outs as drugs, desultory sex, and aimless travel, I am wholeheartedly on their side of the argument, and I hereby cast one vocal vote for Children's Lib.

Missing the Forties

A great deal of inscrutable nonsense has been written lately about that dull and sinister decade, the fifties. We are treated to musicals like *Grease* that celebrate the icky teenage mores of the time, to tuneless rehashes of the ugly, awkward early days of rock, and even to lumpish memoirs of growing up in the placid, turbid Age of Eisenhower.

To anyone who recalls the fifties from anything like a mature viewpoint, though, it was a period of stagnation in our national life—stagnation under which a crop of abominations, to be harvested in the next unhappy decade, malignly grew. Senator Joseph R. McCarthy, the blacklist, and brinkmanship were only the tip of an iceberg of unease—racial, moral, corporate, political—which was to surface in the series of civil commotions which occupied so much of the sixties. The fifties, I think it's fair to say, really represented a regression to the freebooting, laissez-faire social contract of the twenties, when anything went, and went unquestioned —for a while.

The fifties were also a regression, specifically, from the forties, that relatively free and noble decade of which I sing today. In the forties, we had hope, hope strengthened by human efficacy: right was seen to triumph. The sad ebb of a free world which, in the depression and isolation of the thirties, had left Hitler alone too long was overnight replaced by a surge of restitution of our gumption. First, France having fallen with a tragic and farcical crash, England rallied around itself against all expectations, and, by what now seems almost an effort of sheer will, stood off the Germans for a vital eighteen months. In the beginning, the longueurs of the Phony War had seemed more of the drifting, helpless do-nothingism of the thirties; when France fell, we were amply prepared for a quick, meek English debacle to match. But Dunkirk —made possible equally, as we now know, by Hitler's blunder of stopping the Panzers on the Aa and by British pertinacity—came, and brought a miracle that changed our minds. Suddenly Churchill, in what Evelyn Waugh was later to call "sham-Augustan prose," had united Britain behind him—one still remembers Low's emblematic cartoon of the period, "Very Well, Then, Alone"— and a time for cynics had been transformed by some magic of desperation into a time for heroes.

There were plenty of those, and it was with an almost hangdog delight that we followed their exploits day by day. (Though I might say, in extenuation of my enthusiasm, that I was a schoolboy at the time, plenty of adults quite unashamedly celebrated the gallantry of British arms—and, in the Blitz, of the British people, too.) The Battle of Britain was the first great set piece and perhaps the last flowering of single combat as a decisive weapon in history. The young men who beat the Germans off and destroyed the cream of the Luftwaffe were authentic heroes; nobody could gainsay the fact that they had triumphed in a just cause against forbidding odds. There was something touching and heartening in the fragility of their weapons and their lives; war had not quite reached the stage at which a man is simply the actuator of a complex electronic weapons system.

Hope for justice on a human scale flowed from the deeds of men like these, as it did from the deeds of many ordinary British men and women, from the unconquerable people of London to the members of many oddly named military cadres—Secret Operations Executive, Long Range Desert Group, Special Air Service— who carried out hair-raisingly risky forays in the field. Add the scientists and specialists who made brains take the place of matériel in the manufacture of new weapons and new intelligence stratagems, the peacetime magnates who, like Beaverbrook, placed their talents for corporate tyranny at the service of the war effort, and the nearly Quixotic escapers who dug and tunneled out of Colditz and Stalag Luft III, and you have a picture of an entire nation in the grip of a common struggle—and a common ideal. I gasp at the rarity of such a spectacle in our doubt-ridden century; I consider myself lucky to have been a distant witness.

The British example was not only anomalous and inspiriting; it was also contagious. When Pearl Harbor came, we Americans, who had been itching to get into the war, got into it with the kind of patriotic fervor that would strike us as naïve today. It seems to me, though, that this was both commendable and wholesome; after the awful, helpless lethargy of the Depression, in which we found unity only in despair, America needed a common cause like Britain's. And the men who rushed to enlist were, for the most part, not betrayed by the country they wished to serve. The Second World War, unlike the First, was not a bungled butchery (with the exception, of course, of Hitler's Russian adventure); most troops were used with sparing care.

From the beginning, we had our heroes, too. The Bataan march was futile but heroic; the brilliant self-sacrifice of the Navy dive-bomber pilots at Midway was both heroic and effective; thereafter, we never looked back. Of course we made military blunders like the Kasserine Pass and the Anzio-Nettuno beachhead. But these were far outnumbered by successes, both in Europe and the Pacific. For all that the war and its minor discomforts seemed endless and trying to the people at home, there was a genuine pride in the Allied effort. It was, in its way, a *popular* war. We trusted our civilian and military leaders and—strange as it seems today—actually believed what they told us; we would no sooner have questioned the military communiqués in the newspapers or Edward R. Morrow's broadcasts from London than we would have cursed the President. We sang the few—mostly commercial—war songs like "Rodger Young." We flocked to war movies like *Action in the North Atlantic.* It was our war, as the "A" sticker on our car windshield, the ration tokens in our wallet, and the blue star in our window would attest; it was also the war of our gallant allies, the British, the Free French, the Anzacs, the Canadians, the Russians (who had been hastily rehabilitated by the Office of War Information and, quite willingly, by the press), and the underground movements in Occupied Europe. We sat through many toshy movies about these allies, too, but I'm sure we never doubted the bona fides of our Grand Alliance.

There was doubt, to be sure, but it was focused not on the system itself but on individual villains who transgressed against the system: the profiteer, the black-market baron, the unfeeling commander of dogfaces like Bill Mauldin's Willie and Joe, an officer who apparently believed that Rank Has Its Privileges even in wartime. Our faith, our patience, and our tolerance were great; our unity as a people, though less stringently enforced than that of the British, was patent and wonderful.

In this euphoric, purposeful state of mind, it's not surprising that we failed to be stirred to protest by the nearly genocidal bombings of German civilians toward the end of the war, or by the unleashing of the atom bomb itself upon Japan. Today, both acts seem heinous; without wishing to minimize them in any way, though, I should point out that they seemed more than justified at the time. To a people both weary of war and utterly persuaded of the corporate evil of its enemies, these acts seemed almost temperate—a kind of euthanasia to kill the war. Perhaps that's why Harry Truman, surely the least arrogant of our recent wielders of power, consented to the use of atomic weapons without an apparent qualm.

But the war at last was over; we had won, I think it's still fair to say, a peace with honor; and a half decade of great creative potential lay ahead. I feel that we realized much of that potential before the dull, iron fifties clamped down. In Europe, the Marshall Plan showed early promise of reversing the mistakes of Versailles. In the world at large, the United Nations seemed a viable court for the settlement of national grievances. At home, America began the production of consumer goods that would retrieve the losses of the Depression and the war in a new standard of comfort and affluence for virtually the entire population. More: the late forties saw an American resurgence in the arts, no longer a weak echo of the European academy but a new and influential voice in the world. By 1950, to cite a few examples at random, New York had become the world's art capital; the New York school of painters had become internationally important; and, in

Robert Lowell, we had produced an indigenous poet who had no need to cross the Atlantic in order to establish his credentials.

I wax too serious. Surely one of the pervading joys of the forties, early and late, was joy itself—a sense of pleasure and adventure in moving forward together toward some measurable, and soon attainable, goal. We laughed, at the end of the war, in a kind of earned and deserved giddiness, with the whole coruscating future before us, and only the cloud of nuclear weaponry to blemish our clear sky. We thought we could do anything, since so many among us had done almost everything; we were heirs to a smiling and victorious confidence.

Looking about me now at the waste of the fifties and sixties, at the shriveled institutions, shattered credibilities, and shrunken influence of our nation, moving forward haltingly into a new era of utter uncertainty, I can't help humming a bar or two of "As Time Goes By" and missing the forties. More than just a little bit, I fear.

Quare Fellows

It is a mark of maturity in a community when it can produce—and tolerate—eccentrics. America, unlike, say, England, has never been a fertile ground for the production of eccentricity; instead, our country seems to foster extremists and fanatics, a nightmare of another color. But Boston—perhaps because it is both the oldest and the most old-world of American cities—is still a seedbed of the odd, much as it was on my arrival thirty years ago.

Now that I look back on the two-thirds of my life spent in these purlieus, I can see that many, if not most, of my companions were, from the beginning, eccentrics of a broad and gaudy stripe not often met with on American shores. When I was rusticated—urbanized, actually—from college as a disciplinary measure in the spring of 1946, I took a job and a room, which had not seen paint since before the war, in the heart of the shabby, peeling old city. Settling down in my little room in the scabby South End, where the population consisted largely of alcoholic derelicts, I soon fell into what might by courtesy be called an artistic circle. Somewhere around the *fin de siècle,* a group of real or fancied painters had built a string of brick and stone studios along the lower reaches of St. Botolph Street, not far from Copley Square. There was something William Morrisish, something Oscar Wildean, about these solid yet fanciful structures; fifty years later, come down in the world and occupied by impoverished would-be painters, sculptors, and musicians, they were grimy, slatternly, grotesque.

But it was in these houses that I met my first live artists. Most egregious among them were M'Naghten, a hunchbacked dwarf who was the son, it was said, of a noted Boston judge and a music-hall diva; he had been conceived illegitimately, it was further alleged, in the lower berth of a Pullman on a through train to Chicago. Slim, as he was incongruously known, was about four feet five, but his small, lumpy frame was belied by his volcanic mien and temper. His voice was that of Stentor, and when he played his own compositions on the piano, he threw himself at the keys like a left tackle. All of his apparent anger was simply self-assertion; once you had disarmed him simply by waiting for the fireworks show to sputter out, he became as friendly and as unassuming as a dog. Only his family—if that George Price ménage could so be called—perpetually quivered as if in the gale of his wrath. His common-law wife, a painter called Denise, whose classic Greek left profile was hideously marred by a giant congenital strawberry mark, walked in fear of Slim—except on those almost annual occasions when she left his bed and board to conceive a child by some other man. Since Slim was said to be impotent, these doings may not have troubled him; in any case, he was as angrily watchful of the numerous kids' well-being as he was of his own. The oldest child, Procne (all of the children had classical names), now half a head taller than Slim himself, would obey him unquestioningly in all things, as would her mother and the younger kids.

Slim may have been master in his own house, but he was perpetually frustrated as an artist. For as long as anyone could remember, he had been composing a piano concerto, a work that was to make his fame. But poverty—he subsisted as a remittance man, on handouts from a half brother who was a respectable banker and wished to keep Slim's puny skeleton in the closet—an out-of-tune Knabe piano, and a houseful of yowling kids conspired to keep Slim and his muse apart; it may be that, in her case, he was impotent as well. At any rate, during my tenure in the circle, I heard the first movement several times, the second not at all. Slim was apparently a one-movement composer. This did not stop him, though, from composing a ballet suite based loosely on themes from the concerto and attempting to stage it with the help of two other members of the circle: Llewellyn (or Lulu) Bowditch, a tall, blue-faced poet who was both a schizophrenic and a hashish addict, and Morrie Fields, a tiny but nobly muscled ballet dancer with burning black eyes and no discernible mentality whatever. Together, these three sketched out the music and choreography of the ballet, which was to be a hymn to hash, a testimonial from a satisfied user. To my surprise, if to nobody else's, the project actually took shape; the only question that remained was when and where to stage the première performance.

This detail was resolved by Lulu, whose very proper Boston mother belonged to a circle of her own—a group of serious and respectable Christian Scientist ladies who devoted their widowhood to dabbling in the arts. The group—known grandly as the Salon de Boston—had access to a proper theatre where, from time to time, they performed for each other and for their relatives and friends. Lulu was able to secure the theater for the première and the ladies of the Salon for the audience, a double stroke of cunning. On opening night, I read a poem or two as curtain-raiser; I'm sure my dense, clotted, intentionally obscure verse of that period could have meant nothing to those furred and stolid ladies. They warmed up a little more to the second performer, a learned divine with a salt-and-pepper goatee who read, with a hysterically funny lisp, his bird poems, chief among which was "The Warbwer." ("The Bwue Jay" and "The Thwush" were also well applauded.) Next came the *pièce de résistance:* "Cannabis Indica," the ode to hemp, played by Slim, danced by Morrie, and narrated by Lulu, reading his own poem as chorus. The ladies were as mesmerized; they sat, open-mouthed and uncomprehending, as the performers traced the progress of a gigantic high; when Morrie toppled gracefully to the floor at the end, dead of an overdose, they applauded this beautiful message long and manfully.

Sometime after that, the St. Botolph Street circle broke up, following the macabre death of Procne by drowning in a toilet; it was never resolved whether this act was voluntary or otherwise. Slim left, improbably, for Dallas, where, it was later said, he was set up in compositional practice by an oil heiress; Denise, her remaining children in tow, went to New York and became the mistress of an early action painter who thought her strawberry mark a particularly bold use of color; Morrie danced on alone and is still to be seen, steel-gray but blank-brained and fiery-eyed as ever, abroad on Boston streets; Lulu submitted, at his mother's insistence, to a prefrontal lobotomy at the time when those, like bomb shelters, were fashionable, and ended up a vegetable who invariably addressed his mother as "Goose Bag."

Six years later, now graduated from college and returned from a stint of working in New York, I resettled in Boston—and fell at once into another circle. This one was based on what we called Beacon Hill, though it was actually in the West End—the back side of Beacon Hill—that we all lived. I don't know quite how I met these people. Perhaps it was through Mandell, a failed poet at the age of twenty-five who kept an unhappy mistress named Molly Bloomgold and a happy dachshund named Max Welton, "because his brays were bonny." What Mandell—if it was he—introduced me to was a group of young desperadoes whose ringleader was again a cripple. Abe Rosegard was a clubfooted miniature of Edward G. Robinson, a crossgrained spirit both tough and sensitive, both crude and fine. He—and most of the members of his group—were engaged in dropping out of the society, in rebelling, years before the Beats, against their parents and all established values. Abe supported himself in a workaday job as a teacher of auto mechanics in a fly-by-night commercial trade school; after hours, he was the very model of the modern young thug, circa 1954: he drove a black Cadillac, had a black mistress, a singer named Martha Washington, and packed a black .38 revolver under his armpit; in the trunk of his car, he carried a large first-aid kit full of amphetamines and stronger stuff. This fledgling thug was accompanied on his nightly rounds by Benny Malkin, a tall, thin boy with an ambivalent hatred of violence; he had been Section Eighted out of the army in Korea after having been a member of a firing party that executed a deserter. The ranks of the company were further swelled by the presence of a neurasthenic higher-mathematician-cum-classicist named Bodwell and Estrella, his nymphomaniac wife. Once a week or oftener, we gathered for a party; the object of these exercises was to write and produce lewd tape recordings. Abe, among his other accomplishments, was a onetime radio announcer; his professionalism made our taping sessions, on such advanced subjects as the practice of group sex (interlarded with commercials for Pregnot, a vaginal jelly of our own invention), seem startlingly plausible when they were replayed. On weekends, Abe and I drove off at scandalous speeds in his black car, The Billy Sitch, to take in sports-car races, to which we were addicted; in fact, Abe almost got me killed while photographing a three-car crash on a dangerous corner at Watkins Glen in 1954.

Soon after, I moved to Cambridge, and That Old Gang of Mine dispersed. Abe married and remetamorphosed into the nice Jewish boy he had been born as; lately, he has been holding down a highly establishmentarian marketing job with an appliance manufacturer. Malkin indulged his appetite (and repulsion) for violence by becoming PR man for a firm that makes ballistic missiles, and whose activities he privately abhors. Mandell, the failed poet, married an heiress as neurotic as he; they were reputed to have kept a suite at a nearby mental hospital on a permanent lease, so that either or both could pop in at a moment's notice for therapy.

Middle age has touched these and dozens of others among the oddballs I once knew; we have settled down. Does this mean that eccentricity is at an end in Boston? Au contraire. Not long ago I accompanied a new friend of mine, a demi-proper Bostonian named Henry Goddard ("I'm Irish on the chauffeur's side," he says), along with a couple of women we've both known for years, to a new restaurant in Boston. Henry, I should explain, makes his living—when he bothers to send out his bills—as an unconventional psychotherapist. His specialty is troubled teen-agers, and I hear he's a dab hand at bringing them down from a bad trip and explaining the ways of parents to their kith, or kids. He lives in a merchant prince's palace on Beacon Hill with his black housekeeper, an ordained minister, reader, and adviser named Duchess R. Winsor, and succors as many wayward children as ever he can.

This particular evening, Henry was in his best—i.e., most adventurous—restaurant-going mood. (He is frequently known to inspect the kitchens of restaurants where he dines, fraternizing with the dishwashers and rolling affectionately on the floor with the restaurant cat, since he adores all animals; in fact, he sends our dog an annual Christmas card.) The meal went fairly swimmingly until, between the drinks and the appetizer, Henry decided to dance to the Muzak in a restaurant where man had never danced before. The waiter intervened; the headwaiter came; the maître d' appeared. All to no avail; Henry finished his dance with one of the ladies who had accompanied us. In the highest of spirits (though perfectly sober; Henry does not need drink to make him high), he attacked and enjoyed the rest of his meal, or most of it. The pie—obviously not a product of the restaurant's own kitchens—aroused his tiny store of ire. We repaired, at his suggestion, to the bar for a post-prandial brandy. There, on duty at his station, was Mine Host, a former linebacker for the Boston Patriots, a hunk of meat so tall his head appeared to be enveloped in perpetual cloud. Henry struck up a dialogue with him, undaunted by the gross disparity in their size. "How'd ya like the dinner?" asked the linebacker. "Fine," responded Henry. "But, Moose, you gotta get rid of that fucking pecan pie!" Mine Host rumbled; fortunately, it was only strangled laughter.

In Boston, some still live. I mean eccentrics, naturally.

Hypmatized

Let us go, then, you and I, hand in hand into the New England summer of 1947, reeking Cheeverishly of mud flats and clam beds at low tide, colored above by the prematurely autumnal blue of the August sky, colored at eye level by the neon swirls and poster-paint squiggles of hot-dog, shooting-gallery, fried-clams signs, dwindling down the stony strand of Revere Beach like barkers into the eastward twilight where the ocean hove.

My dear friend Harry Brorby, the painter, and I had decided we needed a vacation from our summer vacation from school. Drawn, like so many Midwestern young men in those days, to the randy, yet Puritanic, residue of an older New England along its shores—the sagging, weathered ranks of modest cottages, the big gabled shingle houses on the piny points, the commercial tenderloins picked out with sideshow lights in between, the smells of beer and fish—we gravitated to the nearest of these pleasure domes, the people's beach just outside Boston, where old women in babushkas raised their skirts to wet their bare calves in the water, and old men, with their trousers rolled, dared to eat a Joe & Nemo's hot dog while standing knee-deep in the mud-gray brine, and heard, presumably, the juvenile delinquents singing each to each a good deal further out and deeper in.

New England summers take some explaining, too, to those who have not experienced their tentative delights. They are, *au fond,* a tease: summer, but for a few hot, enervating days, never really comes to those northern shores; there is always a knife, a threat of fall, hiding in the skies just overhead, and summer's fruit is gathered furtively, as in a boy's first fumbling sexual encounter. Indeed, there is something covertly sexual about summer at Rye Beach or Nantasket or Rehoboth or Watch Hill; unlike the foisonous strands of Florida and California, where sex, like tropical fruit, is always ripe, to hand, and free for the taking, the beaches of New England create a tense and tantalizing play between the withholding and the granting of love's hasty, sandy favors.

But it was not, this time at least, in hope of any dreamlike pickup and conquest that Harry and I journeyed by whining, wooden, orange streetcar to Revere; we were simply out to sniff the sea and see the sights, to partake of the reassuringly humane low life of the least pretentious of resorts north of Coney Island. We disembarked, as I recall, at the south end of the beach toward the end of a cool, clear August afternoon, when the water temperature might easily, and deliciously, have exceeded that of the air; the lights were coming on, and the beach parties, some fully clothed, some in long, absurd, moth-holed, prewar bathing costumes, were falling back on the line of stands for the refreshment of Croft Cream Ale and cotton candy.

Ambling in a kind of overdrive, propelled by a kindly lassitude that just punted us along, Harry and I, with his painterly eye and my neophytic writerly one, busied ourselves being members of the crowd and simply sharing in the harmless pleasures of a proletarian day at the seaside. We had a couple of cream ales—there was something sealike in that sharp, peevish taste of alcohol held less subtly in suspension than in beer—and a couple of dogs to hold them down, dogs slathered with brilliant ocher ballpark mustard as a base for the white cubes of chopped onion and the sweet emeralds of relish. We squeezed off a couple of quarters' worth of .22 longs at a shooting gallery, pinking the occasional tin duck but not winning a bamboo pennant cane, a Kewpie doll, or even a vermilion Revere Beach balloon tied to a stick. We drifted down the narrow, disaster-courting aisles of a souvenir shack, inspecting the miniature bean pots lettered "You Don't No Beans Til You've Seen Boston," the red-white-and-blue Revere Beach dresser runners, the balsam pillows ("I pine for you"), and the plaster-of-Paris replicas of Boston Light.

Then we moved on, passing a string of semi-winterized taverns with buzzing neon beer signs in their screened windows, a Karmel Korn machine on wheels, and—with an anti-superstitious picking up of pace—the bead-curtained booth of a gypsy fortune-teller. We stopped, for reasons not quite understood by either of us, before a brightly lit and lettered shack proclaiming the presence of Krypto the Hypnotist, Master of Human Suggestion. The primitive art beneath the sign showed Krypto, a goateed Mediterranean in a white, jeweled turban and a blue-black dinner suit, gesturing mesmerically toward the passersby, thus acting as his own inanimate barker. Hypnosis interested both of us; here was a chance to test the skill, or otherwise, of a small-time grifter, or otherwise; we paid our quarter each and passed in through the navy velvet curtain.

Inside, dispelling our ideas of dim-lit drama, was a small, bright, red-and-yellow beaverboard room about ten by twenty-five, with a low stage, or platform, along one twenty-five-foot side. Upon this stage, Krypto—for it must have been he, though this was a young man in his early twenties, dressed in a turtleneck and gray-flannel jacket over chinos and quite unlike his come-on portrait, except for the long, sallow face and neat goatee—exhorted a small, dubious audience of twenty or so, including many sailors (for the fleet was in), to provide a subject for his art. As he fingered various members of the crowd, they fell back in turn, not wishing to chance their luck at Krypto's rather grubby hands. Finally, the moving finger came to me; after a short, acrimonious internal debate, I found myself volunteering as the subject. Why, I'm not quite sure; I think that I felt a little sorry for this quite possibly inept practitioner; having paid my quarter, I felt, too, a kind of complicity, as if I wished him to succeed enough to make his success a mission of my own. So I clambered to the stage.

I should explain that in those days I was as tall as I am now and, at two hundred pounds or so, a good bit heftier; at six feet four, I found myself towering over my would-be hypnotist, who seemed almost toylike now that we stood on the same level. This was adjusted for by our both taking seats—wire-backed soda-par-

lor chairs—facing each other on the stage. The festivities began
with an order for me to empty my mind and concentrate on my
mentor's commands. I must wish, he said, "to be hypmatized" in
order for the thing to come to pass. I was, he assured me repeatedly, becoming drowsy; I was, he added, falling farther and
farther under his spell. He rose sinuously, like a snake charmer's
cobra, the better to enforce his will, and stood over me, making
presumably Svengali-like orchestra-conducting gestures with his
hands, all the while fixing me with what must have been a genuinely hypnotic stare from his brown, liquid, quasi-Oriental eyes.

After about five minutes of this trance-inducing behavior on his
part, I came to the sudden realization that, for reasons traceable
either to his technique or my immalleability, nothing was happen-
ing; quite clearly, it was just not going to take. This was followed
with a rising desire to laugh uproariously at the whole farcical
proceeding, thwarted by an even stronger order from my superego
to play the good subject and see the damned thing through. Just
as I had resolved upon this course—I felt his *honor* was at stake
and must be vindicated—he nearly blew the gaff (and my resolve)
by telling me, "You are now in a psychotic state." Converting an
involuntary snort into a deep-sleeper's sigh, I soldiered on. In my
psychotic state—eyes tightly shut, ticklishly close to gales of mirth
—I gathered that I was to obey his every whim. First, as I recall,
I shuffled somnambulistically across the stage, bearing various
props from one place to another at his direction. The next, and far
tougher, piece of acting called for me to demonstrate that hypnotic
subjects will refuse commands repugnant to their moral sense. A
volunteer—Harry, I could see under my eyelids—was called up
from the audience; I was told that this was my worst enemy and
invited to assault him with a knife. I flexed my left, or stabbing,
hand vengefully, getting into the spirit of the act. A rubber dagger,
of the kind sold to small boys in dime stores, was thrust into it;
I raised my arm high over my head, bringing it down toward where
Harry's innocent chest must have been. Then, in a superb bit of
melodrama, if I say so myself, I faltered, wincing gravely, caused
my hand to shake with a gross tremor two inches from his chest,
and dropped the dagger with the dullest thud I've heard. This
achievement brought a small round of applause, and I was off on

the toughest test of all. I was to make myself rigid—"ab-so-lute-ly ri-gid"—at the hypmatist's command, arranging myself between the two chairs. This might theoretically be possible for a man in Olympic physical condition or one genuinely hypnotized, but it was nearly impossible for me. In short, I sagged.

My involuntary laxity apparently escaped detection; next thing I knew, I was lifted, feet and shoulders, by two volunteer sailors, and carried, like a coffin, twice around the stage. Keeping rigid under these conditions called up the most strenuous and painful physical effort I've ever made; I just barely managed to avoid folding into a V until the blessed moment, when, to a good hand of clapping and a few enthusiastic whistles, I was set down upon a single chair again. Krypto had come through. I was awakened and thanked for my cooperation.

I was stiff when Harry—who had of course realized that I was faking—and I limped, exhausted, to the streetcar. I was also sore for a week afterward. I was sadder and wiser, too. The moral I derived from this experience—and have furbished to a luster ever since—is this: don't do unto strange hypnotists as you would have them do unto you. Stick to the cream ale and the chili dogs and let the occult go hang.

Christmas Story

It was the winter of 1952-1953, and a cold coming we had of it, Red Harris and I. Not that, as I remember, it was a particularly severe winter in statistical terms; it was only that we chose to sell vacuum cleaners in the Godforgotten Northeast Kingdom of Vermont.

Washed out of political life forever by the Eisenhower landslide of November—I had been a minor functionary in the John F. Kennedy-for-Senator campaign, with hopes of a permanent berth somewhere in the Democratic organization—I turned up jobless as the cold closed in and made for the doubtful shelter of the Deshler Vacuum Cleaner Company, of Terre Haute, Indiana, with Offices in All Principal Cities. My application was accepted on the spot, and I found myself being trained to sell "The Cadillac of Cleaners," an improbable basketball-size aluminum sphere on wheels that, with the aid of a tool chest full of attachments, could sand, saw, mix, blend, wax, buff, and even spray paint as well as clean a rug. Or so the instructions claimed.

Actually, as any student of industrial design could readily have confirmed, the Deshler was a survival from the early days of vacuuming, sort of a contemporary antique. The archaism of its engineering was matched by the antiquity of the company's selling methods. We learned little in our two-day, unpaid training course, except to sing special Deshler pep songs, based on old Big Ten football chants, at the opening of each training session, and to brazen our way into the prospect's house with the most glittering of promises and the direst of innuendos. We were not salesmen, we were sanitation men, and we were there to sanitize the prospect's house—no charge, of course—before her wondering eyes.

When we hit the street, with a withering song in our hearts and a blast of November wind in our faces, each man was on his own. And how. Along with Red Harris, a pushing, torch-headed small and wiry young particle, I was assigned to the unpromising *banlieue* of Waltham, Massachusetts, whose celebrated watch factory was then departing the last of its nine lives, leaving the city as depressed—both mentally and fiscally—as any other New England mill town in those dreary days. Seeking safety in numbers, Red and I joined up together as a team, halving our individual calls and commissions, if any, in the greater interest of solidarity.

It was tough sledding, mitigated by an occasional sale to a cretinous couple who should have known better than to get on the never-never for a Deshler, and by interminable cups of nickel coffee in a handy Howard Johnson's.

If nothing else, it taught us technique, though. Glazed into boldness by necessity, we soon learned how to disarm the housewife's faint-hearted objections at the door, and how, once in, to make directly for the bedroom, where we demanded, if necessary, that the bedclothes be pulled back. Once we had the spavined bed stripped naked before us, we proceeded to a medical demonstration roughly as portentous as, say, the discovery of germs. Running the long, jointed arm of the Deshler over the mattress cover with a loud, menacing hum, as of swarming wasps, we covered the entire surface in a trice. Next we opened the dirt bag and shook out the contents—shook them back, in fact, on the mattress cover itself. A pale, pinkish-tan scurf appeared. We asked the housewife if she could identify this late occupant of her marriage bed. Needless to say, she never could. At which point I would cut in, with a menacing Gildersleeve boom, "That, madam, is dead skin!" Shock and mortification, occasionally followed by a sale, more frequently followed by other, tamer demonstrations of sanding, spraying, waxing, and, terminally, carpet-cleaning. If she wouldn't buy on the spot, we asked for a return engagement that evening in the presence of her husband; this request was often granted, and dead skin was produced on cue again in the evening.

What *was* dead skin? Damned if I know. It might have been lint, pajama tailings, house moss, mattress stuffing, or even, God knows, dead skin itself. Though its identity remained obscure to us, it was the high point of our demos—as we called these playlets in the trade—and most of our few sales were traceable to the housewife's horror at the implied suggestion of uncleanliness.

And so, call by call, day by day, week by week, we perfected our talents at the shell game. Alas, we failed to perfect our batting average. Three or four sales per week turned out to be our upper limit; even with the inflated commissions made possible by the Deshler's inflated price (around two hundred dollars, more than twice the price of a good name-brand vacuum cleaner in those days), we could hardly ever count on more than seventy-five dollars apiece each week, out of which came gas, car expenses, food, and all our other ineluctable overheads. Both of us were married, and both were going broke.

Sitting in the Howard Johnson's one icy day when a dusting of snow made skeins across the streets, we hit upon a plan. Red, aggressive in inverse proportion to his height, suggested we light out for virgin territory—northern Vermont, where he himself came from and where he knew every soul in a twenty-mile radius of St. Johnsbury. Those Vermonters, he said, had plenty socked away in their dead-skin-filled mattresses; with Christmas coming, couldn't a local boy and his friend persuade them to part with some of it? A stroke of genius in necessity; we shook hands on the bargain and prepared to leave next day.

I packed a bag and left my car in Red's snowy side driveway next to his two-decker apartment house in an unfashionable part of Natick. We climbed into his spectacularly oxidized, dark blue '46 Torpedo Oldsmobile and were off. This was long before the day of Interstates; most of the roads were winding two-lane by-ways past miles of tumbledown shacks with dead cars and old Maytags in the yard. This was the postwar depression, which still rode New England. It was before the recent era of recovery, and there was little paint or money showing on the houses or in the crabbed towns.

Aldridge, Vermont, was not what I'd expected. It was not a postcard village—all elms and spires and gingerbread houses—but a kind of rustic slum. It served as a dormitory town for the quarry workers in Barre, some twenty-five miles away down Route 302; its mean houses, many of them, were, like Natick's and Waltham's, double- and triple-deckers. Red took me up to a second deck to meet his family: his father, a cadaverous, toothless, gormless old man of forty-five, worn out and phthisic from inhaling rock dust in the quarries; his mother, a fat, pleasant woman who should have looked jolly but looked drained instead. I was to stay with them as a paying guest; they did their decent best to make me feel at home.

But to the hunt. Next day, Red and I unlimbered our Deshler demonstrator and began to call on the modest satraps of the locality. The first week went reasonably well. With Red's entrée and my scholarly exposition of the evils of dead skin, we made four solid sales—all cash, for, as we had supposed, the money was indeed concealed around the house. And these four, concluded with some real goodwill between ourselves and the customers, led to further referrals. We found ourselves calling on Hawkins cousins and Sawyer aunts in outlying towns. And therein lay our downfall. Bucking our way through a middling blizzard one white-on-white morning, Red spun his worn snow tires on a patch of ice and over-revved the weary engine, which promptly registered displeasure by sending No. 2 piston out through the side of the block. Apart from the stiff expense of the repairs, we were without wheels at the apex of the selling season. And we had miles to go before we slept.

We made the best of this contretemps by listing the locals in Aldridge upon whom we could call on foot—not the meanest of feats, considering that the snow was thirty-six inches deep and the thermometer had dropped, after the storm, to a seemingly permanent twenty-four below zero. Walking "over town" to the general store, the breath froze in our noses, and our lungs felt as if they were being pierced with icicles. Nevertheless, we soldiered on, dragging our Deshler and its case of gadgets and hoses behind us through the snow. A couple more sales slowly jelled with repeated callbacks; between bouts of frozen-fingered selling, we languished in the Harrises' kerosene-heated parlor, stoking our personal fires with large, plain meals of cottonwool bread and sticky pasta.

Finally, less than a week before Christmas, we struck at last at our best prospect: a recently widowed Mrs. Willard, the amiable mistress of a large, dust-collecting Victorian ark, who was, reputedly, rich as Croesus. Bracing her in her living room one night, we out-demonstrated our greatest demonstration, forcing the wheezing Deshler to new heights of sanitation. We sprayed moth gas in her closets, cleaned her drapes, waxed her linoleum, beat her old Orientals to within an eighth-inch of their warp and woof. And lo! she was persuaded. We walked out of her house that freezing night with a signed contract and a small deposit, the rest to be collected in a day or two. At last our trip seemed almost worthwhile: we could return to Boston after the holiday with a couple of hundred dollars each to keep the wolf away.

Then trouble struck. When we got back to the Harrises' one evening, we had an ominous message: a call from Mrs. Willard. A friend, it seems, had heard she was about to buy a Deshler and had advised her to consider an Electrolux instead. The Electrolux man, a sleek deity in a new Pontiac Chieftain, was on his way there now. Would we care to match our machine against his in a competitive demonstration? Of course we would; dragging our Deshler like a travois through the snow, we made our way to Mrs. Willard's white house on the hill. She was a bit embarrassed at the confrontation she had caused; but, she pointed out, it was only fair that she should be able to compare the two machines, and we of course agreed.

Then the slow murder began. The Electrolux man unlimbered his streamlined blue-green machine with its shining wands and politely asked us to go first in cleaning the living-room rug (which we'd already cleaned a couple of days before). We cleaned mightily; we opened our dust bag and showed a pitiful wisp of dust. The Electrolux man set his shining monster sucking at the same square feet of carpet. A moment later he opened his own dust bag, which had previously been empty, to show a fat roll of fresh dirt. The secret was in the extra suction of his more powerful motor, he said (and we believed); to demonstrate this further, he selected a transparent Lucite wand, produced a large, heavy, chromed-steel ball, and proceeded to pick the ball up with the wand and hold it suspended eighteen inches up the wand. He then invited us to do the same. Manfully, Red and I clipped the transparent wand to the Deshler and applied it to the ball. A hiss and gulp; the ball rose leisurely into the tube and then flopped out onto the floor again. The process was repeated. It was no use. We were skunked, whipped like curs, beaten at our own game, vanquished far from home. We returned Mrs. Willard's contract and deposit and slunk, dragging the tonweight of the Deshler, back down the hill toward home.

The next day was Christmas Eve. Red's car was ready; we got in in utter dejection and drove back to Boston. Our first stop was at the Deshler sales office, where we collected our meager winnings and renounced our calling forevermore, giving the rattled sales manager our considered view of his product in front of a raw group of new trainees.

Then, at the fountain of a nearby drugstore, we drank a last cup of watery coffee and shook hands on our decision to go our separate ways in search of something better than Deshler salesmanship. We'd be in touch again when we got situated, both of us vowed. Shortly afterward, but not in time to make that Christmas or New Year's any happier, I finally got a job I'd been after in an advertising agency, and things started to look up. But, of course, I never laid eyes on Red again, though I've often wondered what happened to him.

Merry Christmas, then, Red, wherever you are; you were a good companion and one feisty guy.

Lost Cities

A thousand Jeremiahs tell us—undoubtedly accurately—that we are losing our countryside. Our national parks and national fastnesses are choked with campers. Small towns are overrun with tourist locusts. Navies of powerboats clog our lakes and rivers. Armies of hikers conquer virgin mountains.

But what of our cities, which are already lost to us? What urban adventurer, however foolhardy, would walk out at night to take the air on Riverside Drive, Connecticut Avenue, or Michigan Boulevard? The men and women who furnish our city streets with purposeful motion in the daytime—even then warily—vanish at nightfall into far suburbs or tall buildings, imprisoned behind locks and guards and vicious dogs. Our cities are our jailers; after dark, our demesne is confined to a few small, familiar rooms with the world piped in through the blue eye of TV.

What were our cities to us in the age when we enjoyed the freedom of them day and night? More, I think, than we might at first suppose. America has been a nation of monumentalists, of self-memorializers in living stone. Unlike Europeans, who have always operated under an unspoken obligation to preserve the houses and palaces and offices of their ancestors, Americans began with *tabula rasa*—an open space instead of a city, a forgotten tangle of forebears instead of a family tree. In many ways, they were the first Western men who were truly free to express and perpetuate themselves in the lineaments of their cities. And they did.

Before conformity set in in the last generation, before the freebooting individual gave way to the corporate committee, Americans with power and money committed their fantasies to form. They built cities of palaces bearing their names or the names of their companies, palaces dedicated to the demonstration that a nobody could become a king in his own lifetime. Overcompensating for the humility of their origins—or the origins of their fortunes—they reared fantastical landmarks almost overnight. Depending on the taste or servility of the architects they engaged, these secular fanes and temples ranged from the imposingly ridiculous to the oversized sublime. After the turn of the century, everything was towers, wordless sky-signs designed to advertise the builder's eminence. Louis Sullivan's flat-topped monadnocks gave way to fingers, beacons, spires. The wondrous Standard Oil Building at the Battery and the tall, fat newspaper offices of Park Row were overtopped by the archly Gothic Woolworth Building and soon by many more. In the twenties, boom fever launched hundreds of new ziggurats: the Tribune Tower in Chicago, an enormous Boston Stump, complete with terminal lanthorn; the Penobscot Building in Detroit, a pocket battleship of gray setbacks; and in New York, the Salmon Tower, the Chanin Tower, the Lincoln Tower, and literally above all, the shiny, steel-beaked Chrysler Building.

These buildings were often bad architecture in bad taste. But they transcended that, because they were alive—because they were a piece of living social history, exciting and imposing for all their pompousness (the music that celebrates them, the "busy-city" movie music of the early thirties, is still, for all its unintended irony, alive and moving), and because their presence created a fine tension between them and the monuments of lesser entrepreneurs: the small, unceremonial, individuated houses, apartments, shops, restaurants, and offices that complete a city. The total impression—as John Sloan, Reginald Marsh, and other painters saw and drew—was one of attractive diversity and eclecticism, of human beauty and folly playing themselves on a stage greater, even, than that of the Radio City Music Hall. It was a scene of grave inequity and social injustice, but one in which real people preserved their eccentricity and uniqueness against the pressures of power. The closest literary equivalent to the big-city-scape of the twenties is John Dos Passos' *U.S.A.*, illustrated, significantly, by Reginald Marsh; if a single epithet can describe that book, it is vitality.

When I grew up, in the thirties and forties, the case was altered. The empire-building drive of the twenties had culminated, in New York, in the somber monolith of Rockefeller Center and in the tinsel leanness of the Empire State. The Depression was in progress and the mood of the people had changed from lively expectation to despair and fear. A symbol of the change that I remember was a handsome, twenty-story office tower in Detroit; its rust-and-beige brick exterior had been completed, but the windows were unglazed, and there were no floors inside.

In spite of this pause in our ebullience—a pause from which we may never have recovered—cities were still exciting landscapes when I grew up in them. They were man-made, it's true; but in the making, over a relatively few generations, they became a geological deposit of American taste and aspirations, a living demonstration of the forces that had shaped the recent past and present. All this apart from the sheer beauty, beauty in ugliness, of their soaring juxtapositions: the Sabrett hot-dog man, the smallest known unit of free enterprise, at the heartbreakingly modernique base of the Irving Trust Company on Wall Street, with the brown eighteenth-century eminence of Trinity Church as backdrop. It is not too much to say, in fact, that in the twentieth century we finally learned to be at home in cities just before they were to become unlivable, that we learned to see the cityscape as a curious kind of natural landscape in which all the nature was an extension of human nature. The painters I've mentioned, along with Edward Hopper, Charles Sheeler, and many others, became poets of cityscapes; so did a number of important writers. In Europe, Graham Greene created a despairing elegy out of his vision of Nottingham, which he called Nottwich, and Céline made a decaying, decadent Paris into a vehicle of savage sardonic joy; even "The Waste Land" is a poem, in part, about the dying life of a city. In America, Dos Passos, Fitzgerald, and Thomas Wolfe began the exploration of the beauty, necessity, and *terribilità* of urban life that, in a still darker vein, Saul Bellow, Donald Barthelme, and Philip Roth have continued.

The fact is, of course, that the city is a machine for compressing both people and experience, for multiplying and heightening sensations (in both senses), for speeding and amplifying the impact of life on the individual. Since flesh and blood can withstand only so many stimuli, threats, and shocks without losing their coherence, the city-as-happening has, with the advance of both tension and technology, become simply too much for us: too much life, too much death to imagine or deal with, day after day.

But in the last generation, it was still possible for one—a lucky one with enough youth and health and foolish confidence—to ride, like a surfer, the crest of the wave, to feel himself the confidant and master of a city, to walk the dark streets absorbing sensation with an innocent fearlessness of personal harm. Now that our cities have, so to speak, outgrown us, I think it's important to recall what they meant to us when we could still confront them and change and be changed by them. Take, for instance, a late-summer twilight on West Twentieth Street in Chelsea, circa 1950. The westbound walker saw before him a backlit jumble of modest roof lines, wood water tanks on rooftops, a tangle of ironwork marking the western boundary of the island. Nearer, the wrought-iron rails of brownstone steps, silhouetted by the last light, receded to a vanishing point somewhere on the Jersey shore. At Ninth Avenue, a line of small, shut shops—barbers', butchers', fish merchants'—proceeded shabbily southward. There was an unnatural silence for the city, the silence of people gone away to the mountains and the seashore. The only sounds, besides the passage of occasional taxis, were the lost Latino songs of Puerto Ricans, left behind in the August exodus, singing on front stoops. The only smells, besides an occasional gust of diesel smoke from buses, were the dank, miasmal emanations of Victorian cellars—a universal urban gas, composed of mildew, dead rats, and rotten wood, that I have smelled in many American cities. The total effect was mildly sad, a little sentimental, and remarkably reassuring for its human scale.

Even walking in canyons of skyscrapers was an ironic affirmation. While perhaps condemning the architectural excesses, the solitary walker could, through his patronizing smile, feel some crazy kind of empathy with the force of will that caused these towers to be erected, could be thrilled in secret by the waxing or waning play of light along their flanks and among their overbearing spires. Some structures seemed both massive and imposing and frail and fallible, like the naïvely grand Art-Deco McGraw-Hill Building on West Forty-second Street or the foursquare but fussily ornate New York Central Building—since, alas, overawed by the chesty, graceless Pan Am—at the foot of Park Avenue. And always, in a jaunty, arhythmic figure over the ground bass of the buildings, ran the sights and sounds of ordinary men and women going about their business in the granite forest, like tiny sailors on the deck of some behemoth dreadnought of the Jutland era.

The sounds were astonishingly intimate: the tick of a single pair of heel taps on the pavement half a block away; a truncated gust of laughter from two couples at the entrance to a nightclub; the distant taxi whistle of a doorman; the buzz of a single failing neon sign in a cigar-store window; the angry clipping projected from the entrance to a barber shop; the slow slap of shoeshine cloths in the lobby of an office building; the cross-section of high-pitched babble from the open door of a saloon, rising and fading to silence in a second; a piano, badly and hesitantly played, heard with an almost elfin clarity from some upstairs apartment.

But the mystery and promise was in the smells, especially at night, when much of the population had gone indoors and advertised its presence largely by the aromas of life continuing. Cigar smoke, suggesting an impossible affluence; a hint of perfume, detached from an invisible woman of unimaginable beauty; advertisements for cookery, both the humble cabbage of tenements and the rich, herbal sauces of restaurants; the sudden, raw skunk-smell of gasoline; at subway exits, the compressed amalgam of heat, humidity, sweat, ozone, and oil; over everything, a faint, bitter tang of exhaust; and in the parks—who dares walk in parks at night anywhere anymore?—the contending odors of irrepressible greenery and the surrounding city, still radiating the hot fumes of the day.

That, then, was a little of what cities were thirty or forty years

ago, before their humanity was cruelly superseded by the proliferation of faceless chain stores at street level, obliterating the little,
idiosyncratic shops of small businessmen, and the proliferation of
soulless glass polyhedrons, displaying the corporate compromise
and confusion of modern money power and obliterating the slim
silver-plated pencils of the old entrepreneurs' towers overhead.

The multifarious, splendid, sordid ego-trips that used to be our
cities are vanished, as it were, into thick air.

In the Heart of Downtown, 1935

Look. A woman and her little boy are standing on that corner, waiting for the bus. The neighborhood is drab and down-at-heel —the three-story Victorian frame houses are unpainted, the front yards are littered with discarded washboilers, bedsprings, and bicycle frames half-hidden by the foot-high grass, the slate slabs of the sidewalk are cracked and frost-heaved, a dead marmalade tomcat, already rigid and colonized by bluebottles, dominates the gutter—but the sun is palely cheerful, the air smacks of ozone, and the mother and son are crisply dressed in summer cottons. They—my mother in a natural-straw picture hat with a blue-velvet band, I in my blue summer shorts and a pair of black-leather T-strap shoes not unlike a girl's Mary Janes—are going downtown on a shopping trip. It is the last Saturday in May, 1935.

The double-decker bus, in mud-green Detroit Street Railway livery punctuated by the primary colors of advertising cards, comes by, and we get on. We climb, at my request, to the top deck and sit, at my request, in the right-front seat. The conductor's hand-held coin machine swallows my mother's nickel with a metal gulp—I am too young, at seven, to pay bus fare—and we settle down to watch the skyline grow between the phone poles and the housefronts of our street. One building in particular, a gray granite monadnock with many setbacks and a radio mast atop its highest reaches, soon comes to dominate its flat-topped foothills, and to spell, in the letterless language of children, downtown.

Downtown. We debouch in a vast public square facing the city hall, a building that seems withdrawn behind its sooty, bird-stained face of limestone, studiedly unaware of the crowds of the long-term unemployed who lounge in the sun in its forecourts. These stubbled men, in their rusty bowlers and pale, grease-stained caps and baggy, greenish tweeds, do not alarm us; in spite of the exhortations of a couple of Communist agitators standing on small, portable platforms at the corners of the square, there is no rebellion left in them, and their ranks part for us as we walk up the main street, a short canyon of the city's nice department stores, toward our first appointment at the eye doctor's. (The year before, I had caught scarlet fever from a playmate who had caught it from his dead cousin at an open-coffin funeral; after a terrifying siege of quarantine—my mother and I were locked in the house together, and food and medicine were hauled up in a mushroom basket from outside—I recovered to find that my eyes had been damaged, and that I would have to exercise them to restore the muscle tone.) The doctor's office is high up in a cres-cent-fronted white-brick building of 1910, whose towering lobby is lit by electric flambeaux and by a huge frosted skylight eleven stories above. The elevators—delicate wrought-iron cages en-closed in the wrought-iron cages of their shafts—are visible through the whole of their ascent, since the upper floors are reached only through their back doors; it is startling to see real, ordinary businessmen and pretty women moving up and down in their black-bordered cubes ten stories above the lobby floor.

The doctor's offices are cool, brown-paneled, high-ceilinged, quiet except for a few traffic sounds from the street below. He seats me in a chair—I can smell a sweetly sinister licorice, only later identified as Sen-Sen, on his breath—and adjusts the exercise machine. I am to uncross my eyes enough to put a hand-colored parrot in his old-fashioned cage. I strain; the parrot moves, but not enough; I try again, but he will not go in. It's tiring, like twenty pushups, but I keep at it for ten minutes. I'm making prog-ress, the doctor says, though it's not, literally, visible to me. We thank him, make the next appointment, and take our leave.

The street is busy now. The surviving stores—those that have weathered the first five years of the Depression—seem to be attracting lookers, if not buyers. Each shop still clings to a double character of its own and of its trade, left over from the past.

The high-class pharmacy where my mother stops for Seidlitz powders smells of herbs and pharmaceuticals—indeed, the only thing it sells—and of melting sealing wax. The neat salesclerks make a little ritual of wrapping each purchase in a square of white, crackling butcher paper and sealing it with a stick of cinna-bar-red wax, heated momentarily over a shielded, hissing gas flame on the counter. The fashionable jeweler's where my mother leaves a ring to be cleaned cultivates an atmosphere of leisured privacy, as if every customer were to be waited on alone by a principal of the firm; her tiny request is gravely considered by the old clerk in morning trousers, a price murmured, a date promised. The great twenty-story department store—the wonder of those parts—where we are to buy me, on sale, some winter shoes and knickers, is miraculously spit-and-polish, fulfilling its great-merchant image as impeccably as any Harrod's: the marble floors are antiseptically dustless, the walnut counters glow with polish and their beveled glasses glisten, the magnificent black elevator ladies call departments with imperious assurance and restrain their passengers from the cruel bronze compressed-air-operated gates, the fluted, brass-bound drinking fountains (in two sizes, man and child) spout limpid water from their white-porcelain bubblers, the call gongs utter signals, the pneumatic tubes hiss and fall home with a clunk, and a tall, handsome floorwalker with a red-carnation buttonhole polices every precinct of the store. The salespeople, too, seem equally conscious of their mission; a squat man in a shiny d.b. sharkskin equably engages my mother in a twenty-minute discursion on the philosophy of foot growth and persuades her to buy me shoes a half-size larger than she'd planned; the boys'-shirt-department lady refuses to sell us a slightly soiled blouse; the knicker salesman takes infinite pains over an alteration in the waistline of a four-dollar pair of pants. Having served us before, he calls me by name.

A break for lunch. Down in the street, we walk to the nearest of a chain of ice-cream parlors—it's that or one of a chain of clean little one-arm cafeterias, tiled to the ceiling in dazzling white, but today we feel like ice cream—and walk into a dense and stunning atmosphere of chocolate fudge. At the long green-marble counter, we order hot-fudge sundaes and chicken-salad sandwiches, which come wrapped in neatly tucked and folded wax paper and cost twenty cents. My mother pays the ninety-cent check, leaves the waitress a dime, and we go next door to a matinee at a movie house with red plush seats and a ceiling with moving clouds and winking stars; we see Will Rogers in a revival of *A Connecticut Yankee at King Arthur's Court*. The movie is fun for a seven-year-old; I am particularly delighted by a wave of Knights of the Table Round, mounted on Baby Austins and charging up a hillside to the Yankee's rescue.

Finally, grocery shopping. The sun throws longer shadows as we walk to a large, echoing, clerestory farmers' market a block or two from the theater. My mother buys cut-to-order pork chops, a stewing chicken for fricassee, home-baked beans (ladled from a huge earthenware *pot-au-feu* into a trick cardboard box with a wire handle), farmer's cheese, German potato salad, fresh eggs, and, at a family bakery, unsliced rye bread and a dozen date-filled hermits. I carry one small bag, she carries two big ones as we return to the bus stop, past the less nice stores of the city's second street, with their hand-lettered signs of bargains, sales, and clearances. Radio shops broadcast "Smoke Gets in Your Eyes" out over their transoms. Now newsboys hardly older than I am—but seeming more alive than I am—come skipping up the street from the corner where a truck has dumped their evening papers, yelling some headline about Mussolini. They are joined by people leaving work: slightly threadbare clerks and businessmen with cracked brown briefcases, young typists and filing clerks in mock-silk blouses and bright-red lipstick, messengers and office boys in baggy cardigans, knickers, knee socks, and scuffed and dusty shoes.

On the lower deck of the bus home, we are silent. The sun stipples my mother's cheek when it breaks out from between the buildings on the west side of the street. We are peaceably exhausted, worn out with the wonder, promise, and fulfillment of what Petula Clark was to sing thirty years later (long after the center failed to hold) as "Downtown"—the social, cultural, material exchange of a city, for which it and its mutually dependent outriders existed.

That night, I fell asleep to further assurances of community, the comfy, lonely whistles of trains going their appointed, human rounds; dreamt, in the small hours, of a fleet of Baby Austins, a community of rescue, charging up a hill; woke, on Sunday, to the cacophonous harmony of a community of bells—Catholic, Protestant, Polish, Irish, A.M.E.—across the city.

Adoptive Son

If I had to castigate modern parents for one besetting sin (though, I hasten to add, I'm glad that's not my job), it would be faulty root supply. At a time when a strict and tight-knit code of personal, political, and religious ethics is no longer automatically provided to—indeed, foisted on—children by their parents, it is left largely to a sense of place to furnish the young with roots. Yet, while American communities, the suburbs in particular, are becoming more homogeneous than ever before, the average American family moves more frequently than ever before; in those suburbs, I've read, one out of three families moves in any given year.

Thus the poor, bewildered children must see their lengthening childhood as a series of shots of turning moving-van wheels superimposed on a montage of nearly identical Golf Club Drives and Autumn Lanes, in the manner of old movies. There is no rock and hard place for the imagination to be caught between, no snag of difference or distinction on which to impale the growing mind. Kids must surely be growing up in a vast, anonymous American back yard, with a fuming barbecue on one side and a gently sloshing, chlorine-smelling swimming pool on the other.

I avoided all this—and I may be a member of the last generation to have done so—by the simple expedient of being sent to college in a city that, unlike my birthplace, possessed a soul and conscience and modus operandi that were totally its own. I came from Detroit, a town progressively engulfed in the consequences of its own affluent aggrandizement even when I lived there: to create a ring of superior suburbs, the core city was being melted down into a factory-dotted slum. My parents, who were constitutionally opposed to the idea of property, fearing its potential stranglehold on their freedom, never owned a house while we lived there. Instead, they rented run-down but commodious buildings which could house both my father's business and our living quarters. This neatly avoided the problem of living in the suburbs and at the same time put me in more than nodding touch with the heart of a city which, though in many ways typical of its midwestern counterparts, still had the vestiges of individuality about it, unlike its surrounding Grosse Pointes and Bloomfield Hills.

Still, I lacked more than the merest trace of a sense of belonging until, in 1944, I made the trip east to Boston. Actually, I made it twice; reversing the order in which history is supposed to repeat itself, the first visit was farce, the second, drama. Sometime in August of that year, I completed a bicycle trip across Canada with an unexpected train ride. Somewhere far up Route 201 in northern Maine—I think between two hamlets called Caratunk and The Forks—I was so careless as to let my canteen fall into the back wheel of my bike, bending enough spokes so that it was rendered instantly unridable. No spare wheels—especially in that last year of the war, especially in that depopulated land—being available, I was forced to ride a series of mail cars, rattling old woody station wagons driven by female postpersons, down to the railhead, Waterville. There I took a Boston & Maine local for Boston. When I arrived, and after I had transferred my bike and traps from North Station to South and learned that I had some six hours to wait for a Detroit train, I found myself on the town—on, in fact, the joyous Tenderloin of the old Boston, where the fleet was perpetually in and blue battalions of sailors laid siege to the complaisant bars, burlesques, and hotels of Washington Street and Scollay Square.

Though I was a civilian, and a sheltered private-school boy at that, I entered into the spirit of the occasion. Dressed to kill, or at least to maim, in a mock-Shetland jacket of wartime purple tweed (with monster checks) and a pair of green duck pants, I drifted into the Half-Dollar Bar, where I met a sailor, and where we, in turn, picked up two willing Waves. With my age—sixteen —apparently sufficiently camouflaged by my height—six-four—I was accepted by the group, and, after a couple more beers (my first), we headed for, of all things, a movie. Sitting in the balcony of a rococo picture palace of the twenties on Washington Street, I conducted my first awkward efforts at necking while watching a great extravaganza of the period, *Wilson,* with Alexander Knox. When the picture was over, I disentangled myself, literally as well as figuratively, said good-bye, and rode the subway one stop to South Station, where the man in the change booth made a half-hearted (and indignantly rejected) homosexual proposition to me. Soon I was on the westbound train, the quite pleased beneficiary of A Broadening Experience. I knew really nothing about Boston; I did know that I could function there in my own style, whatever that was.

The second visit came in November (colleges opened late in those days because of an accelerated degree program with three terms a year). My train dropped me at Back Bay Station this time; the palsied 1941 Plymouth cab took me to Cambridge through a city the very opposite of the one I had visited in August. It was a somber day, with thin, slate-colored clouds sometimes letting through flat blades of sun; though the grass was still green on the malls and lawns and riverbanks, it was unmistakably the start of winter. The cab flapped through the buttoned-up Back Bay, a precinct of order and legislated peace; up the regulate river on which no boat moved; into the thicket of spires I recognized for Cambridge. I was away; I was, for the first time, home.

The rules of the game in college, in Cambridge, and, by extension, in Boston, supplied the backbone I had been wanting, the body of law I needed to flout or adhere to, the soil for my roots. I was astonished on the one hand by the freedom of my new existence (I could get drunk, cut classes, or see girls if I wanted to), and by my responsibilities on the other (I was expected to win and keep the goodwill of my roommates, to meet the minimum standards of my teachers, and to comport myself so as to avoid utter disgrace). But I was more surprised—and much more moved—by the two great human, or rather ethnic, forces that shaped and fixed the whole city of Boston and its environs. On the one side was the codex of the Yankees, still very much in evidence: a survival of Puritan sobriety and duty, an enforcement of British understatement, a commitment to the plain, the drab, the serviceable, out of which, if watched and watered, the flower of achievement would eventually spring. On the other was the world view of the more recent immigrants, led by the Irish: the idea of the city not as a sacred trust to be conveyed undiminished to the next generation, but as an apple, or oyster, to be gathered and consumed for one's own betterment and pleasure. Unlike the flint-eyed Brahmins, these people were soft-eyed and softhearted; having had nothing, it was easy come, easy go for them; indulging themselves, they found it easy, as the Puritans did not, to indulge and pardon others.

And yet, though there was every likelihood that these two factions should meet with a clash over the eventual ownership of Boston, somehow they did not: though the spirited fight for the control of the city, politically speaking, had ended with the immigrants in secure possession a generation before my arrival, both sides had continued to hold their views undaunted by failure or success. Thus they preserved two cities for my delectation and instruction: the Brahmin Boston of granite trust companies and strait brick town houses, to which, as an outsider, I could not be invited; and the Irish Boston of ramshackle public buildings, public bars, and private houses, in all of which I was at least hypothetically welcome. And in their unwillingness—inability, really—to accept change, to deal with the onset of the present, these factions also managed effectively to exclude the wave of progress and newness and homogeneity which by then was sweeping all before it across the American continent. Boston remained Boston, with its tang of saltwater flats and coffee roasting; though feebler now, it is still itself today.

Two people came to symbolize these two sides of Boston, these two cities, for me. One was an early roommate of mine, a tall, courtly, withdrawn youth who was so steeped in the Brahmin tradition that he sometimes seemed barely able to function in the real world. His real loves, his paradigms of Yankee achievement, resided in the far mountains of New England, where there were birds to watch, not as an amateur but as an ornithologist, and mountains to scale, not as a weekend camper but as an engineer of cirques and cols and chimneys. Minot and I did not converse to speak of, pun intended; but he fascinated me (as much as, I am sure, my fecklessness fascinated him) for his otherwhereness, for the elusive whereabouts of his whole, feeling heart. It was—it had to be—in the highlands, where the hermit thrush sings to its kind, Minot included.

My other exemplar was Mrs. Shannon, my maid, or biddie, as maids were unkindly called by the young college gentlemen of those days. Mrs. Shannon was as patient and thoughtful as she was determined to best the disorder of my rooms; on cold, dank mornings when the factory sirens would wake me from God knows what drunken sleep, she would soothe me with an invariably cheerful word; though I was given to understand, with frequent sighs, that her husband, Francis, was an invalid, an alcoholic, a lazy layabout, or worse, this really saintly woman continued to cherish her good fortune in being able to support him with the sweat of her pale brow. To me she was helpful, sensible, motherly, always forgiving: a kind of foster mother in my strange home, and one who never demanded the things my real mother did.

Though I traveled far, if not always fast, in the years that followed, I never saw any reason to reconsider my vision of Boston as bound up in those two people. In college, I moved through rooms as full of the dry detritus of Anglo-Saxon learning—and as shabbily comfortable—as an Oxford tutor's study; thrown out of college to rusticate, I fell gratefully into the bosom of that Irish Boston where I was helped up, placed on the city payroll, and sent to do a minute job of work (and earn a minuscule day's pay) among the elective and appointive officials, their names sounding like the refrain to an Irish reel, who made the city move on its stately, if corrupted, way. So the movements alternated: I returned to college, to that super-preppie world of masters, deans, and scholars; after a short, unhappy stint in New

York, I came back to Boston, where I joined the first senatorial campaign of John F. Kennedy and rejoined the Joycean stream of life prefigured by pious Mrs. Shannon.

Since then, I've hung around here, always adoptive, never adopted, always an outsider, never a member of either community. But always, also, rewarded by these two worlds that won't quite have me, perhaps the ideal position for a writer to be in. And, oh, yes, of course I've felt accepted in some ways: the local papers have noticed my writings and doings, I've met and gotten to know a number of *echt* Bostonians of both persuasions, and there have even been times when I've felt—and felt proud to feel—that this was my own, my native (in every sense but literally born-in) city.

It takes thousands of meetings, partings, exchanges, and walks across the same uneven bricks to foment a sense of belonging of this kind. Though I can never belong like a Minot or a Shannon, I can kid myself quite easily into thinking this place home. And in its willful stubbornness to be itself, to resist forever the temptation, the desire, the command of the society to be like someplace else, this is a good city—unlike most other cities—in which to strike down roots, even quasi-imaginary ones, into the resistant, rocky soil. Or so I think, some thirty years after becoming a mock-Bostonian.

A Day in the City, 1970

Up at ten after long night's talk with New Canaan host and hostess. Cutting up old touches (con man's argot, that). Shower. Shave. Dress. November morn. Rime of frost on still-green grass outside. Eat big breakfast fixed by host. Smoke, talk. Who's for New York? Everybody.

Pile into host's huge Plymouth station wagon. Down thumping slabs of Merritt Parkway. Trees in median almost full-grown. Saplings when I was a kid. Road seemed wider then. Down twisting Hutchinson River Parkway, another wonder of the 30s. Lanes hardly one car wide. Still lots of trees in Westchester. Down Thruway to Major Deegan. Crags topped with fantastical high rises, housing projects, pillared institutions. Tangle of Harlem River ramps and bridges at Throgs Neck. Arcs and diagonals of ramps like GM World of Tomorrow at World's Fair, 1939. South Bronx buildings, all brick, tumble down to river's edge. Dale Oldsmobile, Stadium Motel. Down East River Drive. Dynasties of Queens on left, gutted cars in dead-end streets on right. Hospital complex. Low-income housing. Playgrounds; kids with footballs. Windowless shells of tenements in East Hundreds followed by luxury-apartment towers clinging to eastern cliffs of island. Turn off Drive in Fifties.

Across town: double-parkers, women walking poodles, town houses with miraculous cream fronts, boys on delivery trikes, many tiny ethnic restaurants. New buildings still going up in spite of slump; who rents all those square feet of space?

Up Madison. More old buildings here. Fewer stone facings, more brick fronts. Adland upstairs, ads' grist downstairs: clothes, cutlery, cameras, blunt, unsettling. Into the Whitney; an Eakins' show. *William H. Macdowell,* artist's father-in-law. *Mrs. Samuel Murray,* cool and plain. *Mrs. Thomas Eakins,* older, more heroically aware of death. The subjects, poised in the pain and assurance of their Victorian stations, look out at the viewers, mobile, frivolous, anxious, self-concerned, the nineteenth century judging the twentieth.

The last portrait: *Dr. Edward Anthony Spitzka,* 1913. Terrifying. Eyes dark blanks. Cheeks raw gouges. Unfinished, the art historians say, because of Eakins' failing eyesight and waning health. But almost the beginning of a new style, a new statement of life and its consequences.

Down in the elevator. Lunch in the Museum cafeteria. Decent and cheap, especially for New York. A tour of a prefab contemporary house set up in the courtyard. Junk-art furniture. Junk-art art. Cramped Pullman kitchen. Dark, small-windowed bedroom. Sterile white walls. Insult to human dignity.

Into the car; back to East River Drive via 42nd Street. Past the UN, its timeless monolith already dating badly. Past Stuyvesant Town, now middle-aged and sooty. Under the bridges, recoiling from the mass of wrecked cars at the base of the Manhattan, nodding with the pleasure of unchange in the sunlight on the cables of the Brooklyn. Past Park Row, its newspapers long gone, its buildings still the same. Down under Battery Park, up on the West Side Highway, confronted by the absurdly high twin red-and-silver towers of the World Trade Center, still being built. No spires, no masts, no setbacks: only the almost infinite tapering up of parallel lines, ugly, unnerving, and repeated for overemphasis.

We dive into the financial district. Streets of unremembered narrowness; buildings with granite flanks of unremembered size. On Cortlandt Street, a drunken red-haired mulatto woman in a green top and tangerine bellbottoms tacks up the sidewalk, accosts a black man on the corner of Broadway, who turns her down. Streets otherwise empty; Saturday afternoon. Trinity aloof and deserted. No soul on Wall Street the day after a twenty-one-million-share trading day. No one on Pine Street. No one in Fraunces Tavern. Peace.

Up the West Side again, by the scattered ruin of Washington Market, and into the Village. Dense crowds here: the Village of the forties and fifties exploding in quantity, not in kind. More of the same: more chair stores, door stores, junk shops, antique shops, food shops, jewelry stores, clothing stores, off-off theaters, restaurants, bars. More artists, writers, painters, students, hangers-on, neat pretty girls, sloppy pretty girls. More cars. More motorbikes. More trucks. More cop cars. On Sixth below Eighth Street, a solid block of sidewalk hawkers selling leather goods, bomb-shaped candles, hashish pipes, art jewelry, head goods. Most hawkers young, male, skinny, bearded, hillbilly-hatted, in blue jeans. Most customers the same.

We park and walk through Washington Square. Old Village hand—horn-rims, pipe in belt, space shoes—picks us up, points out sights, recommends restaurants. We tell him we're going to Lüchow's. "Tourists! Peasants!" he says, inoffensively, and loses self in crowd. Lüchow's. Glad to see us: No reservation needed. Seated at once in front room. Room half empty, but still early. String band in back room plays waltzes, alternates with German brass band. Reminds me of uniformed German bands tramping through slums, playing for pennies during Depression, when I was a kid. We drink, watch diners drifting in. Odd mixture: few tourists, many aspiring young couples in far-out clothes but far from with it, many middle-aged, middle-class foursomes running to fat and running to mod. Next to us, four older businessmen —needle trades? retailers?—settling down to serious drinking, talk, heavy eating. We order fairly elaborate meals at quite moderate prices. The food comes; it's good and we're hungry. We eat too much, then eat too-rich desserts.

Out on the sidewalk. Academy of Music, where I used to watch real vaudeville twenty years ago. Klein's. On the Square. The Square itself, an American Hyde Park packed with dissident speakers till a few years ago. Now quiet, except for the cars. Not many passersby. Chill air laced with smog. I cough.

Into the car again; up Fourth Avenue, retitled Park Avenue

South but no more gracious for that. Around Gramercy Park, not a hair changed in three decades and quiet as the graves of its old architects. Uptown to Grand Central, a frieze of ill-assorted flashing and unwinking lights. Across 42nd Street again and up the Drive. United Nations Plaza wheels away, followed by Sutton Place and Gracie Mansion, embowered in leafless trees. East Harlem follows. At the northeast tip of the island, I look back. A million lights reflecting green on the low cloud. All of the towers we once looked up to now oppressing us. I face front again, looking backward less and less these days, looking forward to a nightcap in the transient camp of Fairfield County. It's been a long day in the city.

Int'l Jet Set
Hits Watkins Glen

I'm glad I was born soon enough to have seen the American small town, if not at its height, at least in the early days of decline into its present forlorn status as a conduit for cars and people, all headed for some Big City over the horizon. The small town was not always a stultifying trap for bright young people to escape from; in the years before wartime travel ("How're you gonna keep 'em down on the farm/After they've seen Paree?") and the scorn of the Menckens and Sinclair Lewises made the cities a magnet for farm boys and girls, the town of five to twenty thousand was a self-sufficient little city-state of its own.

The main street of those Midwestern towns I remember from the thirties varied little from one place to another: there were always a number of brick Victorian buildings, labeled "Richards Block" or "Denman Block," which housed, downstairs, the chief emporia of the town—the stores which made it a shire town for the surrounding farmlands. Each of these stores was run according to a very exact idea of the rules of its particular game. A hardware store, for instance, had to be densely hung inside with edged tools—scythes, sickles, saws—of all descriptions. It had to smell like oil, like metal, and often like the sacks of fertilizer stacked in the back room. It had to have unstained wood floors, sometimes sprinkled with sawdust, and high cabinets of small drawers containing bolts, screws, nails, and small plumbing accessories. It had to be owned and run by a middle-aged man in a blue apron, assisted by one up-and-coming young man and one part-time boy in his middle teens. It had to sell for cash on the barrelhead, and it did.

The drugstore was a horse of a different color (and odor), but it was circumscribed by equally strict rules. Often, in the thirties, it boasted one of the few neon signs seen on Main Street, usually a blazing vermilion vertical down the side of the building, spelling out "Nyal" or "Rexall" and sometimes the pharmacist's name as well. The window displays, as opposed to the workaday pumps and pipe fittings of the hardware store's unchanging (and fly-specked) windows, were quasi works of art. Loose swags and taut diagonals of pleated crêpe paper in jungle hues formed a nest for the product of the month, often a patent medicine or a new tooth powder; over the crêpe and cardboard burned the store's invariable trademark, a pair of glass urns filled with red and blue colored water and lighted from behind. Inside, the store, except in the poorest towns, was rather splendid: after you recovered, reeling slightly, from the rich, mingled fumes of iodoform, chocolate soda syrup, and the essence of a thousand biologicals, you strode across the marble floor to the marble soda fountain (for a malt or phosphate) or to the pharmacist's counter at the back, behind which were ranged multiple rows of functional apothecary jars. Here you would ask the white-coated (and often rimless-spectacled) druggist for aspirin or Four-Way Cold Tablets or Bromo-Seltzer, or perhaps for paramedical advice, which he was glad to give. (When "a lady" fainted "right on the street" in those days, she was carried directly to the drugstore and ministered to by the druggist, who was often known as "Doc.")

And the grocery store. Tan-and-white striped awnings outside, even in the winter. White Salada Tea lettering on the windows. Inside them, pyramids of cans and sometimes fresh grapefruit in tea-rose tissue wrappers. Inside the store itself, dark oiled softwood floors, a central space surrounded by counters, pickle barrels, cookie and cracker bins. Behind the counters, tall shelves of canned goods, dry groceries, and perhaps a white-enameled butcher's cold case across the back. Baskets of fresh fruits and vegetables (in season). Behind the counters, the grocer, in a striped apron, the butcher, in a bloody white one (and sometimes a surviving straw hat, yellow with age and perspiration), and two or three assistants, rushing like mad to pull the customers' orders down with long, spring-loaded hooks from the top shelves. On the phone—a tall black upright one with a new-fangled dial on the base—the grocer himself or an assistant, taking a telephone order from a nearby customer. Standing by, the boy (in sweater and knickers) who would deliver it. Over all, the smell of coffee grinding and maybe a whiff of fresh celery, too.

Down the street, the other shops and offices that made the town sufficient unto itself and to its trading area: upstairs, behind gold signs in windows, lawyers', doctors', and dentists' offices, as well as Odd Fellows', Elks', and Red Men's halls. Free-standing, in a small grass plot ringed by a black iron fence, the spired and turreted Town Hall, or Town Hall-cum-Courthouse. And, oh yes, the Civil War statue and two gape-throated cannon with their pyramid of cannonballs. Down by the tracks, the depot and freight house, the angular feed-and-grain, topped by a checkered Purina Chow's sign, and the turpentine-scented lumberyard. And then a long double row of neat white houses, often with large gingerbread carriage sheds behind, extending out Main Street to the end of town. Three or four blocks, perhaps.

These towns are by and large gone in 1974, their old stores shut up with dusty windows, or combined, two or three at a time, to make a superette, a W. T. Grant store, or a sub-and-pizza parlor. The business has moved to the big shopping center on the Interstate or to the city over the horizon, and the depopulated old towns drift along toward oblivion, centers of nothing in the middle of nowhere.

But I can think of one exception. Watkins Glen, New York, a nineteenth-century town at the foot of Seneca, the longest of the Finger Lakes, has suddenly been moved through a hundred years of time and plunked down, willy-nilly, in the middle of the seventies. Watkins, as it is called by natives (visitors, for some reason, refer to it as The Glen), enjoyed a modest Victorian fame as a honeymoon resort, largely because of the spectacular gorge on the outskirts of town from which it takes its name. Though it sits in beautiful country—the high, rolling plateaus between the lakes, studded with vineyards and commanding fine views of the lakes themselves—it is a pawky, homely town. Most of the buildings on the main street (which is also New York State Route 414, connecting Geneva to the north with Elmira to the south) were built between 1850 and 1890; they are unambitious piles of brick two stories high, and they still—even unto the 1970s—house such small-town throwbacks as an old-time soda parlor (complete with a tall sign picked out in individual electric bulbs), a storefront bakery, a yellow-clapboard Red Men's Hall, and a tiny Dodge dealership crammed into one small store, not to mention an equally tiny dime store and an old-fashioned grocery across the street from the ancient (but thriving) Hotel Jefferson.

What happened to give Watkins Glen a new lease on its old life was neither suburbanization (there is no large city near enough) nor the location of a new plant in the town, but the location of a major auto race on a course laid out on the plateau above the town. In 1948, the first so-called Watkins Glen Grand Prix—a sports-car race featuring a motley bunch of hybrid cars—was run on a course which included the town's main street. After an accident in which a spectator was killed in 1952, the event was moved to an impromptu course on back roads west of town. Later, as The Glen became an important annual event in the Sports Car Club of America's calendar, the course was redesigned and made both faster and safer. By the early sixties, earnest lobbying by the local organizers—and a lack of other suitable facilities—made Watkins Glen the venue for the Grand Prix of the United States, the most important auto race, except for Indy, run in this country. At that point, all hell broke loose. Attracted by substantial purses, the heroes of Europe's Formula One racing circus, accompanied by team managers, mechanics, wives, mistresses, and glamorous Riviera groupies, made en masse for Watkins Glen the first week in October every year. Correspondingly, the unheard-of opportunity to see stars like Graham Hill, Jim Clark, Stirling Moss, and Dan Gurney racing Lotuses, BRM's, Ferraris, and Porsches right in their own back yard brought tens of thousands of Canadian and American enthusiasts streaming into Watkins Glen in sports cars, on motorcycles with blanket rolls on the pillion, in hearses, in trailers, in campers of all shapes and sizes.

A city of a million would have been stymied—and paralyzed —by such an onslaught. Watkins Glen, however, is apparently made of sterner stuff. The town fathers, organized in efficient committees, parceled out the town's better sleeping spaces in hotels and motels to the various racing teams and the horde of journalists; mere spectators were also helped to find rooms in private houses, or, if they preferred, allowed to camp out up at the course. Somehow, everybody got fed and bedded down; on race day, a large and happy crowd watched a well-run event, and everybody drifted home again without riot or rebellion, leaving the burghers of Watkins some million dollars richer for their pains.

Toward the end of the sixties, when the purse for the Grand Prix had jumped to six figures, along with the crowds, there was a short outburst of bottle-breaking by some youths on the main street; this was soon quelled by the local police and sheriff's deputies, and everything went on as scheduled. There was some rowdiness up at the track, too: in a sea of camping kids estimated at over 100,000, there were bound to be a few fistfights, bad trips, and general disturbances. But again, the cheerful cops coped, and nothing got badly out of hand. I haven't been back for the last couple of years, but I hear that the crowds have continued to grow as well as the take. I intend to return— gasoline permitting—because there is nothing remotely like The Glen in race week.

After you get off the New York State Thruway in Geneva, you follow a long, straight road down along the lakeside. When you arrive within the precincts of Watkins Glen, you begin to notice that both lines of traffic are made up of sports cars. In the town itself, the main street is as serene and aloof as ever— but the noise of unmuffled exhausts is slightly deafening. If you stop into Paradiso's restaurant for hot cakes and coffee (a specialty), you hear the chatter of scores of race fans, speculating on the outcome of this year's race. If you check into the Hotel Jefferson (known familiarly to its regulars as The Jeff), you enjoy a surprisingly good meal (roast beef carved to order) and listen to the English, Australian, Argentinian, and Italian nasalities of drivers, girlfriends, and mechanics as they rehash the triumphs and disasters of that day's practice session. Out on the street, you see Stirling Moss, a regular visitor though no longer an active driver, lost in conversation with a spectacular English girl.

The international jet set has indeed hit Watkins Glen. And Watkins Glen, being York State, shrewd, and sensible, has remained exactly what it was: a slightly forlorn American small town. But quite a rich one now.

The Old Farmer's
Almanac, 1872

The homely publications of a hundred years ago have a message for us. The *Official Railway Guide* of June, 1868, for example, tells me the disheartening news that my regular twenty-seven-mile commute took ten minutes less one hundred and four years ago than it does today. And the 1872 *Old Farmer's Almanac,* which I picked up in a New Hampshire secondhand store some years ago, bears even odder tidings.

If you consult the *Almanac* today, you know that behind its familiar yellow cover is a thick pack of oddments—snippets of astrology, weather prognostications, old rhymes and jokes, a spate of small-space ads for trusses, roach-killer, and fish lures, and on pages that deal with the months of the year ahead, a series of nostalgic, neatly written "Farmer's Calendars."

Things were different in 1872. The *Almanac* was thin—a mere fifty-two pages—and the only ads inside its peach covers (the original yellow was dropped for a time in the middle of the nineteenth century) touted Hallet & Davis pianos (endorsed by "F. Liszt, the First Pianist in the World"), Webb & Twombly's Premium Chocolates (which "have taken the highest award at every Fair in which they have been exhibited"), Wheeler & Wilson's Sewing Machines, Worcester's Quarto Dictionary (with a testimonial from Edward Everett), and the wares of Henry C. Sawyer, whose Waltham Book Store also sold stationery, wall-paper, silverplate, luggage, desks, Bibles, brushes, combs, perfumery, soap, pocket knives and scissors, fans for ladies, umbrellas, picture frames, and, of course, the *Almanac*.

But it is the editorial matter of the old *Almanac* that startles the modern reader. Beginning soberly with a table of Meetings of Friends in New England and a list of salaries of executive officers of the United States ("Ulysses S. Grant, Ill., Pres., $25,000; Hamilton Fish, N.Y., Sec. State, $8,000"), it goes on through a page of astronomical data and rosters of New England colleges and registers in bankruptcy to an early crescendo: the spreads for the months of the year. Each is laid out much as it is today: a table of astronomical calculations on the left, a rather sketchy forecast and the "Farmer's Calendar" on the right. But these "Farmer's Calendars" are nothing like the rather bland, pleasant little essays of today. Each of them preaches and rails at the farmer to keep a better farm and live a better life; the Protestant ethic rears its minatory head in January and harangues the reader through the waxing and the waning year. The nameless scourge of slothful husbandmen begins the cycle, after a terse New Year's greeting, well into his evangelical stride: "Make up your mind therefore to be better and to do better, to aim higher and to have nobler ends in view. . . . Let us sit down by the crackling fire and lay out plans for the year. I suppose you have done the chores, of course, fed the cattle and the pigs, and cleaned up the barn. No use to sit down till the chores are done. . . ." In February, he has progressed a step further in his righteous indignation at his captive parishioners; now he begins by berating them: "Snug up about the barn this winter. Shut the door and the windows. Cold won't make cattle tough. . . . I wouldn't give a fig for a man who can't turn his mind to little things. All your luck in farming hangs on the chores at this season."

In March, he is quick to turn on the hapless, snowbound farmer who grouses about the weather. "No use to fret about the storm and the snow. Keep your temper is a good rule on the farm. This way of finding fault with heaven and earth won't do. . . . It's a pity you don't raise more roots. Hadn't you better look about for a spot to put in an acre of mangolds and another of swedes?"

The Old Farmer takes the offensive early and keeps the pressure up; the shiftless reader won't get a breather, even in springtime: "All plant life is on the spring now, and animal life too, as to that matter. And so you'd better spring around, John, if you want to see your barn well filled in the fall. Yoke up and go at it with your fine and sprightly team. . . . The fact is, there is no end to the work this month, and no time to lose in standing around or leaning over the wall with a gossiping neighbor." And: "It is of no use to find fault with work. We ought to thank our stars that we are able to work."

As the summer ends, the taskmaster's lips are thinner than ever: "Now that the dog star rages, why don't you give the dog a bullet [presumably a pill of dog-days medicine], the boy a hoe, the girl the knitting needles. No work, no eating, is the rule, you know. Can't afford to keep drones on the farm." In September, to keep the enervated farmer on the qui vive, the *Almanac* lays out an impressive list of chores, including removing stones from fields to be tilled. "I hope you got out those rocks. . . . It is a shiftless way to lay down a lot with the bushes growing along the walls. Why don't you dig them out, and clean up the lot?" In October, he notes, with relish, that "there is enough to do to keep us on the jog all this month;" in November, after a peremptory reference to Thanksgiving, he's off again about stalling the cattle every night, fall sowing and plowing, and trimming the grapevines. Even in December—notably, there's no mention of Christmas—he's harping about the grapevines again, as well as pruning the fruit trees, making an inventory of stock and tools on the farm ("the sooner you set about it, the better you will be off"), and generally preparing for the worst: "Spruce up and get ready for a hard winter."

The rest of the *Almanac* is similarly grim; it dispels a number of common notions among farmers about cabbage, kitchen gardens, grass for horses, and food for stock, calls attention to the adulteration of commercial fertilizers, cautions the reader about transplanting evergreens ("it is a mistake to suppose that the same rules apply to evergreens as to deciduous trees"), and sagely discusses the pitfalls of stock-breeding farms. Then a little light relief: three pages of poetry, anecdotes, and puzzles, most of them not so light, at that. One poem, a tearjerker, was "found under the pillow of a soldier who died in a hospital near Port Royal, South Carolina." "Selections" include Scott's "O, what a tangled web we weave/When first we practise to deceive;" the jokes include this epitaph: "I was well—wished to be better—read medical books—took medicine—and died."

The 1872 *Almanac* ends there, with the exception of a few population tables (according to the census of 1870, there were 38,555,983 people in the United States, of whom 942,292 lived in New York City and 4,382,759 in New York State; California could boast a mere 560,247), weather tables, tide tables, and post office regulations (first-class letters, 3 cents per half ounce). It ends with a sort of a whimper and a curious feeling of oppression in the reader, as if he had just been through that exhausting year with the poor, bone-weary farmer. It ends, finally, with a question forming in the modern reader's mind: Were the good old days that bad? In an age when we are daily and sorely tried by all sorts of mind-boggling disasters and injustices, when we daily repair to the past for reassurance and refreshment, is it possible that we are really better off than our forebears, and that our carefully cultivated nostalgia is founded on a mirage? On the evidence of the 1872 *Almanac,* that could well be. The stern preachments of the anonymous author of the "Farmer's Calendar" are not mere mouthings; it seems clear that the struggling farmer of a century ago really needed these appeals to his pride and his sense of duty in order to get on with the back-breaking, dawn-to-dusk job of cultivating his garden. It was a savage life of imponderables—blizzards, floods, crop failures, insect plagues, human and animal diseases for which there were no known cures—and only the most bitterly Calvinistic outlook could prepare one to compete in what had, eventually, to be a losing race. There was no social security in those days, no government price supports, no anesthesia, and above all no leisure. The farmer had literally nothing to look forward to except the fruits of a job well done and another day, week, month, and year of unremitting toil to keep ahead of a hostile nature.

To us, seated in our warm houses on our choreless days off from work, knitted to all our friends by the telephone, possessed of cars to take us across the county or across the country as the whim strikes us, disposing of a hundred diversions to beguile our leisure, protected by effective medical care (for those, at least, who can afford it), assured of a cash competence in our retirement, this stark world of a hundred years ago is hard indeed to believe in—which is one of the reasons why we believe in a gilded age when all the world was young, when cares were few, when love was true, when, over the river and through the woods, grandmother's house was filled with goodwill, provender, and jollity. What a shame the truth was otherwise.

Going Home, 1945

Home is so sad. It stays as it was left . . .
—PHILIP LARKIN

I. GETTING THERE

1. NIGHT

"En route aboard the Twentieth Century
Limited," says the club-car notepaper.
With a glad cry, I take a seat and write
Six crested notes to six deserving friends
Who need a lesson in my eminence,
Or on whose female persons I have vain
Designs. Speaking of female persons, who
Is that old-fashioned girl three seats away,
With maraschino-cherry lips and teeth
As white as lemon pith, with ice-blue eyes
And amber Bourbon hair? Must be Bryn Mawr.
Above my station, which is G.C.T.,
And, at the other end, Fort Street. I cock
An innocent index at the bar waiter,
And call, in a bass tenor, for a Scotch
And branch water. (I hope that branch water
Is carried on crack trains. I think of it
In pear-shaped bottles, like Perrier.) The black
White-coated waiter makes ironically
Over my disarray. "Mix, sir?" "Uh-huh,"

I grunt. Branch water gets no rise,
Not even one eyelid bat, from Bryn Mawr.
I give up and tack back to my roomette,
Where Webster waits to take me by the throat
And threaten me to sleep. "Or with his nails
He'll dig them up again." Amen. I doze,
Until, in the marshalling yards of Buffalo,
The nails of couplings dig me up again.
Up the trick curtain; under it, the moon
Face of the station clock beams a huge One
Into my dilatory pupil. Sleep
Returns for his lost westbound passenger
And hustles him aboard. They couple up
Another Hudson 4-6-4 and I awake
Again. The clock says two. We're off. Good night.

2. DAWN

Morning is not a matter of whiskbroom
Paradiddles on sack-suit shoulders; not
A throb of chocolate voices in the men's
Washroom; not an aubade of good cigars
Smoking on sink rims while their masters shave
In undershirts, pending suspenders; not
Steam rising from the ranks of sinks where jokes
Go off so limply at this hour — "Mister,
Your sign fell down!" (Laughter) — and one man drinks
Rye by himself in a toilet stall; morning is not
That any more at all, but a shave alone
In my roomette and a walk to the dining car,
And breakfast in silence on the Century.

3. NOON

Nous sommes arrivés. The old Lafayette
Coach which my dad affects awaits without,
While my dim mother pins me in a grip
Of flesh and blood. Just two semesters stand

Between me and these twin authorities,
The moon and sun, ruling me night and day
In opposition and conjunction. Now
I stoop to inspect their tiny orrery,
Worked by a crank from higher up, a god
From the Machine-Design Department. We
Climb in the fatal car and head for home
Through widened streets lined with diminished shops,
Patrolled by shrivelled people, shrunken kids,
And miniature dogs. Waste paper blows
For miles along the thoroughfares toward
The straightedge of the horizon, where the world,
Seeing me entering my father's house,
Awaits my resurrection in the fall.

II. AT HOME

1. THE ROOM

The next of kin is marched into a dark,
North-oriented room where trumpet vines
And overhanging eaves restrain the light,
There to confront the body of his past:
A matter of identity. Look, those
Are spectacles that were his eyes. That book
Was his vocabulary. That wall map
(Out of the *Geographic*) was his world.
That copy of "Jane's Fighting Ships" was all
His insular defense. Those model planes—
Stormovik, Stuka, ME-109—
Were his air arm, which tirelessly traversed
The compass rose around its dusty strings.
Who was this recent tenant of my room?
Intelligence demands an answer. "Why,
I never saw the boy before in my life."

2. THE FOLKS

My father casts a stone whose ripples ride
Almost to my unhearing aid, the ear.
My answering fire likewise falls short. Between
Us lies no-generation's land, a waste
Of time. Barbed wire and trenches separate
The conscript class of 1895
From that of 1928. I see
My father, in a tall examination room
Gaslit by fishtail burners, demonstrate
The differential calculus; he sees
Me boozing with low types in Central Square
And touching tasty women on the quick.
(Not such a bad idea, Dad, after all.)
Had he his way, his little mathemat
Would be devouring sums and public praise
Like any Univac; and had I mine,
My dad and I would be out on the town,
Like as a brother act in our black ties,
Clubbable, bibulous, sly, debonair.
Fat chance of that. Across the timing gap
No blue spark fires. We talk in circles which
Are not contiguous. It is too bad
Our purposes for others founder on
Their purposes for us. Now, take my dad.

3. THE DATE

Hat holds me at an angle to survey
My metamorphosis from local boy
To Eastern College Man. Light years away,
Her once and future beaux from Tech and State
Back, blinded, into corners of the room,
Bedazzled by my meteoric rise.
All night, respectfully, their voices flat
As the land's lie, they ask me what it's like
Back there, incredulously fingering
My J. Press jacket, softly crying "Cool!"

Like pigeons. And the girls! Such nattering—
Which even bird conventions cannot touch—
Alarms my keeper, Hat, to vigilance
Over her showpiece, lest I taste too much
Of all I'm offered. But it doesn't matter;
The *pièce re résistance* is Harriet later.

4. THE CHUM

It's Harvard vs. Williams at the D.-
A.C. Out of my corner armchair, I
Dance nimbly to clasp hands with Richie B.
Mackenzie, my old challenger. Now he,
The shorter fighter, boards his bicycle,
And pedals up to me. Right cross; we shake,
Break clean. On to the greater battle, where
The muffled musketry of cutlery
Rattles a rapid fire above the dull
Trench-mortar thuds of crockery. "A dry
One with a twist." "Bourbon and branch water."
"Blue points." "Cracked crab." "The grayling amandine."
"Filet mignon. Pommes allumettes." "Roquefort."
"Blue cheese." "Rosé?" "Rosé." "There's no place like—"
"Cambridge. Boy, what a wild—" "Woman I met
At Bennington." "I'll tell the world they put
Out. Why—" "They don't pass out, I'll never know."
"Two great big townies—" "Landed on their ear
Outside the bar. From Rensselaer." "No kid?"
"I swear." "Rum cake." "Profiteroles."
"Cointreau." "Martell." "Gentlemen's grades. Three 'C's,
A 'D'." "Still worse—two 'D's. On pro." "No kid?"
"I'll pay." "Let me." "I'll pay." "Let me." "O.K."
The winner and still champion is me.

5. THE TOWN

In this al fresco gallery of Sheelers—
Replete with stacks and tipples, ramps and hoppers,

Vents, derricks, ducts, louvers, and intercoolers—
I wander lonely as a cloud. Here is the beauty
Of this ridiculous, gas-smelling city.
Not those gilt towers stuck up so proudly
To spell a skyline, not those too loudly
Dulcet and unobtrusively huge houses
Dotting the northern suburbs. No, the heart
Of it is where its masters' love is:
In the cold-rolling mills, annealing rooms,
Pickling and plating vats, blast furnaces,
Drop-forging shops, final-assembly lines:
Wherever angular, ideal machines,
Formed seamlessly of unalloyed desire,
Strike worthless stereotypes out of the fire.

6. THE ROOM, 8/31

Lieutenant Kije, for the twentieth time
On record, tramps the dogged August night
In glacé top boots, jangling all his high
Orders of Irony and Satire. My
Suffering mother passes through the wall
A muffled *cri de coeur:* "Turn that thing down,"
To which I courteously defer. The summer stands
Suspended in its bowl, and also runs
At a great rate down the drain somehow, dragging
Me into fall. There still remain these nights
Of close restraint in heat, a camisole
Of dampness wired for the amazingly
Loud sound of streetcars roller-skating; for
The shocking sight of their electric-blue
Stars overhead; for their galvanic smell
Of ozone; and the unforgettable scent
Of air-conditioned drugstores, where the pure
Acid of citrus cuts across the fat
Riches of chocolate, subjugates perfume
(Evening in Paris), soap, iodoform.
Back in my heated room with the night game

And Nine Elizabethan Dramatists,
I chill myself with Webster. In the twelfth,
August strikes out and thunders to the showers.

III. AWAY

1. PACKING

Admit the sophomore's impediments
In the Caesarean sense: the stuff I lug
Wisely and foolishly out of the breach
In mother's privet hedge, in father's picket fence.
Item: one pair of officer's pink pants
Left over from R.O.T.C.; one tam
Worn by the Pictou Highlanders and me;
One six-foot Princeton scarf; one pair sweatpants;
Two white bucks aged to gray; one copy each
of "Dubliners," "Wind in the Willows," "Kim,"
"Tropic of Cancer," "House at Pooh Corner," "Teen-
Age Etiquette," "Ulysses," "Leaves of Grass,"
"A Child's Garden of Verses," "Four Quartets,"
"Tarr," "Peter Rabbit," "Lady Chatterley;"
One Remington Electric Shaver; six
Giant Almond Hershey Bars; one roll of Tums;
One jar of Mum; one tube of Pepsodent;
One guest bar of Camay; two Trojans; three
Packs of Balkan Sobranie cigarettes;
A secret diary (three entries), and
A tangled mass too numerous to list.
I genuflect on the stuffed leatherette
Until the straining snap locks creak and catch;
Then I pick up my bags, one in each hand,
And take the first step to Jerusalem,
New England's green and pleasant land.

2. PARTING

"Caoutchouc," I comment, flexing my big feet
In their new gum-boots. "Are you catching cold?"
Mother demands. "Uh, no. Just practicing
A new word." "Good. Do you have everything?"
"Uh, yes. Umbrella, earmuffs, undershirts—"
"The marmalade!" "Oh, hell!" "Your grandmother
Will just be sick. She got it from Dundee."
"Ship it." "It's glass. I can't." "Here comes the train.
Son, have a good year," my poor father says.
His eyes belie his smile. But he's a good,
Though steady, loser. Now, fraternally,
He takes my hand in the firm, funny grip
Of the Order of Fathers and Sons. My mother plants
A moist and plosive kiss across my ear,
Mumbles, and sheds a shiny patent tear.

3. STARTING

Gathering way, we step out of the station
Gingerly, silver showing at the forefoot
Of the long engine, and a curl of cream
Whipped at her whistle. How superior
It is to pass clean through the roots of each
Bystander's real life and leave the city
In the lurch like a wife. My guilt is packed
In with my sweatshirts in the baggage car;
I travel light. Brick tenements sprint by,
All up to here with melodrama, kids,
Mice, misery. I blink and miss a block,
Yawn and omit a mile. Now the Toltec
Pyramids of plants appear and pivot by.
Soon rolling mills give way to fields of rye.
It's reading period: "Wish me good speed;
For I am going into a wilderness."
The sun goes west; the sky goes black; it is
Full tide 'tween night and day. Just in the nick,

Bosola, in a mist, I know not how,
Receives his mortal wound at cocktail time.
I home in on the club car, straightening
The rucked-up jacket I've been reading in,
And take a seat with *Fortune* on my knee.
The waiter fetches Scotch and branch water.
Say, who's that Highland tycoon's fetching daughter
In a dress-Stewart skirt, with Shetland hair,
Eyes like a loch, breasts like a ben? She's mine,
Assuming I can take a dare. With luck,
From now until tomorrow is today,
From here over the hills and far away,
We'll kiss and play and possibly make free,
En route aboard the Twentieth Century.

ii
The Legacy of Literature or Where I Belong

Starting a Magazine

"Let's start a magazine," wrote e. e. cummings, ironically, for the first issue of *Contact* in 1932:

"let's start a magazine

to hell with literature
we want something redblooded

lousy with pure
reeking with stark
and fearlessly obscene

but really clean
get what I mean
let's not spoil it
let's make it serious

something authentic and delirious
you know something genuine like a mark
in a toilet

graced with guts and gutted
with grace"

squeeze your nuts and open your face

"Let's start a magazine," said my friend Albert Cook to me and a gaggle of other feckless undergraduates in a messy room at

Harvard in the summer of 1947. (Come to think of it, I wasn't an undergraduate at the time; I had been thrown out of college to make way for returning veterans the summer before, and I would not be readmitted until the spring of 1948.) Among those present at the *accouchement,* besides Cook, were Jonathan Peale Bishop, Thomas McFarland, Aaron Rosen and Stanley Moss.

Our ostensible (and only avowed) reason for enlisting our lives, our fortunes, and our sacred honor in a new publishing venture was, as the preface to the first issue stated, to "fight tooth and nail the prevailing tendency among advance-guard quarterlies to become journals of current intellectual fashion," to be "predominantly a creative magazine." Our real reasons were, of course, that we wanted to see our own names in print, that we had time on our hands, and that we had discovered an angel (known, in the abstruse technical jargon of the publishing trade, as "a sucker") who would put up the necessary cash. We were also rather sneakily motivated by the local, but relatively dazzling, success of *Wake,* a postwar Cambridge literary magazine whose editors, being of another clique, would not publish our contributions. *Wake's* biggest hit had been an issue devoted almost exclusively to Cummings; we took grumpy note of this in our preface by proclaiming that "we will never publish a perfunctory article because its subject has wide current appeal. Nor will we collect testimonials, biographical fragments, and pictures of a single author in order to produce a lucrative collector's item."

"Never," in little-magazine publishing, is a highly relative term, like "lifetime guarantee" in advertising, and in our case "never" lasted for exactly two issues, after which our angel and our ambitions simultaneously died. *Halcyon,* the name we had chosen because, according to us, it suggested "flight—toward perception, not from life; freedom from fashion and bickering; the calm of austere critical standards; a leaning toward the classic and symbolic in art," was, of course, fun while it lasted. It was, for one thing, our ticket of admission to the Grand Theater of Postwar Literary Operations, that Comédie Américaine that Auden had declined and snubbed so lovingly in "Under Which Lyre," the 1946 Phi Beta Kappa poem at Harvard:

Lone scholars, sniping from the walls
Of learned periodicals,
  Our facts defend,
Our intellectual marines,
Landing in little magazines
  Capture a trend.

The founding of *Halcyon* enabled us to be—and not just think ourselves—active participants in the battle Auden so accurately described: the conflict, then just beginning, between the Apollonians, dull academics, administrators, order-makers, exegetes, and the Hermetics, disorderly, idiosyncratic free creative spirits. We were, of course, in Hermes' army (no two uniforms alike), and we took second place to nobody in our broad and frequent snook-cocking at Apollo's fat Establishment. As we might not have acknowledged quite so quickly, we were also second to none in our haste to correspond and hobnob with our betters. While we were enjoined by our manifesto from publishing an Eliot issue or a Stevens issue, for example, there was nothing to prevent us from swamping the great and near-great with scores of letters beseeching them for samples of their work, and that's exactly what we did.

To our delight, those buttonholed, though presumably weary of being panhandled by literary street urchins, kicked through graciously, most of them, with poems and stories. As a result, our first issue, dated Winter, 1948, carried contributions by Cummings (take that, *Wake!*), Howard Nemerov, Richmond Lattimore, Marya Zaturenska, Oscar Williams, and Harry Brown, and our second added Stevens (two really first-rate poems), William Abrahams, and the painter Morris Graves to the list.

It was great fun getting actual letters addressed to us from these people (I still have a rightfully exasperated note from Cummings, asking for author's proofs), but the headiest part—roughly equivalent to chugalugging a toothbrush glassful of vodka neat—was seeing our names cheek by jowl with theirs on the contents page. Sandwiched securely between James Merrill and Marya Zaturenska and set in the same size type as they, I was a happy man. And that was what it was really all about, publishing a little magazine: the sense of being part of a tradition, of carrying forward the serious and noble work of *The Exile, Hound & Horn, transition, The Double Dealer,* of becoming by fiat, by our own act of linking our names in print with theirs, the legitimate heirs of Cummings and Eliot and Stevens and Pound.

That was the major statement, the big orchestral motive of our ambitions. But there was an almost equally pleasant minor theme in the dash and ease of the literary life. We were no longer rather grubby college boys beset by poverty, pimples, poor grades, and uncomplaisant girls; at a stroke of the press, so to speak, we became editors, creators, critics, *littérateurs*. We were of the company, instantly, of Allen Tate and Edmund Wilson; we were, inevitably, to be the Audens and Isherwoods of our generation, twenty years on. Every cup of cheap Chianti we drank was consecrated, every word we spoke was a fragment of oral autobiography, every halting word we wrote was secular writ. We were painting our self-portraits as future literary figures, and it was a full-time job.

For all the hours of ample and idle talk, for all the posturing and play-acting, though, there was something of value in *Halcyon* for each of us. We learned a lot about our limitations as writers, editors, and people (speaking for myself, I discovered that I was an unformed writer, an incredibly disorganized editor, and a potentially dishonorable person, since I misappropriated part of the magazine's remaining funds in a fit of fiscal desperation after *Halcyon* ceased publishing and suffered excruciating pangs of guilt for months afterward), but we also found there was at least a chance that we might be real writers and editors under all that makeup, that there might be a real literary face, quite different from the one we had imagined, beneath the mask. In short, it was, after all, a broadening and salutary experience, and I commend it without reservation to those beardless (or, rather, bearded) young who even now sit around littered college rooms smoking joints, drinking California red, and saying to each other, with a wild surmise, "Let's start a magazine."

Confessions of a
Second-Class Citizen

I hate to admit it, but I'm one of a small, elect group of men and women in this country—maybe there are a thousand of us, all told—who are bound for oblivion on a one-way, nonstop ticket. Our crime against the state, or status quo, is that all of us have written one or more works of "serious" verse or fiction—that is, books that fall outside the pale of popularization by the mass media. Such books, no matter how objectively meritorious, are a positive offense to The Way Things Are; incapable of fitting into any of the usual pigeonholes of sensation or controversiality, they are rejected by the machine and cast into the outer darkness of unspeakableness, where, from the instant of publication, they are never spoken of again. Well, hardly ever.

A case in point, intended not to air a personal grievance but to exemplify what little magazines used to call "the writer's situation:" my third book of verse was published. It got uniformly excellent reviews—from daily newspapers in Buffalo, N.Y., Boston, Mass., Richmond, Va., Long Beach, Calif., and as many as two other places. It was completely ignored by all the "important" review media, from *Publishers Weekly* to the *New York Times* (daily *and* Sunday) and the *New York Review of Books* (which, to the best of my knowledge, reviewed fewer than a score of new books of American verse, and those mostly by supremely well-established writers, during all of 1971). In spite of this, my book managed to sell a couple of thousand copies, a figure which is considered pretty good for a book of verse, thanks to my publisher's generosity in making both hard- and soft-cover editions available simultaneously. Still, this total is fairly pathetic when compared with the 10,000-copy sale of the average topical nonfiction title.

What goes on here? First, there are undoubtedly a lot of good new poets and novelists around; an old friend of mine, the former head of the English department at Buffalo, recently remarked that there are more good poets in this country today than at any previous time and place in history, and I'm sure this valid observation applies to novelists as well, not to mention the clever, growing band of young short-story writers. Second, and even more curious, there really is an audience for new poetry and fiction out there—an audience, I'd guess, that is larger than anybody has yet suspected. On college campuses there must be, at a conservative estimate, half a million students with a serious appetite for serious literature by unknown but promising poets and novelists. Among recent graduates and faculty members—people in their twenties and early thirties—there must be at least another half million. Say a million prospects, all told. Less than one half of one percent of the U.S. population, but still a formidable market. Why aren't the publishers and the book reviewers reaching them with news about new talent?

For several reasons. Though the publishers are reasonably willing to publish and take losses on new work—the ancient code of honor of their half-art, half-business compels the better houses to print a certain amount of literature beside the best sellers as a form of conscience money—the age-old customs of the trade have effectively stopped them from promoting it. Inasmuch as first novels and books of verse are considered "prestige" books, it is automatically assumed that they cannot sell. In other industries, such an assumption would not be made; instead, the people responsible for launching a new product would perform sufficient research to determine the size and whereabouts of its potential market before they made the decision to proceed.

By contrast, I have never heard of a book publisher investing a dime for research of any kind before launching a new book, or even a whole series of new books. I'd bet, for instance, that the highly praiseworthy program of Knopf "puppies"—a series of short novels by young, "undiscovered" writers—was undertaken without much more than an educated guess that it would be successful; I'll be surprised, and pleased, if Knopf corrects me on this statement. (Later: I stand uncorrected. Having checked with a spokesman at Knopf—a very progressive spokesman for what is regarded as a very progressive publishing house—I was not surprised to hear that no research preceded the launching of the "puppies." The reasons adduced by Knopf were (1) that advertising can't help sell books that won't sell anyway, (2) that a busy publisher often gets too close to the trees to stand back and look at the forest, (3) that you can't spend research money on books with an $800 advertising budget, and (4) since the *New York Times Book Review* is far and away the most effective advertising medium for selling books, the research would not provide a useful media alternative. There was also a tendency to laugh at my naïve suggestion that books, like other products, might benefit by research, or that there might be an unexplored alternative to the present mode of desultory, look-alike book advertising. I can't, at the moment, prove that I'm right, but I can't believe that a situation governed solely by trade convention should, or will, go eternally unchallenged. (Think what might happen to the sale of verse and fiction by unknowns if, even without a penny of research or a substantial investment in advertising, a publisher were to make 10-minute tape cassettes of new authors reading from their own work available—free—to college radio stations, and to arrange college reading tours by these same writers.)

Historically, book publishers have always proceeded on intuition alone in deciding what would sell; in so doing, they have placed themselves at the mercy of the inscrutable marketplace, vastly overprinting books whose topical lure they have, gambler-like, overestimated, cruelly underprinting "sleepers" for which, had they known it, there was a sizable and eager audience awaiting.

But the heaviest burden must rest on the reviewers. It used to be that the books with the heaviest advertising got the most reviews, on the old-line newspaper publisher's principle that ad revenue justifies editorial support. This is not so true today; most newspapers, with the exception of a few major metropolitan dailies, receive so little book advertising that their review activity is minimal. Either they engage a few local teachers, librarians, or their own staffers—who may range from highly literate to absolute zero—to write a once-a-week daily review and two or three on Sunday, or they employ a book editor who does it all himself, with equally variable results. But since the advertising category is negligible, most newspapers give the book page the shortest possible shrift.

This means that the publishers must look to the few national media that more or less conscientiously review books for whatever attention their first novels and books of verse may receive. Unfortunately, they will find that, when it comes to meritorious work by unknown writers, most of these influential media are unable or unwilling to do it justice. In the first place, of course, it would be utterly impossible for any medium to read all the potentially worthy new work published each year and then report on the best of it. Nearly 40,000 new trade books are published in a given year, of which a very high proportion must be evanescent trash; nevertheless, even the *Times,* which manages to review some 3000 books a year in its daily and Sunday pages, still misses many first-rate titles by new authors. But there are many other and more subtle pressures on the reviewer; for one thing, the few book pages or book sections that still carry sizable amounts of book advertising may feel that the books thus advertised—the "big" books of the season, at least in terms of sales—may justify a review, either because the advertiser expects it or, perversely, because the new best seller deserves to be put down (thus enhancing the publication's, and the reviewer's, reputation for literary purity and/or incorruptibility). A recent example: one of the daily reviewers of the *New York Times* was so conscious of this tendency to demolish big, popular names that he devoted an entire column to a kidding discussion of how best to put down Irving Wallace's new novel, *The Word.* But isn't the best way to dismiss such a book simply to ignore it, and to devote the space instead to a good book by somebody the reader never heard of?

On the newsmagazines, the reviewer's problem is often further confounded by (1) the pressure on his little space by the news-minded front-of-the-book editors, and (2) their desire for a bright, flippant homogeneity throughout the magazine. Thus, they will not look kindly on a long, serious review of an unknown; they'd rather see a wicked, witty knifing of some fat target of opportunity (poor Mr. Wallace again) or a lyric celebration of the Big New Name of the Season (since reviewers, for all their restrictions, are still expected to discover talent, they sometimes take the safest way by jumping, three or four times a year, on a bandwagon somebody else has started). The Big New Names suffer from this sudden celebrity; early overpraise can be damaging to their second books, which will often be dismissed as untrue to their authors' early promise by the very critics who discovered them.

Another problem is the dearth of trained reviewers. In England, a large cadre of literate critics keeps the weeklies—the *TLS,* the *New Statesman,* the *Spectator,* and the Sunday papers—filled with lively, able, well-written criticism of worthwhile books; in this country, those publications which carry the largest number of reviews often have to fall back on young, untried academics who are likely to savage their elders and betters—a classic example was the arrogant dismissal of Saul Bellow's *Mr. Sammler's Planet* by a young English professor in the *New York Times Book Review* —since they tend to reserve the senior, well-established critics for front-page reviews of big, "important" books by equally established writers. (Since the Bellow book should, by rights, have been considered "important" and deserving of a page-one review by a first-rank critic, one wonders what editorial accident or animus led to this unfortunate result.) This is a little tragedy in itself; our best-equipped critics should be encouraged to devote at least a part of their reviewing time to the discovery and celebration of genuine new talent, and publications of the prestige of the *Times Book Review* or the *New York Review of Books* should be capable of establishing a regular department in which new work is given the attention it so desperately needs.

A third problem—the mention of the *New York Review* brings it up sharply—is the *politicization* of book reviewing today. We are living, indeed, in times of almost apocalyptic change, and books that plumb that change, its course, speed, and direction, deserve serious and comprehensive coverage; but surely this should not occur at the expense of literature, and surely many marginal or derivative books on politics are not worthy of the extensive attention they now receive. This problem is exacerbated by the tendency of many excellent critics to man the ideological barricades in print, laying aside irrelevant things—great verse and fiction—until the battle shall be won.

Finally, there is the problem of *literary* politics. Much has been said on that subject, most of it true; I'll simply content myself with observing that American literature has an Old Boy Network that would put England's to shame, and that Old Boys are by definition inimical to Young Boys, unless they be Protégés.

It is a sad mess. But there are remedies. A number of the larger book publishers have, for better or worse, been taken over by still larger communications companies in recent years. These companies market their products and services in a more or less ordered, rational, and accountable way; it is to be expected that they will supplant the old seat-of-the-pants marketing methods of the publishers with more modern techniques of research and product planning. This could, of course, have the negative effect of ending the publication of all poor-selling books, irrespective of their literary merit; it is more likely, I devoutly hope, to discover the waiting audience for works of literature and begin to tap it in earnest. And if and when publishers begin to back serious verse and fiction with advertising and publicity to bring it to the attention of its natural prospects in the colleges and the cities, I believe the book-review media will take the point and increase their attention to new work, too.

In fact, I think the change may even come in my own lifetime. When my sixth, and final, book of verse, *Seven Last Words,* is published, I confidently predict that it will be reviewed in the *Times* and will sell 10,000 copies. But that, of course, won't be till 1984.

Going Public

When Norman Mailer astonishingly, and pointlessly, allowed himself to be demolished by Gore Vidal on the *Dick Cavett Show,* the long-deteriorating relationship between American writers and their fans—you'll note I avoid calling them readers—hit some kind of an all-time low. Mr. Mailer, as you'll recall, showed up for this grudge match slightly the worse for wear, having, as he cheerfully admitted, visited a nearby watering place just before the show. Mr. Vidal, no man to pull his punches against a disabled opponent, waded in unmercifully, reducing Mr. Mailer to an appeal for a vote of confidence from the studio audience, an appeal which was loudly and scornfully rejected; the man who lays legitimate claim to being one of our most important novelists found himself on the receiving end of a chorus of boos from a few hundred kids in the studio. This visibly upset Janet Flanner, who was making a rare television appearance and who perhaps believed, with many of us, that a writer has no business going public.

Going public. What do I mean by that? Essentially, what I'm talking about is a separation between the private persona—the individual who sits alone at his typewriter, composing the work that in a sense he exists for—and the public personality, a coarse distortion of some of his salient characteristics into a marketable commodity for the mass media. This personality is closely akin to that of other celebrities, such as show-business people, in that it is simplified—popularized, either by the writer himself or by the intellectual limitations of mass communication—for easy recognition and consumption, rather like the one-dimensional characters in cheap fiction who used to be identified by a single attribute—cowardice or gluttony—or a single repeated turn of phrase.

It's all very well, however, for a *performer* to be so identified; we expect Jack Benny to be miserly, Groucho Marx to be lecherous, Woody Allen to be pusillanimously concupiscent precisely because each of these stage attributes is an integral part of his *shtick,* or act, which we do not impute to him in his private life. For a nonperformer it's another matter, though; if a writer represents himself in public as a tosspot, a racist, a womanizer, or a glutton—to take a few foibles at random—we have every right to assume that these are his private attributes as well. Thus a writer goes public at his peril; whatever simplified self-image he projects to an audience, he is likely to be judged by that image in the future, to the detriment of the way his work is read —and sometimes to the detriment of the work itself.

Writing is a neurotic phenomenon. It springs from a kind of objectivity or insight generated by the attempt to mediate between the two extremes of the neurotic state of mind: supreme self-confidence and utter hopelessness. In the beginning, a young man or woman writes to establish a tangible identity, a credible persona somewhere between that of Sad Sack and that of Superman. The writing itself is a tightrope act, a feat of delicate balance, and its integrity, its equilibrium, is easily disturbed by extremes of public rejection—or acceptance. On the whole, I think it is probably better for a writer to go relatively unnoticed than to be acclaimed at the beginning of his career. Early acclaim is awfully hard to deal with, especially for a person in his twenties; given the terrible efficacy of flattery, it is likely that he will begin to believe that he is loved not for his writing but for himself. When that happens, the writing suffers; the writer is elbowed out of the room so that the performer may primp, before a many-lighted mirror, for his next appearance on the stage. In the truest sense, he becomes his admirers, as Auden wrote of Yeats upon his death; the private writer dies, and his place is taken by a public man who lives to gratify his audience.

America has a long history of lionizing its writers, turning them into caricatures of circus animals conditioned to do tricks in public, to give the gallery a specious peek at greatness. Mark Twain—white hair, white moustache, white flannels—was the first of these tame lions, and it is a tribute to the toughness of his early training (and the absence of mass media in his lifetime) that he was not as seriously deflected from his real work as some who came after him. Henry James was too cerebral and probably too private to become a personality; though, in his last years, he bitterly regretted the failure of the New York Edition of his novels to become a popular success, he had already achieved the greatest triumph an American writer can hope for: a long life of continuous creative development, a literary life with a second act—and a third. And, finally, an imperishable place on the bookshelves of posterity. But both Twain and James flourished before the days of personal publicity, the media hype, and mass communication.

Not so Scott Fitzgerald, the first important American writer demonstrably ruined by celebrity; the advent of sensational journalism and multimillion circulations barely preceded—and set the stage for—his popular eminence and personal downfall. A dazzling success in his early twenties, Fitzgerald was quickly and cruelly—with his own connivance, to be sure—turned into crude copy for the tabloids. Delighted to be designated as the spokesman of the Jazz Age, he lived the role to the hilt, depleting his physical and financial resources and depriving himself of the sobriety and solitude a writer needs to work. His gift burned out with the Jazz Age, perhaps appropriately; I am not one of those who believe that *The Last Tycoon* was the bright beginning of a second act.

In the thirties, of course, poor Hemingway became the trashiest elements of his character—the man's man, the big-game hunter, the torero manqué. Painfully, he came to believe this debased version of himself; more painfully still, his writing showed it. I won't dwell on this oft-told story of decline—really a tragedy, for Hemingway was, at his best, a master—except to say that *Across the*

River and into the Trees curiously and heartbreakingly reflects the cancerous proliferation of these paltry ideals of machismo in the writer's mind.

Now there's a new pride—or shamelessness—of literary lions on the scene, men who are recognized as "famous writers" by millions who, assuredly, have never read a word they wrote. Mr. Mailer has reacted to his celebrity by riding off in all directions—reporting, movie-making, politics—with varying degrees of success. Fortunately, and exceptionally for a man in his position, he seems to have kept himself as writer alive and well and working in some compartment of his life, as evidenced by *The Armies of the Night* and *Miami and the Siege of Chicago,* though *Of a Fire on the Moon* and *The Prisoner of Sex,* his latest opera, could be taken to show a falling off of quality. Mr. Vidal, always threatening to become a novelist of the first rank, now seems too happily settled into his role of man-about-town and public controversialist to make that final effort. And Mr. Capote, whose taste for the limelight was advertised early and often by the notorious jacket portrait on his first novel, *Other Voices, Other Rooms,* some twenty-five years ago, has become a kind of leader-cum-mascot of New York café society; it remains to be seen whether he will at last produce a first-class work of fiction. Messrs. Vonnegut and Dickey have also become public figures of a somewhat smaller order of magnitude, perhaps because their franchise resides more clearly with the young.

It's interesting to note that this list of literary superstars contains, at the time of this writing, nobody under forty; dare one hope that the younger writers take a dim view of the blandishments of the media and prefer to stay at home and knit their art, or is it simply that none of them has the personal charisma to make the big-time grade? I'd like to think that the former is the truth; that the ethic of "making it" publicly and ostentatiously died with the previous generation, and that today's young literary men and women have learned a lesson from their elders—the lesson of privacy, of protecting and husbanding one's secret art.

Writing, to make a homely analogy, is the art of throwing hard —and accurately. A young writer, like a young pitcher, is strong but wild; his speed is blinding, but he'll often miss the plate.

Over the next ten to twenty years, he must perfect his aim while maintaining his power; beyond that, he must make craft and cunning take the place of youthful strength if he is to go on to a complete fulfillment. What I'm talking about is not just idle self-expression; it is the pursuit of perfection. Like a pitcher or a concert pianist who wishes to reach the top of his profession, a writer must take this high aim seriously. He must practice; he must work hard; he must sacrifice mere pleasure to the demands of art; he must be, in a sense, both single-minded and monastic. Unless he is a polymath of the most formidable proportions, he cannot afford or support a second career as a public figure. Even if it did not turn his head, even if it did not dilute the power of his talent, such a career would simply demand too much of his time and attention to permit his work to go forward at its proper pace.

In a word, the serious writer must take serious vows if he is to concentrate on his chief aim. A vow of silence, except through his work. A vow of consistency, sticking with writing to the exclusion of other fields. A vow of ego-chastity, abstaining from adulation. A vow of solitude, or at least long periods of privacy. A vow of self-regard, placing the self as writer before the self as personality.

I'm being a little ironically moralistic here; of course the writer should not become an anchorite; of course he should socialize; of course he should enjoy the respect of his family and his friends; of course he should have the pleasure of being lionized by his readers, his lecture audiences, and his students. After all, he's entitled, as long as he pays his dues by continuing to cultivate the one and only garden he grows well.

Reviewer's Dues

Perhaps because I started out as a poet, and poets' responsibilities are—and should be—mostly to themselves, I find it difficult to master each new kind of writing I'm confronted with. In school, I took quite naturally to verse, but my prose papers, essays, and thesis (what a terrible thesis it was!) were knotty, spastic, dense, and freighted far more heavily with words than with ideas.

For some reason—possibly because my father was an advertising man and I more or less grew up in the business—I didn't find it quite as difficult to solve the problems of print copywriting when I first went to work, in 1953, for an advertising agency; but I came a long-term cropper on television when I essayed that slippery medium, and it wasn't for years that I could turn out a creditable sixty-second script.

At the hoary age of forty, I became—because I suddenly wanted to—a book reviewer. To my surprise, I found it an almost intolerable burden and a long-acting pain. After years of stumping and (I hoped) dazzling other people with anything I cared to try in verse, I was now faced with the opposite situation; the biter had been bit. Now it was my sworn and bounden duty to penetrate and unravel the obscurities of other writers' methods and messages, to dissipate the wet and inky smokescreen in which the wily squid conceals himself, and to set the delicate skeleton of the author's true design in so many words before my readers. Besides being hard, grueling detective work, this was both scary and risky; armed only with a shaky analytic gift and my spotty, idio-syncratic store of reading, I was laying my sacred honor on the line each time I tried to pick another literary lock in public.

For the first couple of years, I heaved, floundered, and rolled like a drowning man in the trough of my overweening ambition. I drove myself to write reviews like an aristocrat driving himself to the gallows, with superficial sangfroid as thin as onionskin and a real clutch of fear each time I sat down at the typewriter.

Then, mercifully, I began to learn the ropes, to rise out of my funk (or muck sweat, as the English say), and look a little more objectively around me. I discovered that reviewing was not simply something that a soi-distant literary man did to fill time, amplify his tiny reputation, and (of course) earn a little money. *Au contraire.* Reviewing, it was slowly and astoundingly revealed to me, was a vocation, a craft, a difficult discipline, with its own rules and customs, with a set of commandments and a rigid protocol. Mostly by making painful mistakes and leaping brashly into pit-falls, I began to amass some notion of the shape of a reviewer's obligations to himself, to the author he reviews, to his editor, to his readers.

In short, I became aware of the moral imperatives of book reviewing. Funny as that may sound in a literary world raddled by cliques and claques and politics, by back-scratching and back-stabbing, by overpraise and undernotice, I now believe that the would-be conscientious reviewer must be guided by a long list of stern prohibitions if he is to keep faith with himself and his various consumers. In the interests of controversy (and, I hope, of air-clearing), I set these down herewith.

1. Never review the work of a friend. All sorts of disasters are implicit here; a man and his work should be separate in the re-viewer's mind, and the work should be his only subject. If you know the man at all well, you become confused and diffident; your praise becomes fulsome, and you fail to convey the real merits and demerits of the book to the poor reader. The hardest review I ever wrote was of the (quite good) novel of a friend four years ago. Never again.

2. Never review the work of an enemy. Unless you fancy your-self as a public assassin, a sort of licensed literary hit man, you

will instinctively avoid this poisonous practice like the plague it
is. Corollary: never consent to be a hatchet man. If Editor **X**
knows you are an old enemy of Novelist Y, he may (and shame
on him, but it happens all the time) call on you to review Y's
latest book. Beware, on pain of losing your credibility.

3. Never review a book in a field you don't know or care
about. Once or twice I've been touted onto titles far from my
beaten track. The resulting reviews were teeth-grindingly difficult
to write and rotten in the bargain. Unless you're a regular polymath, stick to your own last.

4. Never climb on bandwagons. You are not being paid to
subscribe to a consensus, nor will your reader thank you for it.
If a book has been generally praised (or damned), you add nothing to anybody's understanding by praising (or damning) it in
the same terms. Only if you have read the book with care and
found something fresh to comment on should you attempt a review. Otherwise, find something else (how about the work of an
unknown?) to write about. Or skip it; you'll earn that money you
need for a new 500-mm. mirror lens somewhere else.

5. Never read other reviews before you write your own. This
is a tough rule to follow, because all reviewers are naturally curious about the reception of Z's latest book. Nonetheless, you can't
help being subtly influenced by what John Leonard (or whoever)
has to say. Eschew!

6. Never read the jacket copy or the publisher's handout before reading and reviewing a book. Jacket copy (I know; I used
to write it) is almost invariably misleading and inaccurate. The
poor (literally: these downtrodden souls are, along with retail
copywriters, the most underpaid people in advertising) writer is
probably working from a summary compiled by the sales department, not from a firsthand reading of the book. The handouts are
more of the same, only flackier.

7. Never review a book you haven't read at least once. Believe
it or not, some reviewers merely skim a book (or even depend
on, horrors, the jacket copy) before reviewing it. Not only is
this a flagrant abdication of responsibility; there is always the
lurking danger of missing a vital clue in the text and making a

public spectacle of yourself. It should happen frequently to all such lazy reviewers.

8. Never review a book you haven't understood. If *you* haven't figured out what the author is up to, there's simply no way you can convey it to your reader. Reread the book; if necessary, read some of the author's other books; if you still don't know, forget it. The cardinal sin here is to go right ahead and condemn a half-understood book on the covert grounds that you haven't found its combination.

9. Never review your own ideas instead of the author's. Unless you're the ranking pundit in the field and you have a scholarly bone to pick with the author, you have no right to use the book under inspection as a springboard for a trumpet voluntary of your own.

10. Never fail to give the reader a judgment and a recommendation on the book. And tell why. A reviewer is really a humble consumer adviser; his main job is to tell the public what to read and what to skip. It's an important job because nobody can possibly keep up with all the books being published today.

11. Never neglect new writers. First novelists, in particular, get passed over too frequently for several reasons. The obvious reason is that Norman Mailer's new novel is better copy than Hannah Furlong's maiden effort. The less obvious reason is that it's much harder for a reviewer to get an intelligent fix on an unknown. In short, it's harder work to review a debutant.

12. Never assume that a writer is predictable. This is, in a way, the converse of the previous proposition. Part of the pleasure of picking up a new book by a writer you've read before is *knowing* what you're about to read—the themes, the style, the old, familiar tricks. But what if the novelist has *grown;* what if he does something daring and unexpected? That's when a lot of reviewers, myself included, are tempted to put him down for not rewriting himself. The only answer is to approach the book with great caution and read it on its own merits, forgetting what has gone before.

13. Never forget to summarize the story or the argument. What's more maddening than a review that rhapsodizes (or bitches) for two thousand words about the author's style, his

technique, his place in letters without ever giving us a clue to the nature of the story, beyond the mention of an incident or two?

14. Never, on the other hand, write a review that is merely a plot summary and nothing more. This happens surprisingly often, especially in newspaper reviews. The reader of the review deserves a judgment, a rating, not simply a recapitulation.

15. Never impale a serious writer on his minor errors. Nobody's perfect, as the old gag line says, and, given the susceptibility of even the most powerful piece of work to ridicule, it is frighteningly easy for the reviewer to have his fun at the author's expense and end up distorting the value and import of the book. (Example: I recently read a good novel in which the author consistently misused the word "fulsome" and mixed up "she" and "her." It would have been an act of willful irresponsibility to take the author to task for these small miscues, which were also his editor's fault.)

16. Never write critical jargon. The day of the New Criticism, for all its goods, is mercifully past, and so, I'd hope, is the compulsion of some reviewers to pose and posture as anointed gospelers of the true and beautiful. The reviewer who writes for a general-circulation newspaper or magazine should have his typewriter unplugged if he persists in pedagogeries.

17. Never fail to take chances in judgment. Because it forces you to enter the mind of another on his own terms, reviewing is literally mind-expanding. Often the reviewer is astonished at his new conclusions and afraid to put them down on paper. This is a mistake; one of the highest critical acts is to arrive at a new understanding and communicate it to the reader.

18. Never pick a barn-door target to jeer at. Not long ago, one of the daily reviewers in the *New York Times* wasted an entire column on the new novel by one of the Irving Wallaces. Irving Stone? Jacqueline Susann? Or whoever. Anyway, it was painfully easy—shooting fish in a barrel—and painfully unworthy of the reviewer's taste and talent. He might far better have reviewed a good first novel.

19. Never play the shark among little fishes. Being a reviewer does not entitle you to savage the beginner, the fumbler, the less-

than-accomplished writer. A sincere and decent effort demands a sincere and decent response. If you've ever struggled to write a book yourself, you know the vast amounts of pain and love it takes. To put down an honest attempt in gloating arrogance is to deal a crippling blow to a nascent career of possible promise.

20. Never compete with your subject. A reviewer is not, at least during his hours as reviewer, a rival of the person he's reviewing. If he sees flaws in the work under inspection, he should report them, but he should not give vent to a long harangue on how *he* would have written the book. (If his hubris is that keen, perhaps he should take time off and write a book himself.)

In a word, then, the sins and temptations of reviewers are legion. As an incumbent sinner, I have more often than I like to think about been brought up short by the realization of my own weaknesses. Thus the list above. While I know I don't have the constancy and fortitude to follow it to the letter, I try to bear it in mind, like a catechism, when I sit down to write about another person's work. It is the least I can do for another poor sufferer who has taken the supreme risk of letting his dreams and talents go forth between covers, and for all those poor sufferers who simply like to read, and who rely, for better or worse, on the dim and uncertain skills of reviewers for a guide through the maze of new titles in their bright, unrevealing jackets on the shelves.

Plastic English

A couple of us old foreign-car nuts, who remember the long-gone era of aromatic leather interiors and burl-walnut facias—dashboards to you—with some respect for the craftsmanship they implied, broke into recent titters and guffaws when we read the results of a *Road & Track* owners' survey in which the partisans of a certain Japanese make agreed that its best features included the *interior*—a miracle of mass-produced plastic, undoubtedly untouched by human hands. This led us to further not-so-risible conjectures on the rising tolerance, even appetite, for plastic in all our artifacts and ways. In the elevator and the supermarket and the airport waiting room, we are lulled and stupefied by plastic music; on the Interstates, we ingest plastic food; when we read a magazine or newspaper or watch TV, a flood of plastic English assaults our eyes and ears.

I am using "plastic" in an exact sense here; let me quote from a dictionary definition of the word written some years before the introduction of what we now call plastic itself: "plastic, *adj.* . . . 6. *Physics.* Capable of being deformed continuously and permanently in any direction without rupture, under a stress exceeding the yield value." Under the stress of an unholy impulsion to power and wealth, far exceeding the yield value in humanitarian terms, the pace and tone and environment of our life, and especially the language we speak and read, have suffered a sea change into something cheap and strange, something alien, something continuously and permanently deformed, something, in fact, plastic.

There is not a single heathen tongue; rather, there are many, a babel of multicolored plastic languages under the general rubric we call English. They are the jargons, or argots, of many disciplines, if I may use the noble word "discipline" in such a laughably antithetical way: science, scholarship, advertising, journalism, politics, and many more. They have one thing in common, though; all of these debased and isolable forms of the mother tongue attempt to paper over an unpalatable truth and/or to advance the career of the speaker (or the issue, cause, or product he is agent for) by a kind of verbal sleight of hand, a one-upmanship of which the reader or listener is victim.

I am not in the least embarrassed that this jeremiad over the imminent dissolution of the language has had many earlier prophets than myself; specifically, I am proud to revive a protest made so tellingly, some twenty-six years ago, by George Orwell in his essay, "Politics and the English Language." Orwell concerned himself with the "swindles and perversions" of the language of his time on the grounds that imprecision of thought leads to sloppy, self-indulgent language, which leads in turn to even sloppier, lazier thinking; to make his point, he adduced several horrible examples of writing current in the England of 1946. I'd like to do the same, citing some samples from the America of 1972 and adding notes on their pathology.

1. "A Toast to a New Breed of Brides. Elegantly individual. Stark with savvy. Inclined toward the sublime simplicity of an exciting new designer, Michele Piccione of Rome. Above—a bow'd belle of wool and silk . . . beyond—a marvelous wool mood-maker with soft wedding hood. Lean, lovely ideas, both. . . ."

The first thought is, how *can* they, in this day and age? But this emetic Bergdorf's ad, in the Sunday *New York Times,* is perfectly representative of thousands of its kind, running daily and weekly hairless cheek by bloody jowl with reports from My Lai, Attica, Jackson State, Watts, and the streets a few blocks to the north of Bergdorf's. Surely no member of that "new breed of brides" is so anchoritic as to swirl through life like a deb of the twenties? But, ah: light dawns. This particular ad is addressed to their poor, rich mothers, still hoping for a swatch of grace and harmless flummery in a darkening hour of muggings in tower elevators. That doesn't, however, explicate all the other sick, tired fashion ads aimed at their dancing daughters. Is there a conspiracy between fashion copywriters and fashion consumers to shut out the rest of the menacing world? Perhaps; much plastic English is on the secret service of her majesty, nepenthe.

2. ". . . Monod is constrained to use the word 'teleonomy,' which stands for living 'objects endowed with a purpose or project,' and which includes the genetic replication of such purpose. Yet in no way is this to be confused with 'teleology' *à la* Aristotle, or with final causation, and certainly not with 'animism,' which is the projection of organic teleonomy into the universe itself. This is the author's *bête noire,* and his stable extends from Plato through Leibniz and Hegel, down to dialectical materialism. . . ."

An animistic *bête noire* in a stable? *À la* Aristotle? This short chunk from a brief review of Monod's *Chance and Necessity* in the *Antioch Review* is a fair example, not in the least atypical, of the state of the art of scholarly prose, complete with the warts of terminological jugglery, foreign phrases sprinkled *ad libitum,* as here, and impacted metaphor. While it does not begin to compare with Orwell's superb example of same from the works of Harold Laski, it is sufficient unto the day. The purpose, clearly, is to anoint the author as an academic mensch.

3. "Just finished 'Life Story.' It really was a hit to my head. You know, it was really refreshing and cosmic. I was a pancake until last year, but guess I missed my chance to tell you about it. . . ."

So a recent letter to the editors of *Rolling Stone. Two* "really"s and one "you know." Par for the course. In an age of lowered barriers, the ultimate creative experience—literary, physical, spiritual—is open to all those who can afford the dues: the price of a rock album and a pledge of allegiance to the lockstep argot of the young. Yet they are—and I'm not kidding—the hope of the world, and if they ever learn to individuate themselves and their language they may be quite unstoppable.

4. "Over the past 50 years, the Mafia has been convulsed by

eight major gang wars, most of them wrenching it further into the twentieth century.

"Each war was set off by personal ambitions and jealousies. Each one shook the organization to its foundations and spilled gallons of blood unnecessarily. But in a historical perspective, each war can be seen as a confrontation between the old order and the new, the old-timers and the Young Turks."

This introit from the recent *New York* Magazine series by Nicholas Gage on the Mafia raises all sorts of yellowing ghosts. The *American Weekly*. The *Daily Graphic*. James Wechsler's cephalically muscular recreations of the twenties. Walter Winchell's voice-over introductions to *The Untouchables*. Apparently color—the color of blood—laced with fancyisms like "historical perspective" and action words like "convulsed" and "wrenching" and Newspeakisms like "confrontation" may be folded together into a reasonable facsimile of the New Journalism *(sic)*. A remarkable recycling of an apparently non-biodegradable, to use another nonce word, plastic.

5. "We look on the decision-making process as a very important component of the overall deterrence package."

The speaker is Admiral Thomas Moorer, chairman of the Joint Chiefs of Staff. The sentence is not really meaningless; freely translated, that is, stripped of its soothing coating of interchangeable euphemisms—what Orwell called *"phrases* tacked together like the sections of a prefabricated hen-house"—it means, as Robert Sherrill wrote recently in the *New York Times* Magazine, "that, while everyone else from New York to San Diego may be wiped out en masse, the enemy would tremble to know that Washington's bureaucrats and politicians had survived and were making decisions just as well as always."

Other officialese, of course, is intended to mean just nothing; Melvin Laird is sardonically saluted by Sherrill in the same article for his adroitly unresponsive answers to the questions of congressional committees. And some public language is intended to turn black into white, hey presto!, before the astonished voter's eyes. Thus Senator Hugh Scott's call for the Nobel Peace Prize for President Nixon, which Tom Wicker nominated for the "Orwell Award," on the grounds that Scott "had come about as close as anyone could to the ideal Newspeak formulation, 'War is Peace.' "

6. "In North Vietnam, in the period from 1954 to 1956 . . . a minimum of 500,000 were murdered, assassinated . . . in the event that the United States followed the course of action recommended by some of those who have voted for the so-called end-the-war resolution in the Senate . . . it would mean that there would be visited upon South Vietnam the same atrocities that were visited upon North Vietnam, with perhaps at least one million marked for assassination. . . . That would be the height of immorality to impose on the 17 million people of South Vietnam a Communist government with the bloodbath that would follow. . . ." Thus President Nixon in a press conference.

Later, in the same conference: "This question I noticed has been reflected on by some lower-level officials in the Government, but not because Secretary Rogers and I have talked about this matter and Dr. Kissinger and I, not by us."

It's nice to watch a real master at work. In the first set of quotations President Nixon is, as Tom Wicker has said, grossly inflating the number of casualties in North Vietnam in 1954-1956, a figure usually set at 10,000 to 15,000 and never higher than 50,000, in order to set the stage for what Wicker called the President's "nearly singlehanded discovery of the coming bloodbath" involving the wildly speculative figure of a million South Vietnamese. This in the context of a conference in which he accused the Secretary-General of the United Nations of "a hypocritical double standard" on the subject of the bombing of North Vietnamese dikes.

In the second quotation Mr. Nixon is simply retreating into what Oliver Jensen once happily dubbed Eisenhowese: an inscrutably inarticulate utterance in public.

This gross manufacture of plastic English for self-seeking ends in high places is especially worrying because it implies that a speaker who, like the cuttlefish, shrouds himself in inky opacities has no real knowledge of his whereabouts, and, lost in the stylish practice of duplicities, can no longer distinguish a real right from a real wrong. But, naggingly, this plastic deformation of language for selfish purposes is pandemic now: it pops up in the slovenly shortcuts of all kinds of lazy, self-indulgent writing—"Yes, ma'am," with its needful pause and broadening apostrophe, is increasingly rendered as the nuanceless, and downright wrong, "Yes mam."

All sorts of special pleaders, however just their cause, begin to sound, in the ripeness and density of their trite political catchphrases, like American Communists of the thirties. Women's Liberation, which now prefers to be called "the movement," for one, has turned its useful dialogue with its exploiters into a useless monologue by settling for such thoughtless formulas as "male chauvinist." On another front, such movements distort and corrupt further the language already savaged by the Establishment politicians when they conspire to eliminate the innocuous, and correct, locution, "Everyone knows *he* has to decide for *himself*," and to substitute the odious Newspeakism "chairperson" for the sufficiently separate—and equal—"chairman" and "chairwoman."

A plague on plastic prefab houses, and on the widespread debasement of our only valid (*there's* a nonce word; even in an article like this, I can't eliminate them all) tool for change: independent thought, expressed in individual language. For what does it profit a man if he gains a whole new world, but loses the soul of his moral authority: his ideas and the fragile, precious, idiosyncratic words he clothes them in?

The Constant Rereader's Five-Foot Shelf

Picking up a new book—or a hitherto unread one—is not, for me at least, an unmixed pleasure. Long before I became an I hope conscientious book reviewer, I had regarded each new volume, its cargo of experience filtered through ego secreted between bland, protective boards, with wariness. At best it would turn out to be a botch that proclaimed itself in the initial pages, obviating further reading; at worst, it would tease me with hinted-at but unrealized potentialities until THE END; and somewhere in between, and maybe worse than worst, it would remain tantalizingly unclassifiable throughout its length, a Damoclean indictment of my possible shallowness as a reader. Once in a great while, though, I pick up a new book that is none of these things, but proclaims itself instead as a prime candidate for that relatively tiny library of books I reread as often as once a year for the unfailing pleasure of their mastery in whatever they set out to do.

Thus rereading is, for me, the most satisfying, if not the most profitable, kind of reading; and, in the hope that you may share some of my predilections, I unhesitatingly commend to you the mixed and sometimes startling contents of my rereader's five-foot shelf. It begins, on the left (so to speak, for of course these books are not literally ranged in this order in my *soi-disant* library), on the high ground of poetry. I am like Dennis Barlow in *The Loved One* in that rhythms from the anthologies (and many individual books of verse) move softly through my mind, and it is an incomparable anodyne to revisit them and find them as magically potent as ever, there on their yellowing pages. Life falls away; today's headlines fade to whiteness; this rereading is unconsciously triangulated with my life's associations at the time of the last rereading and the one before that and the lowest harmonic of the first reading, when I was seduced and surrendered. Skelton, Wyatt, Sidney leap and sizzle to life at the touch of an eye in their collision between courtly guile and pastoral innocence. Donne's tough-minded, skew-metered lyrics speak the modern tongue. Jonson's songs create their own gorgeous, unheard music. Herbert's devotions mediate, with grave loveliness, between God and man.

I should confess here that there are some books, in every genre and in every period, that I find too daunting because too dazzling, in intellect or execution, to be as easily reread. Shakespeare is almost too rich, in his insistence on ultimates in diction, wordplay, characterization, and dramatic event, to reread meditatively; he alarms and excites the reader into understandings each time new, and to reread him is for me not a casual revisiting but an expedition up Everest, crampons, pitons, oxygen, rations, rope, and all. Ditto Milton, in another sense. Ditto Pope, in still another.

But I can return, not as a pilgrim but as a familiar, almost a friend, to the verse of Dryden and Swift, Gay and D'Urfey, Blake and Wordsworth, Coleridge and Keats. Among the Victorians my closest poetic aquaintances are strange bedfellows: Gilbert and Hopkins. In the twentieth century, I reread most or all of Eliot, really *il miglior fabbro,* most of Auden, especially the "Songs and Musical Pieces," some of them among the greatest lyrics in the language; most of Cummings, most of Stevens, most of Ransom, much of Hart Crane, much of Robert Lowell, all of Philip Larkin, that Midlands existentialist. And I should perhaps include Harold Pinter, whose purpose is so obviously poetic, so clearly to create a new metric notation out of the spoken word and the equally spoken silence. Besides these masters, there are all sorts of poets whose great individual poems I reread as often as I can: Graves's "Warning to Children," Wilfred Owen's flawed sonnet, "Hospital Barge at Cérisy," MacNeice's "Eclogue by a Five-Barred Gate," Hugh MacDiarmid's "Of John Davidson," Patrick Kavanagh's "The Hospital," James Dickey's "The Celebration," and two stunning, because totally unexpected, war poems: Norman Nicholson's "Early March, 1941," and Henry Reed's "The Naming of Parts." And innumerable others.

But it is fiction that is the most rereadable kind of writing of all. Perhaps that's because a novel or a book of short stories by one writer possesses enough sheer *duration*—as opposed to a poem or even a play—to capture and reward the rereader's attention over a span of hours or days, to permit him to re-evaluate the work—and himself as reader, critic, and person in progress—in full and at length. Thus, rereading Defoe holds an untarnished eighteenth-century mirror up to our times in general and to me in particular, both as I am now and, more subtly, as I was when I last read Defoe in, say, 1965. Likewise, Jane Austen makes a devastating comment not only on the continuity of human nature but on the shocking present disrepair of our civility and our morals, a comment more devastating today than even five years ago. Dickens casts before him the deepening shadow—a prophetic utterance, really—of our urban disarray, much more pointedly now, in our mushrooming jungle of cities, than in Ike Eisenhower's glorious days.

As we come closer, the comment often becomes even sharper and more biting. The novels of the twenties and thirties and forties, once read for their light on people and places other than our own, or for new views of our own, now often become fingers pointing toward our time and at us, once disparate pieces that now fit together into a disconcerting pattern of judgment on our time and place and person. Fitzgerald's and Faulkner's early novels and Hemingway's early stories—in each case, I think, their best and most representative work—all enumerate the disjunctions in our way of life that have brought us to our present state. Passos' *U.S.A.* is, in fact, a schematic diagram of the drives and tensions that have resulted in today's inequities, as well as a picture of a period that is worth rereading for historical or nostalgic reasons alone. Even the great entertainments of the period from 1920 to 1950 (by entertainments I mean fiction read primarily for pleasure, not for serious intellectual or moral instruction) deal meaningfully with the dominant twentieth-century theme of the lone moral man and his temptations and vicissitudes in a world that, like his body, is failing and dying around him: the bitterness of Ring Lardner's view of the human condition, as savage as Swift's, the acidity of Perelman's satires on idiocy in everyday life, the disillusionment and loss of the heroes of such differing writers as Hammett, Chandler, Ambler, Household, Greene, and Waugh have all become, irrespective of literary aims and achievements, works of instruction about the way we live now. I read and reread them with a double perspective, with mental bifocals, so to speak, finding felicity in the play of diction and humor and action, finding disturbance and truth and saneness in the contrapuntal moral question.

Conversely, avowedly didactic fiction must be read, like the novels of George Orwell, for its unsettling message, but it may also be read for its pleasures of evocation. In *Coming up for Air,* Orwell brilliantly evokes two stages in the destruction of the English countryside: the end of the era of unmetaled roads at the turn of the century and the beginning of megalopolis in the thirties. Even the most contemporary of novels can, indeed, provide this multiple frame of reference. Saul Bellow's *Mr. Sammler's Planet,* to take one example, may be profitably reread on several levels. It is at once a swingeing moral comment on our times, the story of a lone moral man against a society run amok, a telling picture of New York today, a social comedy, and a remarkable piece of writing in itself. It makes my day, week, month, and year when I come across a novel like this one, because I know I will add it to my five-foot shelf to reread another year.

Not that all rereading should be, or is, the discharge of an ethical and literary duty, however rewarding its aesthetic side effects. I regularly revisit a whole spectrum of books and shorter pieces which are, at least in a technical sense, not even literature at all. Reference books, for instance. It is no mean trick for a compiler or lexicographer to contrive to give us a lively sense of his own personality and prejudices while satisfying our thirst for hard facts arranged in alphabetical order, and it is with a great sense of love and homage that I repeatedly browse through the works of Fowler and Partridge when I'm not looking up anything at all. Partridge's keen and good-humored judgments and guesses on the provenance of slang and Fowler's finely aimed, arrogant scorn of pomposity never fail to cheer me up. By the same token, I can lose myself for hours in the *Times of London Atlas* or in the pages of Mencken's *American Language,* whose author admittedly allows himself more scope for personal exhibitionism than the three foregoing.

For solace in dark hours—all right, for pure escape—I also return to a small collection of surefire palliatives in three special fields I'm interested in: cars, railroads, and military history. If you care about cars, you will already have read Charles Jarrott's classic book of recollections about long-distance road racing on the Continent in the earliest years of the century, Henry Manney's sprightly commentaries (in an inimitable transatlantic style) on cars and racing in *Road & Track,* and L.J.K. Setright's magisterial reflections, replete with comic asides and classical references, in the British magazine *Car.* If you are a railway fancier, I hope you will run down L.T.C. Rolt's mindbendingly fascinating *Red for Danger,* a history of British railway accidents and railway safety, and Stewart Holbrook's nourishingly anecdotal *Story of American Railroads.*

If you read about wars, you will probably return with some frequency to the works of Cyril Falls and Sir Basil Liddell Hart, Robert Graves's *Goodbye to All That,* Siegfried Sassoon's *Memoirs of an Infantry Officer,* and, on the technical side, such books as *Jane's Fighting Ships* (editions of 1914 and 1939, for preference) and *All the World's Aircraft* (1939 again) and Constance Babington-Smith's history of British test-flying, *Testing Time.* My own extra-special interest, for some reason, is in escape literature, which I mean quite literally: books like *Escape from Colditz* and *The Wooden Horse,* besides being true thrillers of a sort, seem to deal again with the single moral man in a hostile world—only this time he has a chance to be heroic, to make good his escape against all odds.

What have I left out of my rereading list? A great many things, for lack of space. All the foreign writers, from Ronsard to Chekhov, who have made a special impression on me. A long list of Irish, English, and American novelists, from James and Joyce to Philip Roth and Kingsley Amis. A double handful of short-story writers, from Katherine Mansfield to O'Hara, Cheever, Updike,

Salinger, and Barthelme. Two critics in particular—Pritchett for England, Wilson for America—who seem to me to have said more about our time more gracefully and sanely than anybody else (read Edmund Wilson's *New Republic* pieces of the twenties, both literary and otherwise; they're still as much alive, like his recent Talcottville variations, as anything else written in this century). A small, distinguished company of poets under fifty: Hecht, Merrill, Moss, Dunn, Wilbur, Starbuck, Heaney, Kennedy, a few more. And a grab bag of books in many categories—Betjeman's verse and architectural commentary, *Ian Nairn's London,* Sylvia Brooke's deliciously eccentric autobiography, *Queen of the Headhunters,* a group of recent novels by young writers, headed by Thomas McGuane and Ann Richardson Roiphe.

A list of books that you reread is like a clearing in the forest: a level, clean, well-lighted place where you set down your burdens and set up your home, your identity, your concerns, your continuity in a world that is at best indifferent, at worst malign. Since you, the reader, are that hero of modern literature, the existential loner, the smallest denominator of moral force, it behooves you to take counsel, sustenance, and solace from the writers who have been writing about you these hundred or five hundred years, to sequester yourself with their books and read and reread them to get a fix on yourself and a purchase on the world that will, with luck, like the house in the clearing, last you for life.

"Never Such Innocence":
July, 1914

It's hard to remember that less than a lifetime ago—within the lifetimes, in fact, of our fathers and grandfathers, some of whom still live—the world was such a different place.

In England, at the height of empire in the height of summer, 1914, people moved in their appointed, time-honored places as they and their ancestors had for generations: the "horseman" in East Suffolk, plowing his niggardly, unthankful farmer's field with a hard-learned care for the accuracy of a furrow that was art; the craftsmen sewing more stitches per inch into a pony harness than ever were strictly necessary; the railway servants, signalers and footplatemen alike, putting their spotless and beautifully painted expresses and goods trains into their destinations on the tick of the appointed time; small merchants taking infinite pride in the quality of their beer or lamb or nails or cabbages and in the spanking turnout of their shops; city clerks looking ahead to meticulous service and a painfully slow rise to a chief clerkship; Fabian ladies and gentlemen debating the course of the world with all the time in the world, and with infinite kindness and courtesy; vicars and dons and doctors making their self-assured way as unquestioned mentors to men; and aristocrats conserving or squandering capital and tradition, according to their wont.

In a flash—the distant flash of Princip's gun—all that was altered forever, and the world was plunged into the modern age of disillusion, suspicion, assassination, and war. The serenity of that final summer of peace has perhaps been exaggerated in retrospect, as we tend to exaggerate the tranquillity of a remembered happy childhood; with the big battalions forming up on both sides of the Channel, with new navies of dreadnoughts standing, steam up, in the roads at Kiel and Scapa Flow, it cannot have been quite as still and sunny and murmurless—except for the summer wind in the wheat and the copses—as that.

But by contrast with what almost immediately followed, it must always have been a season symbolized—as George Steiner has recently reminded us—by Christopher Tietjens' magic dogcart ride with Valentine Wannop through a nightlong mist on the Kentish downs in Ford Madox Ford's *Some Do Not . . .*

All this is brought to mind, nearly sixty years after the fact, by some books I've recently read or reread. As one might suspect, that sudden change from boundless peace to endless war, from innocence—Philip Larkin ends his celebrated poem "MCMXIV": "Never such innocence again"—to complicity in sin, has been well memorialized by English writers.

Editor Kenneth Giniger, in association with Stackpole Books, has recently reissued a whole series of narratives of the First World War. Two of the most striking—both from the English point of view—are Siegfried Sassoon's *The Memoirs of George Sherston* and Cecil Lewis' *Sagittarius Rising*. They couldn't be more different: Sassoon takes his hero, or antihero, a thinly disguised version of Siegfried Sassoon, from a happy prewar career as a fox hunter to the pity and misery of the Somme, where he becomes a prototypical war protester and is returned, not unkindly, to a shell-shock hospital in Scotland; Lewis takes himself, for his book is avowedly autobiographical, from public-schoolboy keenness to early maturity as a flight commander in the Royal Flying Corps. Sassoon, like Robert Graves, his fellow Royal Welch Fusilier, in *Good-bye to All That,* achieves a bitter indictment of the hidebound masters of the war—but his weapon is innocence: his own and that of the boys around him, both officers and other ranks, who die for nothing. His *saeva indignatio* in the cause of decency and human sweetness is balanced by Lewis' demonstration of that peculiarly English sweetness in action. A deadkeen pilot, intoxicated with flight and separated from the horrors of the trenches by a mile of sky, Lewis developed a saving belief in his own invulnerability and lived through the war, increasingly showing that innocent steadfastness that must have been such a dominant trait of Edwardian England. His writing is less accomplished than Sassoon's—it tends to purple in the flying passages—but it is charged with such exhilaration and such moving youngness as to make *Sagittarius Rising* an invaluable book.

Add to these two books two more, and you will have a rounded picture of what we have lost in two generations, and of the magnitude, both psychic and numerical, of losses in the First World War. Martin Middlebrook's history, *First Day on the Somme,* tells, for the most part quite unsentimentally, what happened on July 1, 1916. Two years after the final summer of peace, the regrouped British Army, pushed hard by the French to take the pressure off Verdun, mounted a battle that epitomizes all the failures of leadership on both sides of the Western Front. Though British casualties had been heavy in such earlier fights as Loos, stringent recruiting efforts had raised a New Army of men who shared the patriotic spirit of the earlier recruits of August, 1914. These touchingly named battalions—the Salford Pals, the Glasgow Tramways, the Newcastle Commercials, the Glasgow Boys' Brigade, the Hull Tradesmen, the Hull Sportsmen—stood beside the Regulars and Territorials in seventeen divisions assigned to break the German line on a front of some twenty miles.

A long but ineffective artillery barrage preceded the battle; when the British troops went over the top, not at dawn but at 7:30 on the morning of July 1, they were immediately decimated —and more than decimated—by large numbers of surviving German machine-gun posts. British (and German) bravery was beyond praise; even the rawest New Army formations proceeded, at a walking pace (some idiot had decided that the supposedly annihilating bombardment precluded the necessity to run), toward their objectives, sometimes losing their entire force before reaching them. Obedience to orders was, in the main, undeviating. Unfortunately, the orders were suitable only for suicide units. At the end of the first day of the Somme, the British had taken almost sixty thousand casualties, more than in any battle before or since. And the Somme went on. It ended on November 14. Total casu-

alties on the British side numbered over 400,000; the gain in
ground was six inutile miles, four short of the first day's objective.

Years later, one of the survivors, his bitterness undiminished,
told Martin Middlebrook, "I cursed, and still do, the generals who
caused us to suffer such torture, living in filth, eating filth, and
then, death or injury just to boost their ego."

This brings us to the last book, the *Selected Poems* of Siegfried
Sassoon. (Shamefully, Sassoon's verse is now out of print in this
country.) I have enormous respect for the war poems of Wilfred
Owen, who died, heartbreakingly, while leading his company of
Manchesters across the Sambre Canal on—how awful—November 4, 1918, seven days before the armistice, but I find him, on
balance, a little more self-conscious, a little less heartfelt, than
Sassoon. In the *Selected Poems,* Sassoon is not always technically
impeccable or as toughly unsentimental as we might wish a modern poet to be. Nonetheless, there are a dozen or so poems which,
though flawed, must take their place among the great war poems
of the ages.

"The Redeemer," which—again that trumpet note of innocence
—likens a poor private shouldering a load of planks in the
trenches to Christ, walks a tightrope of bathos but at last, barely
and triumphantly, comes right and whole. "Blighters," which con-
trasts a patriotic wartime musical—"We're sure the Kaiser loves
our dear old Tanks"—with the conditions of death on the Somme,
has the real subversive bite of Louis MacNeice's "Bagpipe Music."
"The Rear-Guard" tells, with infinite repulsion, the story of an
officer who discovers that an apparently sleeping man in a deserted
dugout is actually long dead and retreats upward to the trench,
"Unloading hell behind him step by step." "Fight to a Finish" is
the most hostile of all Sassoon's seditious antiwar poems: it begins
with a victory parade and ends with the returning troops, still
armed, turning their bayonets first on the "Yellow-Pressmen" who
sold the war to the English people and then on "those Junkers"
in Parliament.

Finally, one poem, "The One-Legged Man," deserves to be
quoted because it delineates the loss of innocence, the rise of selfishness, even the rightness of selfishness for those who had made
the whole journey from illimitable peace to hideous war and back

to a partial and uneasy peace again: "Propped on a stick he viewed the August weald; . . ./ How right it seemed that he should reach the span/ Of comfortable years allowed to man!/ Splendid to eat and sleep and choose a wife,/ Safe with his wound, a citizen of life./ He hobbled blithely through the garden gate,/ And thought, 'Thank God they had to amputate!' "

Beyond the poetry and the pity, there is a lesson for us in this disillusion of a generation of young men.

During the First World War, a kind of emotional Gresham's Law was at work: the Edwardian currency of great expectations —innocence, decency, justice, equality—was driven out by the false money of cruelty, greed, and injustice in the conduct of the war. Nor could the good currency be restored; once those young men had seen the miseries and stupidities of a war far more degrading than Goya's at firsthand, they could never again expect a better world than the one they got: unemployment, the Crash, the dole, the rise of Hitler, the decline of England, even in victory. In fact, it might even be said that the brutal excesses of the First World War were the enabling act—in the subconscious minds of men—for all the Katyns and Belsens that were to follow.

Evelyn Waugh:
The Height of His Powers

Nineteen seventy-two marks the thirtieth anniversary of the publication of a novel that nobody seems to read these days, a novel of breathtaking symmetry, grace, craft, and discipline, a novel from which many of our younger writers of self-indulgent, sprawling, amorphous fiction could learn the structure of their art.

It is generally and uncritically accepted these days that *A Handful of Dust* (1934) was the greatest of Evelyn Waugh's novels, fulfilling the early promise of *Decline and Fall* (1928), and that his career as a writer gradually ran downhill from there. There is some truth to this, but it falsifies the value of a writer whose creative life, unlike that of so many twentieth-century writers, possessed not only a first act but a second and third as well. The first act, whose theme was a dazzling, sardonic irreverence toward the crumbling Empire between the wars, came to an end in 1942; the second, more dourly preoccupied with the Second War and its fatal consequences for the English upper class—with the striking, farcical exception of *The Loved One* (1948)—ended with the completion of the *Sword of Honour* trilogy in 1962; the third, short and glorious, overlapped the second, including the brilliant *Ordeal of Gilbert Pinfold* (1957) and the unfinished autobiography, *A Little Learning* (1964).

Speaking for myself, I would rank *Decline and Fall* and *Pinfold,* for their very different but equally genuine qualities as art, with *A Handful of Dust,* placing *Vile Bodies* (1930) and *The Loved*

One somewhat lower in the scale. *The Sword of Honour* books would seem to come next, followed by *Scoop* (1938), and such dilute and repetitious work as *Black Mischief* (1932) and the embarrassingly wish-fulfilling (though often beautifully written) *Brideshead Revisited* (1945) at the bottom of the list.

If you haven't as yet recalled the title of the 1942 novel this column is about, perhaps my point about its undeserved obscurity has been made. In any case, not to temporize longer, its title is *Put Out More Flags* (available in paperback), and it is the best record I have read of England in the first year of the Second War. In it, at the very height of his powers, Waugh somehow fuses the savage, deadly comedy of his earlier books with the ominous seriousness of his later ones. The abrupt and arbitrary rises and falls in his earlier characters' fortunes recur in *Put Out More Flags,* but here they are seen not as the operation of the author's whim but as a logical—or illogical—consequence of the war, itself a consequence of Waugh's upper-class characters' failure to deal effectively with Hitler in the thirties. In other words, this is the first of Waugh's novels to relate his people directly to history, to the worldwide consequences of their actions and omissions. It may also be the last; the *Sword of Honour* sequence, for all its sedulous following of the course of the war, is really the subjective, even paranoid, history of a single individual, Guy Crouchback, who feels increasingly disillusioned and betrayed by the alliance with Russia and the triumph, with Western assistance, of what can only be called "godless Communism." Because of this bias, Waugh loses his own objectivity in the later trilogy, turning characters who should have been rounded and alive into flat saints (Mr. Crouchback) and villains (Frank de Souza).

But *Put Out More Flags* is not like that. It rejoices in its author's skill at developing living characters, understanding them, sympathizing with them, however repellent they might have been to the later Waugh. Character after character from his earlier books deepens and broadens when faced with the reality of war. Alastair Digby-Vaine-Trumpington, who appears in *Decline and Fall* as the sort of feckless student who might have inspired Sir John Betjeman's "Varsity Students' Rag"—"And then we smash'd up ev'rything, and what was the funniest part/ We smashed some rotten old pictures which were priceless works of art"—has by now matured into a serious, uxorious, quietly heroic young man who volunteers for the army as a private and refuses officers' training. Likewise, Peter Pastmaster, the son of the scandalous Margot Metroland, shows a new sense of responsibility, marrying thoughtfully—more about his intended later—and volunteering for hazardous duty with the Commandos. It is a measure of Waugh's art that we accept these metamorphoses of stock figures into real people without demur. But the greatest proof of his skill lies in another group of characters upon whom the larger part of the action turns: Ambrose Silk, Basil Seal, his sister, Barbara, and his mistress, Angela Lyne.

In Ambrose Silk, Waugh does something quite astonishing for him: he creates a detailed, sympathetic, understanding picture of what would, in his earlier (and perhaps his later) books, have been merely a figure of fun—a homosexual, half-Jewish intellectual who hangs out with the odds and sods of London bohemianism. But there is nothing merely funny about Waugh's portrait of Silk, who is immediately established as a first-rate writer and the unhappy victim of his sexual conflicts:

> A pansy. An old queen. A habit of dress, a tone of voice, an elegant, humorous deportment that had been admired and imitated, a swift, epicene felicity of wit, the art of dazzling and confusing those he despised—these had been his; and now they were the current exchange of comedians; there were only a few restaurants, now, which he could frequent without fear of ridicule, and there he was surrounded, as though by distorting mirrors, with gross reflections and caricatures of himself.

Nor is there anything merely funny about Basil Seal, the black sheep and remittance man of *Black Mischief,* who reappears here in deeper, more sinister colors as a man who "rejoiced, always, in the spectacle of women at a disadvantage: thus he would watch, in the asparagus season, a dribble of melted butter on a woman's chin, marring her beauty and making her ridiculous, while she would still talk and smile and turn her head, not knowing how she appeared to him," as, in his own words, "one of those people one heard about in 1919: the hard-faced men who did well out of the war."

Basil does well out of the war, up to a point: he unhesitatingly takes advantage of his sister's latently incestuous attraction for him—the scenes in which this attraction surfaces, played out in chilling nursery talk between Basil and Barbara, are among the best expositions of sibling love I've ever encountered—makes money and gains a temporary mistress out of a scheme in which he must find a country billet for three appallingly uncouth *évacué* children, and earns himself a reputation as a spy-catcher for the War Office by turning in poor Ambrose, now the editor of a literary magazine, as a crypto-fascist.

But out of this apparent continuation of his old self-serving career grows a new character: suddenly confronted with the imminent ruin of Angela Lyne, his former mistress, who is drinking herself to death out of loneliness, he does the first real volteface of his life by returning to her, cajoling her back to health, marrying her, and himself joining the Commandos. This change of spots is made entirely plausible by the grainy, palpable reality of the two women in Basil's life: Barbara, spellbound now as twenty years before by her brother's sexual power over her; Angela, rich, fashionable, withdrawn, despairing, preoccupied with death, an embodiment of the woman in *The Waste Land* who says, "My nerves are bad to-night."

Very few male novelists can draw women well; Waugh is a towering exception. His Angela personifies all the vain (in both senses) smartness of the years between the wars; the waste of her life symbolizes the waste of the old values of upper-class England; her words when Basil tells her, in proposing, that he will be a terrible husband forecast the future of that class and place: "Yes, darling, don't I know it? But you see one can't expect anything to be perfect now. In the old days if there was one thing wrong it spoiled everything; from now on for all our lives, if there's one thing right the day is made."

But the joys of *Put Out More Flags* do not reside entirely in its major characters, male and female, drawn at full length; for each of these, there are a dozen vignettes of people and places, sketched, it would seem, in a second with an artist's almost contemptuous skill. Thus one of the most enchanting women in fiction, the young Lady Molly Meadowes, who marries Peter Pastmaster, materializes, doughty and adorable, before the reader's eyes in a mere four and a half pages. Thus the fusty, echoing, obfuscatory aura of the great bureaucratic ministries of wartime London is caught forever in a line or two, in a single dizzying stroke of observation. And thus a mosaic is built, a great mural embracing all London, all England, on the brink of the dissolution forever of its old order.

I hope you will give yourself the pleasure of reading—in between the often promising but unfulfilling novels being published now—this triumphant, ordered, perhaps triumphant *because* ordered, exemplar of the art of fiction. If I'm not mistaken, *Put Out More Flags* is the greatest of Evelyn Waugh's great novels. As such, it deserves to be revived and reread as long as we read English.

Edmund Wilson

Time after time, in the years I've been reading Edmund Wilson, since I first discovered his criticism in the *New Yorker* in the fall of 1944, I've been tempted to write him a fan letter; several times, moved by the lucency and prescience of one of his judgments, I've started such a letter; always I've been forestalled by the seeming impudence of the gesture, given Wilson's magisterial eminence; and now it's too late.

Too late, anyway—though I confess I thought of it on hearing of his death—to apostrophize him posthumously with a public version of my letter in these pages. But not too late, perhaps, to memorialize him by making a point or two about his stance and scope that have been missed, so far at least, by his many eulogists.

It is taken as read—and I concur—that Edmund Wilson was the greatest of our critics of this century, and among the three or four greatest—along with T. S. Eliot, Wallace Stevens, and F. Scott Fitzgerald—of our literary men. He has been widely and rightly praised for his long and almost obsessive study of many literatures, including, of course, our own, and for his ability to make enlightening connections between them; for his unsparing spirit of inquiry and the discoveries it led to; and for his destruction of the literary isolationism of this continent. It is not too much to say that he, almost single-handedly, replaced the dim, effete domestic idols of the late genteel tradition with the real giants of modern European literature.

What enabled him to do all this? That point hasn't really been discussed. And it deserves to be, because Wilson is not only a towering figure but also a unique one; nobody, before or since, has possessed quite his quality of, to coin a phrase, involved detachment, quite his ability to render an objective judgment in an issue with which he was concerned as a partisan, quite his talent for lively—even popular—exposition of the most abstruse and arcane subjects.

I think several elements in his character and training made these achievements possible. First, he was a born showman and didact, as his early infatuation with magic suggests; though he was not a public performer on the lecture platform, he must have had a powerful predilection for dazzling and edifying the public through his writings. Second, he was never an academic; he did not wall up his light or circumscribe his experience by retreating into a university. Instead, he remained very much in the world and of it, and his ferocious erudition was tempered and broadened by a continuing acquaintance with all sorts and conditions of men—and an appetite, on the scale of John Dos Passos', for life. Third, as kind of a corollary, his own drive for distinction (and perhaps his educative bent) led him to publish at length in popular journals—the *New Republic* and the *New Yorker* in particular—which would assure him a fairly sizable, though mainly nonacademic, audience. Finally, one condition of publication in magazines like these is the possession of a clear, cogent, untechnical style, free of the jargon of academic criticism; this Wilson developed early.

We have now connected the dots of the puzzle, so to speak, to make an outline portrait of a man who must be virtually *sui generis:* a distinguished scholar—though one who owed allegiance to no established school of criticism—who was also a practicing literary journalist of the first rank (indeed, he was alone in that rank). This remarkable duality of solitariness and popularity must have accounted both for Wilson's remarkable independence of judgment and for the irresistible readability of even his most casual essays. (As evidence of the latter, let me adduce a recent example. I had just begun to read a book I'd been looking forward to with some eagerness, when I decided to glance again at Wilson's *The Bit Between My Teeth* in preparation for this article. So mesmeric was the impact of these critical essays, written between seven and twenty-two years ago, that I found myself rereading the book *in toto* without a thought for the neglected new volume, which deals with the pressing issues of the 1972 elections.)

I turn often to Wilson's collections of critical essays, to his incomplete memoirs, of which *A Prelude* seems the most satisfying, and to his political writings; less often to his flawed and idiosyncratic fiction and his decidedly quirky poetry. But one book I find myself rereading more often than any other of his twenty-odd titles is one that sheds a quite different light on its author and his times, *The American Earthquake*. It is composed of pieces of what the author calls "simple reporting," written between 1923 and 1934 and collected in 1958, and it is quite the best book about that period in America I have ever read. Looking back, it is hard to imagine the Jeffersonian aristocrat Wilson moving among people of all classes, conditions, and regions of the country as a humble reporter; but that is exactly what he did, and with results so telling and moving that they prefigure—and perhaps enable—the later work of a number of lesser writers who have reported firsthand on the situation of ordinary Americans.

The American Earthquake, for all the casualness of its compilation, has a strong and cogent scheme: in the first section, called "The Follies," Wilson deals with the excesses of the Boom; in the second, "The Earthquake," with the consequences of the Crash; in the third, "Dawn of the New Deal," with the painful beginnings of the slow climb back. The first section is all skewed sunshine and driving energy—vignettes of apartment-hunting in New York, Texas Guinan's nightclub, the finale at the Follies, the circus, brownstones coming down and skyscrapers thrusting up, a Princeton reunion, the Gray-Snyder case, and such touching notes on style as this:

> In the billiard parlors of Waterbury and Scranton, young men are wearing the blue shirts and the white-rimmed gray hats of the Prince of Wales; and in the back streets of Newark and Sche-

nectady, little girls in the green hats of Michael Arlen are dancing the Charleston on the pavement.

In the second section, all this forced gaiety and expansion turn to something sour and sinister: we see the political head-quarters in New York on election night, 1930; we watch a deputation of depositors in a failed bank wait on Mayor Jimmy Walker with their demands for restitution; we visit Detroit to talk to the unemployed; we tour rural Kentucky with a Red Cross worker and a county agent; we investigate a rash of suicides in Brooklyn; we are present at the grand opening of the Empire State Building; we interview the survivors of a mine dispute; we attend the infamous Scottsboro case; we inspect the irrelevant nonsensicality of Los Angeles and return to a textile workers' strike in Lawrence, Massachusetts. All of these reports are written with artful simplicity and directness; all of them are fresh and moving now. Two in particular—"Detroit Motors," with its sustained opening section that describes the dismantling and resmelting of junk cars at River Rouge with the cumulative force of some *ballet mécanique,* and "The City of Our Lady the Queen of the Angels," which uses the outrageous wordplays of a Joyce to describe the indescribable—qualify as distinguished literary experiments as well. A few of these outrageous words from the Los Angeles piece—which does for Los Angeles architecture what S. J. Perelman's brilliant and contemporaneous "Scenario" does for the Hollywood vulgate—will show what I mean:

> The residential people of Los Angeles are cultivated enervated people, lovers of mixturesque beauty—and they like to express their emotivation in homes that imaginatively symphonize their favorite historical films. . . . Here you will find a Pekinese pagoda made of fresh and crackly peanut brittle—there a snow-white marshmallow igloo—there a toothsome pink nougat in the Florentine manner, rich with embedded pecans. There rears a pocket-size replica of heraldic Warwick Castle—and there drowses a nausey old nance.

The third section of *The American Earthquake* intensifies this juxtaposition of American banalities—short-fallen dreams like the Radio City Music Hall and the shabby, leftover twenties pomp of the Roosevelt inaugural parade—with American realities: Hull House in 1932, the trial for fraud of the president of the National City Bank, a nasty clash between striking dairy farmers and state troopers in Oriskany, New York, and the faint hopes and floundering confusions of the first years of the New Deal. There are two more personal reports that add a further depth: Wilson's first piece (1933) on a return to the ancestral house in Talcottville, which figures so prominently in his last book, *Upstate,* and "What to Do Till the Doctor Comes," a short story about casual sex and drinking—almost as a memorial to the spirit of the twenties—in New York in 1934.

I can't think of any other book—with the partial exception of *U.S.A.*—that conveys so broadly and fully the aspirations, fears, and failures of those ten years when America thought it had come of age in the world and then discovered otherwise, as it was to discover again in the late sixties. (Some recent events are almost spookily prefigured here: in a report on the address of an American engineer, H. J. Freyn, to the Taylor Society on his experiences in the Soviet Union of the first Five-Year Plan, Wilson seems to suggest that the mass scientific management of the Russians gave rise to an American desire to emulate them, which raises the possibility that the military-industrial complex isolated by Eisenhower, and Emmet Hughes, at the end of the fifties was actually the result of competition with the Soviets dating from the thirties. Again, in a 1957 footnote to an earlier article on the New Deal, Wilson implies that "the irresistible instinct of power to expand itself" led Roosevelt to welcome and even provoke the Second World War, with the consequence that "we turned up after the war occupying or controlling foreign countries all over America, Europe, Asia, and the Middle East. . . . After years of being shocked by the imperialism of others, we are developing a new kind of our own." This seven years before Vietnam became an issue.)

Thus *The American Earthquake* not only provides a detailed and emblematic picture of American life in the Boom and the Depression but also connects that past with the immediate present. In itself, the book is an enduring achievement; above that,

it is a persuasive piece of evidence that points to the chief reason for Wilson's preeminence as a critic not only of arts and
letters but of politics and manners: an experience deeply rooted
in a life beyond the world of books.

Wilson is dead, but, thankfully, we have much more to hear
from him. Roger Straus, his publisher, recently revealed that a
number of volumes of Wilson's journals are still to be edited and
published in the years ahead. It is likely that they will be as
engaging and pungent as his earlier books, but with a stronger
element of the personal. I look forward to them with intolerable
impatience.

W. H. Auden

The day after W. H. Auden's unexpected and untimely death, I was incensed to see a suggestion in the *New York Times* to the effect that the poet's work might not outlive him. Now, I'm prejudiced in favor of Auden—as you will abundantly see in the course of this article—but I think that any objective and fair-minded critic would allow the likelihood that his work, in large part, will go on being read, and go on being influential, for many years to come. And probably permanently. While several obituarists have touched on the coldness and distance of Auden from his work—and, presumably, from his readers—there was much more to his verse, I think, than a cold, clever, star-like glitter. Unlike the more open confessional poets who followed him, he kept his soul well wrapped behind the surface lightning of his poetry; but unlike them, too, he combined a universal feeling for the human condition with his scrupulous, precisian judgments upon it. Like his idol Mozart, he made music that was formally grave and joyous without forsaking the human impulse, the human aspiration, from which it sprang.

But to my prejudice. When, in the early fall of 1945, I sat out on a slate roof at Harvard and composed my first poems, I lacked a corrective influence, a *cher maître* near enough to me in time and circumstance to give my verse that astringent distancing and humane bite that characterize the best of modern poetry. My first poems were turgid, maundering, soft-centered, and fraught with an illicit weight of Elizabethan borrowings. (I've recently looked over a long-buried pile of these juvenilia, and I'm strongly tempted to burn them, on the grounds that they would certainly incriminate me as a boy boob among poets.)

It was not until I discovered Auden that winter that I met my Influence: the stern, minatory figure that, poetically speaking, put iron in my veins, bone in my backbone, and lead in my pencil. I had been moved—and I daresay influenced—by both Yeats and Eliot, but it was Auden who became my closest literary kin (from, of course, my point of view only; I never met Auden, and it's likely that he never heard of me). Like me, he had a boyish love of landscapes and machinery; like me, he had a predilection for the remedies of radical politics; like me, he saw the cataclysm of Europe in this century as an opportunity for romantic adventurism.

More important to my development, perhaps, he was also a virtuoso poet, capable of besieging and capturing the most difficult of traditional forms, from the sestina and the villanelle to the canzone; capable in almost the same breath of mimicking the tempo and language of an American blues or folk song; capable of a Popean delicacy of means or a Swiftian volley of scorn; capable of Anglo-Saxon spareness and Tennysonian orotundity.

When I read his poems, available mainly, in those days, in the slim Faber editions printed in England before the war and purveyed by the Grolier Bookshop in Cambridge, I was not so immediately aware of form; instead, I was galvanized by the content. Auden had drawn his own sketch map of the world between the wars and peopled it with his own creatures, taken from life but transmuted by his art into the stuff of modern myth: secret agents, airmen, conspirators, "short-haired mad executives," losers like Miss Edith Gee, all contorted by the air of between-the-wars into something sinister, significant, political.

When, sitting in a cheap flat on Beacon Hill in Boston shortly after my graduation from college and wondering not very purposefully what to do with the rest of my life, I picked up the first American edition of Auden's *Collected Poetry,* I was powerfully moved by the sweep and span of his work, and not less by his example. He seemed to me then a poet for all conditions and seasons, a man who could write plainly or elaborately, subtly or bluntly, on any given subject or occasion, and all in a flawlessly intelligent poetic diction and syntax of his own.

I vowed—as heartily as I could vow anything in those languid post-graduate days—to follow, at a distance, in his steps, and to try to forge some sort of voice or instrument that would allow me to comment on the world as he had done.

I failed in this; four years later, discouraged by lack of luck in publishing my verse, I stopped writing it for a pause of what amounted to ten years more. But, all through the discouraging fifties and the dawn of the sixties, I remained aware of Auden's course and growth as a poet, of his perfection of an Anglo-American voice, of his long and witty—but always unpompous —descants on his, and man's, changing and static condition. I loved in particular "Under Which Lyre," his Harvard Phi Beta Kappa poem of 1946, in which he effortlessly pilloried the pretensions of students and teachers returning to college after their successful and morally profitable war; many years later, faced with the need to compose a Phi Beta Kappa poem of my own, I toyed with the idea of basing my poem on Auden's model, but, after a few leaden trial balloons, thought better of competing with my master and wrote something else more manageably my own.

I loved, too, in Auden's middle and later years, the cool achievement of "In Praise of Limestone"; the lyric pyrotechnics of such poems as "Prime"; and the chatty animadversions, larded with O.E.D. obscurities, of Auden's nose-thumbingly trivial domestic poems. Though it is likely that he did not grow greatly in scope or stature after 1960—if asked, I'm sure he would have said he did not choose to—he remained the closest thing we had to a universal man of the arts: poet par excellence, critic, librettist, unflappable commentator on the spreading mess the world was in. He was the very model of a grand old man: punctilious, unbellicose, evenhanded, coasting with evident enjoyment down the waning rim of his life and into—well, posterity?

Of course. Returning to my first argument, it is unthinkable that Auden should be lost to the generations ahead because of an imagined aloofness, an imagined lack of human warmth in his verse. Wystan Auden was no more unmoved by the condition of the race than, say, George Orwell; while Orwell used the dogged language of Defoe, lit by the lightning of indignation, to reveal the inequities of our time, Auden couched his caveats and demurrers in a high and glittering lexicon which made use of the whole poetic tradition in English. And some of his most polished, artful poems do not lack for love, for anguished fellow feeling. Let me quote a few of my favorite—and his most moving—examples, all from "Songs and Musical Pieces" in the *Collected Poetry:*

XI
Lay your sleeping head, my love,
Human on my faithless arm;
Time and fevers burn away
Individual beauty from
Thoughtful children, and the grave
Proves the child ephemeral:
But in my arms till break of day
Let the living creature lie,
Mortal, guilty, but to me
The entirely beautiful. . . .

XIII
Let the florid music praise,
    The flute and the trumpet,
Beauty's conquest of your face:
In that land of flesh and bone,
Where from citadels on high
Her imperial standards fly,
        Let the hot sun
        Shine on, shine on.

O but the unloved have had power,
    The weeping and striking,
Always: time will bring their hour;
Their secretive children walk
Through your vigilance of breath

To unpardonable death,
    And my vows break
    Before his look.

XXI
O lurcher-loving collier, black as night,
Follow your love across the smokeless hill;
Your lamp is out and all the cages still;
Course for her heart and do not miss,
For Sunday soon is past and, Kate, fly not so fast,
For Monday comes when none may kiss:
Be marble to his soot, and to his black be white.

The defense rests; I can't think that any finer or more affecting lyrics have been written—or will be written—in this century. Though the weight of his work as a whole is yet to be judged, I can't help believing that Auden belongs to the ages; and great delight may they find in him. The harum-scarum verse plays of the thirties—*The Ascent of F.6* and *The Dog Beneath the Skin* —what a funny and acid picture of Europe's "nightmare of the dark" they will convey to future students. The great elegies to Yeats, Freud, and James—what awesome public monuments they will be in the principal squares of the cities of the intellect a hundred years from now. And the personal, philosophical, ruminative poems, tracing their author's journey deeper into civility and Christianity—what a chart of our intellectual history they will provide our heirs. Above all, what a magnificent body of practice in the art of verse Auden has left us for edification, example, and, yes, again, delight.

When I heard of Auden's death, I was moved at first—as I have been on the deaths of other writers—to compose an elegy of my own for him. But, as in the case of my abortive Phi Beta Kappa poem, I cried off on the grounds that it was impossible to top the master at his own game: reading any elegy of Auden, I myself would be all too likely to say, "Ah, but he would have contrived this better himself."

So I have written instead this fragment of reminiscence of

how his work affected me when I first came upon him, and how it has affected me for the rest of my adult life. Because he *has* lived, in his enduring influence on myself and others, it is safe to say that he *will* live. Of that I am quite sure.

In Bardbury

(For John Malcolm Brinnin)

"This ere is what," says Mr. Carpenter,
The coffin foreman, in a herringbone
Waistcoat and gold-rimmed spectacles obtained
On the National Health, no doubt, "This ere is what—"
And points one digit to a neatly joined
And midget casket, just, to judge from the
Miasma of acetone, neatly cellulosed
In a suitable baby white, "This ere is what
We buried the remains of Mr. Eliot
In out there," pointing to the churchyard of
St. Muse. "And shockin little of im there was:
Two little volumes not ardly bigger than the
Basingstoke telephone book." With which he shook
His ploughshare nose and a colorless drop fell off.
"Now look at this ere:" a rod-long oak box,
Full fathom wide, wood dark as blackbeetles.
"This ere size is the one we ad to use
To plant the Poet Laureate, if you'll excuse
My French. More books than a ole libary."
Thanks, Mr. Carpenter, for the florin tour
Of Plume & Sons' back room. I point my broad-
Stub nose toward the moist, unpainted air
And pad out past the bone booths in their rows
To the green-grown, gray-pocked graveyard right out there,

Patrolled by stick-straight Mr. Sacrister
In his green-grown gray cerement.
"Two new memorials of special note
You'll wish to look at, sir," he says, by rote,
And courteously conducts my crofted arm
To one small marble marker, two by two,
Charged with her arms and "By Appointment to
H. M. the Queen her Poet Laureate."
The tumulus extends five yards in front of it.
A pause. Mist drips from lindens. My guide clears
His throat, discreet. "On this side, sir, we ave
The other monument." A minute's walk.
Above the tiny mound, a tall Trajan's
Column materializes out of moist
And pearl-gray air. A cool Ionic plinth
Incised with one chaste E. A fluted shaft
As great in girth as any tree, which shades
Up into thickening mist and disappears.
"Massive but tasteful, sir, I'd say." The yews
Drizzle in silence on St. Muse.

iii.
Curmudgeonations:
Life in
These Here
United States

A Middle-aged Declaration
of Independence

I've grown damned sick and tired of having the youth culture, whatever that is, rammed down my throat by members of my own generation. I am all for the self-determination of the young; but I am equally in favor of the self-determination of the old, or getting on for old, and I do not think that a mindless and guilt-ridden capitulation to the questionable values of the young will set my people free. Those of us who were born before, say, 1935 have some values and some virtues of our own, and I think it's high time one of us spoke up for them.

In the teeth of a perfect gale of mass-media propaganda to the contrary, I'd like to suggest that the middle generation possesses a greater share of skill, subtlety, discipline, and judgment than its juniors; that the kids could learn from us in these particulars, not we from them; and that there is nothing sadder or more comic than a middle-aged swinger who has sold out to the values of his children.

What brought us to the state of a sort of despised East Germany of the spirit, surrounded by our younger, brighter, more modish neighbors, watching our contemporaries defect across the border to the young Wild West? Largely, I think, a lack of self-respect, without which we could not even hope for the respect of others.

Two world wars and a depression in between destroyed our fathers' arrogant certainties, their rigid religious and ethical systems, their progressive belief in the perfectibility of man; we learned, early on, to withhold judgment, to view with jaundice, to curb enthusiasm, and to duck. To cultivate one's garden—to succeed in our chosen work and to provide amply for our families—seemed a high and worthy goal when we returned to civil life at the end of World War II, and we lost no time in losing ourselves in its tillage, in becoming better providers, materially, at least, than our fathers ever were. So good, in fact, did we become that we provided our children with a leisure we had never had—a leisure they soon employed to catalogue their grievances against us.

When their bill of particulars indicting us was brought in in the early sixties, we were all too ready to incriminate ourselves, to confess our guilt as floridly as a defendant in a Soviet show trial. Yes, we had neglected our children for our work; yes, we had substituted money for love; yes, we had set a bad example; yes, we had espoused, in our preoccupation, the melioristic thought that the world would mend itself by itself without our active help. Given the historical circumstances, it seems likely that our generation, conditioned by ten years of depression and five years of war, could not have conducted itself in any other way; but we were quick to forget, in 1965, that our goal of survival had been an honorable one in 1945, and that we were not monsters but fallible men.

So—rather like the Beautiful Liberals of today, who shudder with masochistic pleasure when they confess their personal complicity in the plight of the black man and the Indian—we sought to expiate our guilt by accepting the whole blame for the problems of our children. From there, it was only one short step to abdicating our self-respect, negating our own values, and embracing, without thought, the intransigent, escapist dreams of the most militant of our children.

Those dreams should indeed be questioned: can an adult of fifty, having seen what we've seen of the world, seriously believe that society can heal its wounds by going on a diet of mind-damaging drugs, ear-shattering music, indiscriminate sex, activist violence, and personal irresponsibility? We must hope that these dreams are a phase the kids will pass through; we must not, on pain of becoming laughingstocks, attempt to ape them.

That is why I am assaulted by mixed feelings—an urge to whinny and an urge to weep—when I see some portly burgher of fifty togged out in beads and flares and sideburns, or when I see a middle-aged mother shame her very proper teeny-bopper daughter with the shortness of her skirts and the thickness of her thighs. Man was not born to be young beyond his time, any more than he was born to fly; the young will not respect us or accept us for forsaking our very real gifts for a raddled imitation of adolescence.

And some of us have gifts our kids have not: gifts they may never be fortunate enough to come by, given the hotting-up of technology and the acceleration of the world past the threshold of human sight and human hearing.

We have the gift of knowing how to read. We were lucky enough to have been born too early to be seduced by television; we can, many of us, still sit down and get as much or more concentrated pleasure from a book than we could from any television show or movie. (A recent case in point: after seeing *Catch-22,* which I thought to be a terrible movie, I reread Joseph Heller's novel and caught myself thinking, "It works much better than the movie—but after all, Heller had his mind and the English language to work with, not just ten million dollars' worth of talent, props, and film stock.")

We have the gift of knowing how to work. Some of us, anyway, have found that it's perhaps the greatest of all pleasures— something you don't find out until you're in your thirties, if then. Work—the subduing of concrete or abstract materials to your will and expertise—is immensely satisfying, one of the three or four things that can certify your value as a human being, that can challenge you to grow, that can ensure your immortality, however humbly.

We have the gift of knowing how to judge. Our checkered experience has given us a sense of likelihood, of probability; we can more accurately assess the chances of any enterprise than most people half our age—unless, of course, we are blinkered by the narrowness of the institutions we work in.

We have the gift of knowing how to remember. Our past is, for all its terrible difficulties, a better past, I think, than the one the kids will have to look back upon; it is an enormous source of strength and pleasure for us, and sometimes, when essential, of escape. If you were in New York in 1945 or Paris in 1946 or Cambridge in 1947, you have something worth remembering, something that can shape the rest of your life for the better.

We have the gift of knowing how to love. Loving has nothing to do with boy-and-girl romances, or at least very little; it is the business of maintaining some kind of decent and mutually rewarding relationship with your wife and your friends through all the vicissitudes of an adult life; it is a perquisite and duty of maturity; it encompasses agreement and argument, understanding and misunderstanding, and a tough and supple solidarity that takes years to build.

We have the gift of knowing how to laugh. We do not—cannot, as proved by the pratfalls of experience—take ourselves as seriously as we did when we were kids, and as the kids do today. Because we have accepted the idea that life is tragic and will remain so, we are free to mock it and ourselves. And if we're smart, we do.

We have the gift of knowing how to live. The luckiest of my contemporaries has developed an eclectic—in the best sense, the sense of a fully developed individuality—set of tastes and preferences in people, in reading, in food, in music, in entertainment, art, and work. Each time our routine touches again on one of these tastes and gratifies it, we are inspirited by the resonance of a pleasure re-enacted, by the allusion to the whole texture of a life.

I don't pretend, of course, that there is anything saintly in these gifts; they do not make us superior, or even successful, men and women. But they do enable us to cope—with failure, disappointment, sickness, death—and to continue to move on, on a reasonably even keel, toward some perhaps minute fulfillment. Middle age is often both battered and bowed, but it contains the great and consolatory seed of reflection and tranquillity, and that game may well be worth the candle.

I have no quarrel with the kids themselves; I do take exception to their means of achieving an end we'd all devoutly wish for, and I gravely doubt they're capable of turning this society around, *pace* Professor Charles A. Reich. But what I'm really exercised about is the endemic self-doubt of my own generation, which has led so many of us, in the highly illusory hope of a modicum of love or respect or even *notice* from the young, to throw ourselves upon their scanty mercy and lose ourselves in a feeble imitation of their way of life.

No, our only salvation, I think, lies in declaring our independence of them and using our accumulated gifts and skills to challenge our system from within. Unlike the kids, we have credit and credibility within the Establishment; we wear its clothes and talk its language; we wield its kind of power; we understand the mechanics of change and how to set them in motion through great coalitions of the adroit, unsentimental middle-aged, like John Gardner's new and promising Common Cause. We can make our greatest contribution to the future—to our kids and *their* kids—by putting our talent and knowledge to work in such practical movements with possible goals, and not by copping out for a trip on the Jefferson Airplane.

Pabulum to the General

It could easily be argued that the American press achieves its finest hours in magazines. Television captures, compresses, and sometimes distorts the news of the moment in pictures that move. Newspapers—in spite of the rare exception, such as the exposé of Watergate—embalm the news of the day in rigid, formal, boring reams of eight-point type. But magazines, often enough to give us hope for our press and our system, lean back against their longer deadlines, survey the Brownian movements of masses of individuals, and reveal the news of the year, the decade, and the century. More, they have often *made* that news—in the sense of discovering trends and making them a matter of public knowledge.

Some examples. In the 1850s, *The Atlantic* provided one of America's first forums for literacy and literature. At the turn of the century, *McClure's* and others attacked the trusts and gave muckraking its good name. In the teens, *Vanity Fair* almost single-handedly created this country's sense of style. In the twenties, *The American Mercury* discovered our insularity and crusaded against it with the weapon of laughter. In the same decade, *Time* found a new way to report the news—a way so terse and breezy that it made ten-day-old stories seem fresher than that morning's turgid headlines—and *The New Yorker* invented a new mode of American cosmopolitanism that fused high wit with high seriousness. In the thirties, *Life* liberated magazine journalism from the dominance of text and made good pictures tell the story. In the forties, *Holiday* proved that a special-interest magazine could be well written, well edited, and well illustrated.

Then came the fifties and sixties and seventies, the season of adversity, decline, and death for many magazines. Television took over the burden, the highly lucrative burden, of advertising mass products to the masses, and magazine revenues fell away. The giants died, one by one. The smaller survivors shrank in circulation and advertising volume. Only the highly specialized hobby magazines—cars, photography, boating—seemed to prosper. Except for a proliferation of skin books, new ventures often died a-borning: the vaunted new *Saturday Review,* under the aegis of Messrs. Veronis and Charney, fell to pieces in a flurry of different editions and conflicting subscription offers like a collapsing house of cards (*Saturday*'s long-time editor Norman Cousins has doggedly striven to fit the pieces back together into a viable publication). And, as the seventies progressed, three more pieces of bad news for magazines loomed on the near horizon. First, postal rates escalated. Second, paper supplies declined, creating a genuine shortage by the end of 1973. Third, the relationship between the press and its readers, hardly affectionate at best, slipped further downhill—with an assist from the late, unlamented Spiro Agnew—by 1972; even the sterling Hawkshaw work at the *Washington Post* failed to redeem the press in the eyes of a disillusioned public after Watergate.

Given all these signs and portents, warnings and omens, it might be thought that any new magazine or newspaper of the seventies would perforce have to be fresh and radical in its approach and subject matter, granitic and unassailable in its integrity. Not at all. *New Times,* the major new magazine entry in 1973, has not, to date, lived up to its prospectus: its stable of writers, redoubtable as they are in theory, have failed to practice their highest art in the pages of the magazine, a failure underscored by listless editing. *W,* the leading new contender in newspaper format, is equally a botch. Hideous typography and color like a maltuned Motorola simply serve to emphasize the thinness of the kitsch therein purveyed: endless beautiful people on an endless voyage to nowhere, about whom nobody who really matters could possibly care.

Hope springs eternal. Nineteen seventy-four begins with two new publications that, despite their designedly dated outlook and content, may well make it on the newsstands and—more importantly—having wisely decided to eschew mail subscriptions, the supermarket checkouts of America. The first is *The National Star,* the initial American product of Rupert Murdoch, the Australian publishing magnate who has made such a splash in London with the *Sun,* the most aggressive of England's scabrous national dailies, whose messy blend of sex, celebrities, and crime is in itself a national scandal. *The National Star* follows closely in the giant steps of its parent publications, measuring up nicely to the highest standards of what Fleet Street calls the tit-and-bum school of journalism. In deference to American Puritanism, however, both t.'s and b.'s are decorously draped in the *Star,* and it follows a number of its Stateside antecedents in its format and features. The granddaddies of all scandal sheets—Hearst's *American Weekly* and Bernarr Macfadden's *Daily Graphic*—are paid homage in the *Star's* tabloid format and its accent on high crimes and high jinks; their daddy, the *Daily News,* is honored in such features as "Liveliest Letters—$2 for your stories" and a spate of test-yourself quizzes ("How to Know If You Are an Alcoholic"). From its lately sanitized contemporary, *The National Enquirer,* the *Star* borrows part of its name and much of its understanding of How Far to Go: though the *Star* contains many an innuendo, there are no out-and-out exposures of dirty words and deeds, nor are particularly gruesome crimes given houseroom.

The result is a totally aimless, totally amiable potpourri of forgettable trivia, an outfall of strained (in both senses) and puréed pabulum designed to divert the presumably mindless general public after a hard day's work ("Chee, Mae, do my feet hurt!"). Some typical headlines tell the curious Anglo-American story of the *Star:* "The Exorcist Makers' Fortune from Horror;" "Meg and Tony Feud Upsets U.S. Tour;" "The New Girl in Lennon's Life;" "The Brave Ones: Together, Teddy and Son Are Winning the

Battle of Their Lives;" "Horror Scopes—an Astrological Look at the Real You;" "Our Daughter's a Streaker;" "Sheep Serum Deaths Probed;" "Scandals of Kids Who Must Slave for Charity." You see what I mean. The real scandal is that foreign capitalists— or any capitalists, for that matter—can start such a cynical rag, whose sole intent is to rip off the weekly quarters of bored and undereducated sensation-seekers. If there were a spark of genuine irreverence or breeziness (or *anything* fresh and recognizably human) to the *Star,* its lucrative sins might be slightly more forgivable. Alas, there is not.

But if the *Star* is just the newest in a series of exploitations of working-class Americans (it's terribly easy to see it unfolded on the rumpled bed of a George Price roomer, next to the Pi-Peer Patent Truss and the empty bottle of Blatz), what are we to think of a glossier but otherwise similar type aimed at the middle class? Saints alive, Joe, please say it isn't so. But, by God, it is. The publishers of plump, stately *Fortune* and wisecracking, fiftyish *Time* have brought forth upon this continent a new abomination, conceived in avarice and dedicated to the proposition that there's one born every minute. Or so it seems when you pick up a copy of *People. People* is an enormous stretch of the People section of *Time,* justly famous for its pithy bits of gossip on the great and near-. In the stretching, something has been lost: notably the astringent, faintly heckling note of *Time. People* is never disrespectful of its subjects; rather, it is blandly deferential. And blandness, nearing banality, is the seeming keystone of the entire enterprise. Instead of rooting out the facts behind the press-release façades, *People* staffers appear merely to be editing those press releases to meet the standards of the magazine's style book: witness the early article on Tricia Nixon which purported to be the inside story of her presumably troubled marriage, as told in an exclusive *People* interview, and turned out to be a standard whitewash-cum-denial written mainly by the White House (according to Maxine Cheshire) and released, to *People'*s evident embarrassment, to a women's magazine as well.

Even the genuinely staff-researched and -written pieces won't set any journalism reviews on fire. A cover story on Martha Mitchell, billed as the inside on "her breakup with John," adds nothing

new to Helen Thomas' dispatches; another on Gerald Ford
manages to bury its tiny scoop—the fact that Ford had promised
his family not to run for office after 1975—in the second-to-last
paragraph, even though it is tantalizingly blazoned on the cover
and in the subhead over the article. Most of the story is tiresome
padding, with such mother-loving quotations from Ford as, "I
don't want to be President because I want *him* to be President,"
and, "I enjoy the press corps. I really do. We have a lot of fun."

But the real sinfulness of *People* lies not in its minute news hole
but in its bankrupt and banal viewpoint. Instead of the fresh, dispu-
tatious sassiness of a *Time* or even a *Sports Illustrated, People*
brings to its subject matter a kind of vitiated, warmed-over *National Star* approach, tricked out in neat, contemporary layouts on
suitably slick paper. There are many pictures and many weakly
punning captions ("Two Picasso Originals Worth $20 Million,"
i.e., Claude and Paloma Picasso; "Get Me a Grant," under a photo
of Cary Grant and his new girlfriend; "A Meany Smile," under—
you guessed it—a smiling George Meany), both reminiscent of
the old *Life,* except for the fact that, while the text is as ignorable
as *Life*'s used to be, the pictures are, too: a page-and-a-half photo
of Gerald Ford holding hands with his wife is hardly the kind of
probing photojournalism we expect from the heirs of Robert Capa
and David Douglas Duncan. But of course we shouldn't expect it:
People was obviously designed with painful care to be empty of
controversy. I append a list of article titles. Some are from *The
National Star,* some from *People.* See if you can guess which is
which. "The Monroe Movie That's Under Wraps;" "The Old
Presley Magic Is Still Packing Them In;" "Mailer's Million—The
Wives Are Waiting;" "A Capitalist Russia Loves;" "Marlo
Thomas Sings Out Against Sexism;" "Batman Joins the Baddies;"
"His Highness on Leave;" "Nixon's Nephew Goes to Work for
Vesco;" "A Mother's War on Crib Death;" "You Gotta Believe
in Tug McGraw;" "Jason Miller: 'Exorcist' Priest Who Quit the
Church;" "The Pain and the Heartbreak End for Al Pacino." OK,
gang? Nos. 1,3,5,7,9, and 11 are, believe it or not, from *People,*
the rest from the *Star.*

I needn't continue. Except to point out that this is a time of
great change and redirection in our society. A time when many

institutions, mostly rightly, are being called into question not by a few dissident intellectuals but by the American millions. A time when the paper shortage—like all the other shortages—is overshadowed by a shortage of integrity. The integrity of the press, like that of the state, is exposed to a new, tough scrutiny, as perhaps it should be. In any case, it is no time to create superficial, frivolous new magazines out of the whole cloth of the profit motive and to aim them at millions of middle-class Americans who should rightfully be preoccupied with more serious issues. The immediate future of America, for one.

Facing the Tube

Mise en scène: a large, cold-looking private hospital room, high up on the east face of a new building. At left, an infinitely adjustable, electrically powered bed, presently unoccupied. Next to it, a Danish-blond chest of drawers designed to hold bright-blue plastic urinals and emesis basins and surmounted by a bright-blue plastic water jug and a bright-blond telephone. At center, a large, unradiant Thermopane picture window, disclosing through its internal Venetian-blind slats a dim, late-afternoon, late-fall cityscape: a hill of serried hospitals interspersed with two- and three-story frame dwelling houses; on its summit, onion domes of a Slavic church, the needle of some sort of monument, and the apotheosis of a city of hospitals, a lone pavilion thrusting its concrete colonnade into the skyline. At right, high up the wall on a swiveling bracket, a large Motorola color television set.

Enter myself, doped up, on a stretcher from the Recovery Room. I am slid into the bed by willing hands. There follow several hours of silence, broken only by the tenth-of-a-decibel drip of the dextrose IV into my feeding arm and the hollow donjon rattle of elevators stopping and flapping open their tin doors in the shaft directly behind the wall of the room. Darkness comes down glumly, evenly, behind the pregnant rain clouds. Mercury-vapor lights pick out the hill of hospitals.

More hours pass, their shuffle interrupted only by the pad of shadowy nurses. At last, close on nine at night, my eyes snap open and my left hand begins its journey. It travels painfully over the covers and out to the boundary of the bed. It pauses, makes a leap in space, and lands clutching the edge of the blond chest of drawers. It closes over a triangular object trailing a long umbilicus and carries it back to the counterpane. Follows a soft click and a long buzz. Then a ghastly gold-and-purple light illuminates the bed, and two coarse female voices begin to decry the irreducibility of "greasy oil." In my hour of need, after a lapse of years, I have returned to the suckling solace of TV.

I don't mean for a minute to sound as if I'm one of those lofty people who's *above* TV. Not a bit of it. For years, I've watched two or three or four shows regularly every week, plus, of course, the news. And occasionally I've seen a movie. But my schedule is such that something had to go, and TV did. Thus, in my hospital bed, I was in the position of an innocent who had never, or almost never, taken television in a massive, concentrated dose. When I did, for inability to lift the juicy, heavy books my friends had sent me and balance them on a fresh incision, my eyes were—literally—opened.

Now I know, for example, what so many critics (and so many ordinary, non-expert people, too) have been crying about. TV—and I'm sorry to be about the last to come to this realization—is almost indescribably terrible. It is a nightmare of tastelessness and condescension, far worse, even, than the insistently repetitious, parrotlike ads of the thirties and forties, which were avowedly aimed at a mythical twelve-year-old mind (advertising, with the exception of quite a lot of TV spots which I'll come to, has largely outgrown this awful, awkward stage). Worse, it is a mirror of the worst and most virulent kind of American mindlessness. Like the thirties movies, but far more neurotically, both programs and commercials portray a simplistic world of gratified winners—handsome, assured—on one side, and frustrated losers—ugly, browbeaten—on the other. In the commercials, the difference is made by the product; in the programs, it is made by superior force —that is, violence—or cunning.

In *The Greening of America,* Charles Reich, who was otherwise often wrong (as the last four years have shown), referred tellingly to TV as a "riot box" which stimulated the aspirations of ghetto people without providing any means—except riot and looting themselves—of gratifying them. Having watched a lot of television for a number of weeks recently, I'd go further than Mr. Reich and say that TV is a vehicle of extreme frustration for most of the people most of the time. In the morning, we watch talk-mistresses, who manage to be simultaneously sycophantic to their guests and patronizing to their audience, roll out a tidbit tray of (sometimes dim) celebrities for our delectation and chastisement (we're dull homebodies who know nothing *in,* and we ought to realize it); later come gruesome game shows (one of them should surely be called *Naked Greed*) which dangle material carrots before the stagestruck noses of the eager child-bride-and-groom competitors and make us shake with vicarious longing for the prize, along with mostly crudely set and acted soaps, which assume that we'll find fellowship in other tangled lives; then comes (after another wodge of game shows) the local and national news, a manful attempt to reduce the *New York Times* to 2500 well-chosen words and an insult to the viewer only in its incompleteness; then the prime-time programs, a sad potpourri of flayed and outworn formulas (sit-com, crime show, drama, variety hour) or, perhaps, a mediocre movie; then the late local news, sports, and weather; then the blandishments of the late night, with sycophantic talkmasters condescending to their audience as they stride—or, more accurately, sit—through a world of small talk and high life with the nominally great.

And all through this outpouring of festering garbage—lit like a searchlight by the most occasional exception, such as *The Graduate* or Brian Moore's Playhouse-90 drama, *Catholics*—runs the mumbling (and sometimes screaming) litany of the commercials. I've already said that advertising has improved in recent years, but the meretriciousness of the networks and the stations in selling too much commercial time—and in permitting four thirty-second spots to be aired in a row, and more during station breaks—destroys not only the integrity, if any, of the programming but also the effectiveness of the better commercials themselves. This problem is exacerbated by the tendency of certain advertisers, whether for reasons of economy or simple obeisance to the old Ted Bates formula of raucous repetitiousness, to run the same threadbare

commercial dozens of times a day for months on end. Notable
offenders in this mind-bruising sadism, which approximates the
Chinese water torture in its effects on the viewer, are Anacin, with
its white-haired Mr. Nice Guy and his chart of pain relievers,
like tiny TV spots, piercing the upper centers of the brain, and
Bayer Aspirin, with its dark-haired Mr. Nice Guy and his big-lie
technique of dealing with the difference in aspirins, which is, of
course, nil. Others who literally make me want to vomit are the
aforementioned All commercial, with its gaggle of greasy-oil
haters, the continuing series of Wisk "ring around the collar" commercials with their hackle-stirring nyah-nyah refrain, the various
dreary tests of the absorbency of paper towels, and all, or almost
all, of the terrible, sexist perfume and men's cologne commercials
which beset us as I write this. (Are American men so insecure
that they feel they must wear some obscene decoction which, as
the day wears on, in the words of another annoying, but now
retired, commercial, makes them smell distinctly like defensive
polecats?) Not to mention the really terrible, because so waste-
fully naïve in their assumptions, Detroit-car commercials that are
still trying to sell us the big old gas hogs (whose chassis engineering hasn't essentially been changed or improved since 1936) on
a platform of sex, showing off, and spurious luxury. Detroit is
even now getting a painful comeuppance—painful to all of us, I
fear—for its rigidity, but it is instructive that our largest and,
presumably, most astute industry proved no more prescient about
the energy mess than the jowly clowns in Washington who guide
our destinies, God help us all.

Some other commercials with hidden agendas also deserve to
be pilloried here. I'm thinking particularly of the insidious sells
aimed at young kids, many of which incite to violence, militarism,
and a dehumanizing kind of mock-humanity (the little girl bud-
dying up, for example, to the Keane-eyed doll that says, lispingly,
"Peekaboo, I see you!"), and almost all of which make kids want
goods like hell, not very healthy in a shrinking empire whose
overindulgence has led to the probability of material scarcity for
decades, and maybe generations, to come.

But it is really the prime-time programs themselves that expose,
and comment on, the grinding bankruptcy of commercial televi-

sion in America. Each year, dutifully, the same tired formulas are stirred in the same old pots, with a few new faces or gimmicks or plot twists thrown in; each year, more and more of these anti-quated and outworn webs for capturing the public attention fall by the wayside. (The 1973-1974 season of new shows has been particularly disastrous for the networks, with anemic ratings and new programs being axed week after week.) How long will the magnates of Manhattan, like the magnates of Detroit, go on play-ing the numbers game, assuming that the only good programming is mass programming, and falling expensively on their faces year after year? How soon before some gutful wonder begins to take a chance on segmented programs, designed not to be all things to all men but some things to some men (like the best, alas *only* the best, of BBC and PBS programming), and, who knows, wins big, like the people who put *All in the Family* on the air?

I'm afraid I can confidently predict that it will be a long, long time before this comes to pass. The networks are desperate enough by now, God wot, to try something new, but their potent inertia will, I'm sure, keep them careening along the same old and pointless path. Nor will the coming economic chill give them the rich coffers to experiment; one blessing of the energy problem will be a notable slackening of paid commercials. But will those gilded barkers at the networks fill the blank time with more pro-gramming? Not a bit of it; they'll simply plug in more staccato, dopey promos for their own forthcoming shows, in the ceaseless rating-point battle with the other networks.

TV was, is, and always will be a matchless opportunity for art, instruction, and edification, as its rare triumphs have so seldom, but so clearly, shown. It is equally pellucid, though, that it will, in this country, continue to evade its opportunities and remain a commercial football for the networks and the advertisers (and one should not let the rich and greedy local stations any more easily off the hook), while the audience and its real-world wants and needs go whistling, and the placid and paunchy FCC twiddles its fat thumbs in gormless Washington.

When I got home from the hospital, pale, wan, and glad to be back among the prosaically functioning, my wife suggested one night that I sit with her and watch some highly heralded new television program. I sat down willingly before our small black-and-white TV set and began to watch. The program started; a starling flight of spots streaked by; and suddenly I was overcome by a nausea of apprehension. I staggered into our bedroom and fell down under a good book. Obviously, I had become a victim, late in life, of acute television poisoning.

The Sex Biz

Time was when a voyeur was a sick—or at least kinky—individual who got his sexual jollies by watching other people doing it, and we felt superior to and sorry for him. Today, willy-nilly (mostly nilly), America is fast becoming a nation of 200 million involuntary peeping toms, a state of affairs I'd like to deplore in the most scathing terms.

Let me begin by saying that I'm not for censorship; this century's classic legal battles for freedom to treat of sex in print and elsewhere were too hard-won and their consummations (no pun intended) were too devoutly to be desired for us to step back now behind a veil of mid-Victorian hypocrisies. At the same time, though, I think that the sanctity of our private lives, not to mention that of our literaure, is being increasingly threatened by the cynical commercial exploitation of secondhand sex.

The sexual life of a human being is a delicate balance between the ideal and the real, between the pragmatic and the impossible, worked out painfully over a period of years—adolescence and early adulthood—until an accommodation, an adjustment that will last for life, is finally arrived at. However imperfect that adjustment, it is at least a partial solution to the problem; it permits us to give and receive love, to build an ongoing family relationship, and to free some of our interests and energies for other concerns, of which excellence in our work is the foremost. Until fairly recently, our sexual expectations were modest enough so that we could accept a partial fulfillment as a condition of life and go on to other things.

Now, though, we are constantly invited by the media to participate voyeuristically in the supposedly ideal sex lives of others, to be intimidated and made guilty by that ideality, and to preoccupy ourselves with our own sexual betterment through any one of the dozens of quick, sure cures that proliferate today as wonder diets used to do.

The first step of this highly commercialized (though not conspiratorial) brainwashing process occurs when we have our sexual expectations raised for us by contact with some magazine or book or movie. *Playboy* is the proto-villain in all of this, the first mass pusher of the drug of sex to the sensually disadvantaged of all ages, the first mass packager of denatured (and dehumanized) female flesh, the first mass marketer of measured doses of addictive sexual sensation, as Walt Disney was the first mass marketer of measured doses of addictive cruelty. Like Disney, *Playboy* went about its dirty work of prettifying, trivializing, and making palatably cute (for example, "Bunny" for paid temptress) a part of the human condition within certain well-defined limits of "decency." Thus it is not alone because of postal regulations that *Playboy* has not, until very recently (and then very timidly), admitted pictorially the existence of pubic hair; it is also partly because *Playboy* needs desperately to be accepted by reader and advertiser alike as an unsubversive, overground publication that is part of the system, and partly because *Playboy's* sick male-chauvinist "philosophy" cannot admit the existence of a woman's sexual power, as signified visibly by pubic hair. In fact, *Playboy's* central marketing strategy is to sell fantasies of women as powerless, grateful sexual slaves to men who have found women far otherwise—strong, demanding, and frightening—in real life.

But if *Playboy* confines itself to selling sanitized masturbatory fantasies, other magazines, books, and movies—for a variety of motives, ranging from literary integrity to naked greed—do not. Perceiving our growing permissiveness, they have rushed to fill the vacuum with millions of feet and words of increasingly "frank" sexual portrayal. Just a few years ago, the movie *Blow-Up* created a small sensation with a single fleeting glimpse of frontal nudity; this year, no self-respecting film would dare make its debut without several long, dull, narcissistic, and often insufferably arty stretches of what John Coleman, the astringent movie critic of the *New Statesman,* has succinctly dubbed "fake fucking." Since this is as true of good movies as of bad, it means literally that we cannot sit through a serious film these days without being made voyeurs of a simulation of somebody else's sex, without becoming a thirdhand party to synthetic intimacy, without sharing a *ménage à trois* with two impersonators. This is all annoying enough, but what's worse, if possible, is that since our stupid bodies respond to these bogus sexual stimuli more readily than our clever brains, the threshold of our sexual expectations is raised without our consent and even against our will; if the rate of divorce among the long (and reasonably happily) married suddenly starts to rise, as a recent Yale study of infidelity among men thirty-five to forty-five suggests it will, these rising expectations will be a prime cause.

Books, like movies, contribute to this general malaise, and works of fiction, with their ability to concentrate *in extenso* on minute descriptions of sex, exacerbate the inadequacies of their readers and increase the dependence of those readers on a vicarious, and hence unreal, experience of sexuality. Since sex is now *de rigueur* in literary as well as admittedly potboiling fiction, it means that the serious reader, like the serious moviegoer, must become a voyeur in spite of himself. From another viewpoint, it makes me fear for the future of our literature, since so many otherwise able writers now modishly throw their talents away in trying to describe the indescribable. Our wisest writers have known for a long time that sex is most effectively treated by indirection, precisely because, in large doses, sexual exposition tends to engage the physiological, not the intellectual, attention of both writer and reader, and thus polarizes and distorts the fabric of the book and the intentions of the author. There is also the danger of becoming ludicrously clinical; as John Cheever remarks in *Some People, Places, & Things That Will Not Appear in My Next Novel,* "Out with this and all other explicit descriptions of sexual commerce, for how can we describe the most exalted experience of our physical lives, as if—jack, wrench, hubcap, and nuts—we were describing the changing of a flat tire?" Finally, there is the peril—again, for both writer and reader—of arrested development, of dwelling eternally in naïve wonderment on the rather simple marvels of the fact that tab A does indeed fit slot B, or what Philip Larkin calls "the printed instructions of sex." "Isn't it time," to quote Cheever again, "that we embraced the indiscretion and inconstancy of the flesh and moved on?"

What we move on to as consumers, though, is more printed instructions: specifically, the great spate of sex manuals loosed on our heads by publishers who get their kicks from grosser profits. Having weathered years of euphemistic explication by the old masters (or Masters) of the sex books like Dr. Theodor Van de Velde and Havelock Ellis and the leering Albert Ellis, we finally broke through to new high ground with the imported *ABZ of Love:* assorted fully illustrated compilations of positions (from which we were surprised and gratified to learn of the existence of added tabs and slots); and, latterly, *The Sensuous Man, The Sensuous Woman,* and *The Couple.* If you doubt that it is a degrading experience to read one of these books with serious intent, spend a half hour with *The Sensuous Woman;* it is exactly like spending half an hour in the home of a semi-literate woman of execrable taste who insists on explaining to you nonstop the provenance and price of each of her possessions. Yet tens of thousands of unfortunates who lack—or think they lack—a full experience of sexuality buy and consume such tawdry slop in the earnest hope of becoming better and more valued people.

Perhaps equally irritating—though probably far less demeaning—is the parallel trend of late toward childish scatology for its own sake in the media. Thus some late talk shows (but not Dick Cavett) would consider themselves incomplete without at least some unhousebroken bathroom references; thus every youth-oriented new movie must show the hero at a urinal or in a toilet stall; thus one William Magruder, an incredible crew-cut apparition out of the late forties, had to certify himself as one of the boys in the otherwise adult purlieus of the Cavett show by defending his stegosaurian brainchild, the SST, with an analogy involving flies and road apples; thus the crude, inane, and boring film, *There Was a Crooked Man,* uses a clutch of those selfsame road

apples as a clue to the direction in which the bad guy has gone.
Ugh.

Our privacy, we are told, is being increasingly invaded by technology and its mechanical and human agents—computers and
snoopers of various kinds. No doubt; but it is equally being invaded by the agents of so-called sexual freedom, the supersales-
men of vicarious experience who would obsess and preoccupy us
with sex in exchange for our money whether we like it or not. I,
for one, do not; I resent and repudiate this no-knock invasion of
an intensely private and personal part of human life with which
I feel perfectly capable, thank you, to cope without the interference of a plague of huckstering busybodies.

After I had written the foregoing, I came upon an article by
Irving Kristol entitled "Pornography, Obscenity and The Case
For Censorship," in the *New York Times Magazine*. Mr. Kristol
argues persuasively for a "liberal censorship" which would distinguish between erotic art and hard pornography; he believes,
following the arguments of Walter Berns in a recent issue of *The
Public Interest,* that pornography, like such outlawed entertainments as bearbaiting and cockfighting, tends to debase and
brutalize the people. He feels that "pornography differs from
erotic art in that its whole purpose is to treat human beings ob-
scenely, to deprive human beings of their specifically human
dimensions." Further, "when sex is public, the viewer does not
see—cannot see—the sentiments and the ideals. He can only see
the animal coupling. . . . When sex is a public spectacle, a human
relationship has been debased into a mere animal connection."
Mr. Kristol also suggests that pornography and obscenity promote
a kind of sexual regression, an infantile sexuality that is "not only
a permanent temptation for the adolescent or even the adult—it
can quite easily become a permanent, self-reinforcing neurosis."
Finally, he adds the valuable insight that, in the arts, "Gresham's
Law can work for books or theater . . . driving out the good,
establishing the debased. . . . A pornographic novel has a far better chance of being published today than a non-pornographic one,
and quite a few pretty good novels are not being published at all
simply because they are not pornographic." All this leads him to
the conclusion that a limited censorship is not only desirable but

essential, because "civilization and humanity, nothing less" are at stake.

As I suggested at the beginning of this article, I can't agree. Much as I sympathize with Mr. Kristol's arguments, I can't believe that such a censorship—apart from being a repellent measure in itself—would work much better in this country than Prohibition in the twenties or marijuana laws today. If there is an intense (and profitable) demand for pornography, there will be an immense supply, no matter how severe the penalties of the law.

No, I think we must seek extralegal redress for this infringement of our personal rights. We can do this in two ways. First, by working through consumerist means and consumer organizations to lodge a loud and continuing protest with the producers and purveyors of obscenity; these methods work, as some large corporations know. Second, those of us who are writers, teachers, community leaders, makers of opinion can bury our outmoded, liberal, laissez-faire ideas about freedom of expression at any cost—and help to cramp and cripple the mass appeal of pornography by making it *démodé,* by pointing out its kitschy insipidity, by exposing its infantilism, by laughing it to scorn.

The Bus Line in the Sky and Other Expensive Indignities

If I were to charge you several hundred dollars for the privilege of standing in line in a humid, crowded terminal, clutching two or three small but exquisitely heavy and awkward bags, in order to spend six or seven hours in the cramped steerage of a rumbling, lurching conveyance to the accompaniment of rattling dishes, screaming infants, flushing toilets, and the squeaking, booming sound track of a mindless PG movie, you would probably punch me in the mouth. With reason.

Yet this sort of humiliating slaveship treatment is what practically every long-distance traveler pays plenty for—in the name of pleasure, escape, and relaxation—today. There is a big bus line in the sky, dedicated to the proposition that Americans will put up good money (or good credit) to be conveyed, in maximum discomfort reminiscent of cross-country bus travel in the thirties or day-coach travel during World War II, to distant places. Nor does their ordeal end when they arrive at the promised (but not delivered) land. The first-class or deluxe hotels are carpeted with the serried BOAC bags of fellow travelers; the white and naked beaches of the tour brochures are discovered to be as populous as Coney Island; the gorgeous tombs and ruins swarm with ant colonies of unquiet Americans, not to mention even more vociferous Germans, Scandinavians, French, and Dutch; the browned-off natives, wearily supplying the immense demand, have little time for charm; at night, the fancy hotel dining rooms serve wizened New York sirloins while their orchestras play deceased Broadway show tunes for the dancing pleasure of couples in mink stoles and royal-blue After Six tuxedos.

Thus the unhurried, edifying exploration of an alien culture has become instead the extension overseas of the worst aspects of our own culture, thinly but impermeably applied to the face of foreign countries. In our own cities, we studiously avoid the loud hotels and tourist traps; abroad, we find them inescapable. Our national genius for marketable simulation—tear down the real thing and build a bigger, better replica—has led us, in collaboration with the dollar-eager foreigners, to turn Europe and the Caribbean into flattened, distorted caricatures of themselves, overlaid by a flattened caricature of our worst excesses of American "good living." Side by side with the domestic fakery of the Moulin Rouge, there is the imported fakery of a New Miami Beach in Paris, just as the flavorless American hotels, already flyspecked by the passage of thousands of junketing Willie Lomans, jostle such institutionalized London landmarks as the Cheshire Cheese and Madame Tussaud's. And the process is even more advanced in such defenseless resorts as Palma, where the Majorcan culture has been virtually effaced by miles and miles of high-rise condominiums, discothèques, and souvenir stands; in the Son Vida, Palma's premier hotel, there are no Majorcan dishes on the menu, and the chief recreations of the American guests are golf (on a bitty nine-hole hotel course) and snacking at the poolside (since there is no beach withing walking distance). To get any idea of Majorca proper, it is necessary to hire a car and driver and take to the inadequate and precipitous mountain roads.

If this is true outside the continental United States, it is doubly true within our borders. It is entirely possible to travel to many American cities without getting any real idea of those cities, their life, or their people. Regional differences are stylized into the cute and kitschy tourist attraction: the Colonial South is embalmed in Williamsburg and Colonial New England in Sturbridge Village; Atlanta, New Orleans, St. Louis, and San Francisco have "redeveloped" areas that are supposed to give a potted, once-over-lightly view of their past; and Los Angeles and Miami have effaced their local character in favor of a tacky, tourist-oriented embodiment of the American dream: Disneyland and the Sunset Strip on one hand, Marineland and the sixty-five miles of condominiums from Palm Beach to Boca Raton on the other.

How did it happen? If I remember rightly, it was Thorstein Veblen who first proposed that the ultimate effect of mass production would be a democratization of taste in which the lowest common denominator of goods and services would eventually be equated with the highest, and the consumption of the rich would differ only in degree—but not in quality—from that of the less affluent. This has largely come to pass. Your ordinary rich man now buys a Cadillac, a mass-produced item only marginally superior in quality to his employee's Chevrolet; since his servants have left him for better-paying, less demeaning work, he relies, like his employee, on labor-saving appliances (and suffers the same service problems with them); his travel dollars, however numerous, do not buy him more peace, more privacy, or more insight into the place he travels to than his employee's dollars do.

While this democratizing of goods and services may have had a salutary effect on plutocracy and elitism, it was also hell on the quality of life, as a peek at commercial TV, an airplane ride, or a visit to Miami or Honolulu will quickly show. It takes a positive effort of will and a strong detective sense to avoid plastic food, plastic living, and plastic entertainment these days—to avoid, in a word, becoming your own credit-card number. There are three logical if unsatisfying reasons for this. First, our masters' assumptions about taste (by our masters, I mean all those often obscure people who are responsible for the form and content of our daily lives). As I pointed out recently, the admen of the thirties and forties operated under the mistaken assumption that "mass" was the opposite of "class," and that in order to sell a product in large quantities it was necessary to make it flashy, cheap, and gaudy, in the manner of trade goods for the natives. This idea—that the mass of the public reveled in the tawdry and even preferred it to the tasteful—unfortunately caught on and infected our whole life. Now the generation that grew up on it have themselves become the tastemakers for the masses—the middle-aged minor executives in half-sleeve shirts, Slim Jim ties, and drip-dry suits who decide to put Muzak in elevators, portion-controlled chicken croquettes on Howard Johnson's menus, laser stripes on muscle-cars, *The Smith Family* on television, and inspirational pep talks on the stereo channels of United airliners. These people are in no sense innovators; they are simply dedicated to giving us more of the same, the safe, the non-wavemaking pap they themselves were reared on.

Unfortunately, though, the annoyance factor of their works is rising perceptibly, year by year, because of two other developments. The first is, simply, population growth. There are more people in elevators, in the lines at movie houses, in the streets, in the parking lots at shopping centers, in the hotels and restaurants we visit on vacation. To the mild affront of Muzak and bland, pastel decor is suddenly added the grave affront of being *herded,* like the sheep it is tacitly assumed we are, into and out of all the small occasions of our lives. The shepherds are the signs and arrows of outrageous fortune, the recorded announcements on busy telephone circuits and moving sidewalks in airports, the live announcements urging us to buy in discount stores and urging us to see the awful movie (at $2.50 extra) on transatlantic airliners. Moving in long, snakelike lines, jostled fore and aft by the bags and packages of our neighbors, we suddenly realize, at the moment that nasal, amplified, inhuman voice cuts in, that we have lost control of our lives and destinies, that, no matter how far we run or how much we spend to escape, our vaunted individuality is a fiction and a joke. At home, we may congratulate ourselves to the skies and hug ourselves with secret, sinful pleasure at our eclectic taste in music, paintings, books, and furniture; abroad—at the shopping plaza or in the Place Pigalle—all our selfish intransigence falls to the ground, and we take our preordained place in those shuffling gray lines of sheep again. (Joseph Reed, a professor of English at Wesleyan University who is also a painter, recently had a one-man show of his meticulous miniatures in London. Each painting depicted some glorious, or vainglorious, public occasion of the last hundred years; in each—a formal diplomatic banquet, a victory parade, the opening of the Burbank Airport, clouded by a phalanx of tiny Ford Trimotors, in 1931—the crowds of people were replaced by swarms of ants. This struck me as a pretty good metaphor for what I'm talking about, except that ants may have too much racial purposiveness to be quite as passive as crowds are today.)

The third thing that makes our subjugation to institutionalized indignity increasingly hard to take is our rising expectations, our growing awareness of an alternative. Though we may have given too many hostages to fortune to break out of our circumscribed lives and join those who have become street people, professional vagabonds, or members of self-sufficient communes—and though we may indeed deplore the damage to their personal development entailed in dropping out—the young, the disaffected, and the intentionally rootless have demonstrated publicly that such an alternative exists, and that mass humiliation need not be our eternal lot.

It is all part of our general subjugation to a machine, a multifarious machine that may simultaneously be a war machine, an economic machine, a teaching machine, a pleasure machine—in short, like Le Corbusier's famous (and I suspect unworkable) house, a machine for living. But if we need a machine for living, then we are living for a machine, pledging our lives, our fortunes, and our sacred honor, if there's any left, to a mechanism and not to life itself. While the logistics of providing a decent, private, edifying life to three billion people are properly staggering, I think we may reasonably fight for—and get—more serious consideration for the human principle in daily life.

In a time when every institution is being openly challenged with increasing vigor and impatience, we must shortly challenge the validity and humanity of those long, gray styrene corridors, resonant with "The Sound of Music," where we wait out our days on our way to the air bus bound for plastic Paris, Palma, Honolulu, and all the other shrines of the inhuman spirit.

Pass the Outrage, Please

This kind of nonsense has got to stop.

Last month, I took one of the editors of this magazine to lunch in Boston at a brand-new restaurant called Mamma Leone's, a gargantuan—750 seats, I think—spin-off of the original Mamma Leone's in New York. (At first blush, a showboat of these proportions seemed a bit overblown even for its proud proprietors, Restaurant Associates; on reflection, though, it appeared a more or less logical extension of some of R.A.'s more garish New York productions.) The Boston version, for all its vastiness, unblushingly featured a cameo portrait of the original Mamma in its ads, which went on to suggest *alla famiglia* feasts of liver-boggling proportions: "Eat & eat & eat," the headlines said.

We arrived at Mamma's around 12:30 P.M. on a weekday; at this point, the restaurant had been in operation for a number of weeks, or well past its shakedown cruise. After disadmiring the décor—lavish marble floors clashing with amateurish frescoes of Vesuvian landscapes and a heavy-handed swagging of red, white, and green in the main dining room—we found ourselves disadmiring the unwillingness of the servitors to serve. The waiters and waitresses, who were present in supernumerary abundance, seemed all to be deeply occupied in side work: flapping tablecloths, filling grated-cheese shakers, avoiding the few customers' eyes. Finally, after about ten minutes, a young man came, making it clear we were not his station, and otherwise pleasantly took our drink order. Interim. Time flowed slower than the Tiber in mid-summer. Then a peasant-costumed waitress, who had been standing thirty feet away and staring at our table for some minutes, lurched across, flipped up the edge of our tablecloth, muttered "Fifty-seven?" with surprise, and decided she was ours to command. We explained about the drinks, which had not yet arrived. She went off—about ten feet off—and remonstrated with the aforesaid young man for usurping her station, eventually returning with our drinks.

My friend tasted his martini, which looked rather special. It was. A cloudy crocus-yellow in color, it appeared to be about one to one. A taste verified this: one part vermouth, one part something suspiciously like water. It was, in a word, undrinkable, except perhaps to watered-vermouth drinkers. We cast about for the waitress to send it back. No waitress. She had retreated into the grotto, or possibly ghetto, behind the frescoes. Another relaxing fifteen-minute wait, spent toying with menus that featured such authentic paisannerie as "Pizza, per slice" and "Meatball Sandwich," along with such more expectable items as manicotti, veal parmigiana, and chicken tetrazzini. At last she returned to take our order: too late to send back the drink, of course. My friend ordered fettucine; I chose veal parmigiana.

Another pause—but this time, I solemnly swear, not more than fifty seconds. Two steaming plates were plunked before us. Cooked to order? In a minute? Visions of radar ranges—something new in Latium—danced in our heads, but only till we tasted our messes (the just word). Then steam tables replaced them in our minds' eyes. My friend's fettucine—which the waitress had permissively pronounced "fettaseeny"—was, in his pithy summation, "blankety." My cutlet could not be disposed of so succinctly: of the texture of an indifferent Egg Foo Yong and delicately smothered in a fire-engine-red and highly American tomato sauce, it evaded classification, perhaps because it was, mercifully, sui generis.

We had to admit the bread—Italian, what else, with sesame seeds—was good, as was the hearty, if tepid, espresso (called "expresso," naturally, by the young waiter, who was mysteriously back). The check was less edifying, considering (a) that I had asked the waitress, in my friend's momentary absence, to deliver it to me, whereupon, on his return, she instantly presented it to him, and (b) that the execrable lunch had come to fifteen dollars, and had featured the first martini that, on his own admission, my friend had ever been unable to finish.

Granted that Boston is a terrible restaurant town, which, if it is ever visited by a convention of Frenchmen, will be razed to the heaving Back Bay mud in minutes; granted that Mamma Leone's, in this incarnation, had not been long in operation; granted that my friend and I are more finicking eaters than most; still it must be said that yellow martinis and steam-table entrées are at best inexcusable, at worst a swindle and an outrage.

If this were an isolated example, we might be more willing to take our gastronomic lumps and sidle dyspeptically away. But it's not. Day after day, eating in restaurants of all kinds and pretensions, Americans are sated with gimmicky décor and starved of decent cookery. On the lowest level, one can cross the country on our magnificent interstates without ever tasting an edible meal in those ghastly roadside HoJos and Savarins serving portion-controlled croquettes under a concession license, with de absentee massa far, far away. Closer to home, the same standardized prole food is readily available on any urban strip of cars and gas and Burger Kings. Despite the cautionary collapse following the great franchise boom of the late sixties, fast-food (ugh!) restaurants still proliferate.

But that's being a bit unfair. There is, after all, some social utility in a quick, unpretentious place that fills your gut for under a dollar, especially if you bring the ravening, undiscriminating kids; and one or two of the chains—notably Friendly Ice Cream, in the Northeast, and Col. Sanders, all over—do dispense some pretty reliable and palatable food. The bone I appositely pick is rather with the more expensive . . . I guess the only sufficiently awful word is "eateries." These, of course, have levels, too.

In the nationwide motel chains, there's always a King Arthur's Court with its attendant Round Table Bar, or, to mix periods, something done with a fine and lavish hand, Olde Stratford Pub or Bit & Bridle or Yankee Tavern. In the worst and most modern, the drinks are mixed by a computerized automaton. They are quite dreadful, but this arrangement has the considerable virtue of permitting The Management to hire a busboy dressed as a bartender instead of the real article. The food in the restaurant is quite dreadful, too. Steak and roast beef are the only remotely possible choices; the steak is one of your few chances to acquaint yourself with the glories of Utility Grade; the King's Own Prime Rib on Groaning Board is cold and gristly. Gravies, like soups, are out of institutional-size cans; salad dressings, slathered on limp, brown lettuce and cellulose hothouse tomatoes, taste of indefinable industrial chemicals forged in Clifton, N.J. Desserts are made by the mile and sawed off by the foot in huge hygienic bakeries, after which they're topped with clouds of tempting hydrogenated vegetable oil, or something worse.

On the walls round about are hung artificial artifacts—huge sommeliers' keys capable of opening the dungeons of the Bastille, shields and targes, halberds, half-suits of sixteenth-century armor, sporting prints brown with old varnish applied just yesterday. Tap the collection and you'll find much of it is either plaster or plastic, suitably sprayed; tap a knowledgeable developer, and you'll find that most of these restaurant and pub décors come out of a fat book of standard interiors, sold by the yard, like fake book-backs, to restaurateurs who don't want to get involved. (I once walked into a new Chinese restaurant that was filled with a floor-to-ceiling fretwork of blinding golden dragons. An architect friend who happened to be with me assured me that this was merely The Mandarin, Interior #1161 in the handy builders' crib book.)

On the chain-motel and shopping-plaza circuit, there is also, and always, Muzak. (The Chinese extravaganza belied its prefab opulence by playing medleys of American show tunes.) This— but not much else—is missing on the next highest level, the chain hotel and independent roadhouse. Here the décor is much the same, though probably a tad more costly, but things look up in two or three respects: the waiters are real, if surly, waiters, the steak and roast beef are Good or Choice, and, alas, the check is larger. If you stick with the beef you're safe, and there's no Muzak to outshout. But the overall effect is deadening, because there's seldom or never an attempt to relate the place to the city it's in, its nature, or its history. Too expensive, I suppose, for a mass-feeding operation whose only goal is profit.

Among the most insidious joints of this class is what might be called the Jock Roadhouse, though it often sits in the center of a city. The J.R. is decorated with trophies, blurry autographed photos of the near-great and ungreat, see-through bar girls, and, infrequently, Thine Host (not mine, by God!), who has been suckered into lending his name as a front for this madness and must sometimes Show His Head and Heart to the People, as they did to King Charles after his execution. If you'd like a little side bet, I'll give you odds the food in the Jock Roadhouse is unspeakable.

Next rung up: the pseudo-classy theme restaurant, like Mamma Leone's. The reasoning here is simple: it takes years of constant personal attention to build a good ethnic restaurant (and this covers a lot of ground, from P. J. Clarke's to L'Armorique to La Bilbaina to the ancient original of Mamma Leone's). Since many people who would like to patronize such a place can't get in, either for reasons of clubbableness or because the place is just too tiny, why not run up a counterfeit or two and see what happens? These ethnic theme places have several things in common: generally tasteful and expensive décor in the appropriate style, though often reproduced instead of real, for obvious reasons; pretty good to very good (but never excellent) food at first, often simmering down to mediocrity soon afterward; a hell of a clever advertising campaign, designed to convince the unwary and the new to town that this is the old, original Hungarian Whatsit, doing business at the same old stand under the management of Franz and Josef since before . . . well, yesterday. A whole cast of folk heroes who never were has been created by the theme-men and the admen: Charley O, Charley Brown, Gatsby (and, for God's sake, Daisy Buchanan, too), the new, phony Mamma (as opposed to the real, old Mamma), and many more. Why, if the food is lacking in individuality, do they survive? Because they're selling *entertainment*—a promise of mood—to undiscriminating people, a lot of whom are socking the check to the expense account, anyway.

One unfortunate effect of this is that it tends to kill the few really good places—the last of the top-class restaurants, run by dedicated people who won't have a bad meal on their conscience, and who must charge accordingly. If you can buy a big, black, shiny car with a pseudo-Rolls-Royce grille for one-third the price of a Rolls, why buy the Rolls? Your neighbors will never know the difference. If you can wine and dine and entertain a client at some splashy place with a menu the size of a surfboard and Second Empire chandeliers (the barmaids are Second Empire French maids, naturally), why seek out a real French restaurant where the menu will be unintelligible and the waiters will snicker at your French?

The massness of everything American is obviously at fault. But it galls "the man who cares" to pay near-class prices for mass feeding, no matter how ingeniously tawdry the décor. Why, then, don't I protest in person at the time of the incident, rather than here and now? Well, a certain American diffidence, a reluctance to make a scene in public, I guess. And maybe a certain sneaking realization that it's part of a social contract that all of us have tacitly signed, that sham and shoddiness (and indigestion) are part of the price we pay for our freedom, mobility, and affluence. But is that game worth the plastic electric candle with fake-plastic wax drips stuck in the fake Chianti bottle on the fake-rococo table? I doubt it.

The B.S. Bicentennial

As it happens, I'm writing this, owing to the exigencies of a dead-line, on the morning of July 4. It is an old-fashioned Fourth if there ever was one: after a few illicit firecrackers down the road last night, the celebratory sounds have faded to a desultory chain saw, the voices of neighbors preparing for a cookout, and a few brave birds—robins, mostly—who are oblivious to the early heat.

Yet I'm reminded, in all this semi-rustic, semi-antique American calm, that just ahead lies the biggest celebration of them all: the bicentennial of these United States. Given the kinds and numbers of problems our country has faced and flubbed over the last decade or two, one might think that the forthcoming jubilee would be subdued, retrospective, elegiac, maybe even prayerful. Given our native bumptiousness and ebullition, though, one might be certain that the party would be big, noisy, brash, and pointless.

And so, I fear, it will, if the mountains of handouts, bulletins, and documents I've been reading lately are any indication. My researches were triggered off by the arrival, a couple of weeks ago, of a large, glossy, red, white, and blue envelope at the offices of *The Atlantic*. "Media kit," it shouted, in Second-Coming type, on the outside; on the inside, it was filled with exhortations to editors to do their part in the bicentennial shivaree. Entitled "How To Reach And Involve American Newspaper, Magazine And

Periodical Readers In The American Revolution Bicentennial," the central brochure began by quoting the President ("By working together to meet this unique challenge, we can make 1976 as memorable as was the year 1776—for America, and for the world") and went on to explain that, since "now more than ever, the American people look to you to lead them on into history and even greater understanding and achievement," the print media can "initiate projects and activities that involve the lives of your readers and contribute greatly to the success of the Bicentennial and this Nation." (Capitals theirs; the authors of this brochure are great on caps, conferring them on such innocent, plebeian words as Country, Print Media, Commemoration, Century, Citizen, Channel, and Quality of American Life.) The brochure then goes on to suggest some hot new bicentennial ideas for jaded editors who wish to Do Their Part, including "articles on long-time residents . . . photo stories on Bicentennial projects which can demonstrate in a particularly graphic manner [what else?] 'good works by good citizens' . . . articles directed to strengthen individual pride in one's particular cultural heritage and to demonstrate to every Citizen that every cultural community has contributed equally to American history and life [which is surely patently untrue] . . . sponsoring of Bicentennial-related contests —Essay Contests on 'Freedom of the Press,' 'How My Community Can Get Involved in the American Revolution Bicentennial,' " and so on. If the ideas seem a little, shall we say, thin and uninspired, that's only because they are. And the authors winningly admit it at once: "This list of suggested activities is by no means complete. Make any changes you feel are necessary," they add in controlled desperation.

The rest of the kit consists of a second equally glossy red, white, and blue brochure, equally full of sound if not fury, entitled "Your Opportunity To Get Involved In The Spirit of '76." It promises, among other things, that "if all of us start now and act together, major steps can be taken by the time of our Bicentennial to begin to solve the energy crisis, and at the same time satisfy our human need for a healthy and pleasing natural environment . . . we can step up the work to eliminate urban blight . . . assure the improved public transportation . . . be a long way down the road toward ending lingering discrimination . . . formulate better plans to educate our Youth . . . help instill deepening respect for Law and Order." All, one assumes, on local initiatives without federal funding, since none is mentioned. Besides these generalities, the kit includes, for some reason, a blank sheet of stationery edged in the national colors and a selection of ad mats of the bicentennial symbol, a fat, blunt-pointed star.

Speaking as an old-time medialogue, an ancient stager in the PR wars, I found all this redolent of bureaucracy, of wasteful, inefficient fuzziness, of, in an awful phrase, committee work. And so it is. The media kits, disseminated to more than twenty-one thousand broadcast and printed media (down to the level of tiny weekly newspapers) at a cost to you and me of a mere $4.51 per copy, are the creation of the American Revolution Bicentennial Commission, a model of modern Washington bureaucracy. More than a model: a paragon. Since its founding in 1966, the Commission expended tens of millions of tax dollars without apparent result; so gross did the stink become, in fact, that three congressmen, led by Emanuel Celler, fought for a detailed investigation of the Commission and its operations. Out of this came a plan, endorsed by the President, to reorganize the body, turning it into the American Revolution Bicentennial Administration, whatever that means.

Besides the disillusioned congressmen, the ARBC had been monitored by John Harr, the editor of a New Jersey-based *American Bicentennial Newsletter,* who, from an independent position, had blown the whistle on the unwieldy, leaderless Commission and many of its works. Early and often, Harr called attention to the "essential unworkability of the Commission structure" and to the ARBC's failure, in the words of the House Judiciary Committee, "to give direction either to itself or to its staff," with the result that it was still engaged in "debating its own role" after six years of existence. He also ventilated the ARBC's dubious hiring practices—one employee who earns $33,260 per year was paid $10,512 in his previous job; the politically inspired tendency of the Commission to phase itself out at the end of the second Nixon Administration, rather than continue its work throughout the entire bicentennial period, which ends with the anniversary of the founding of the Republic in 1989; the scuttling of the so-called "Jonsson Plan," named for the go-getting former mayor of Dallas, which would have translated the bicentennial blarney into real community action in many American cities; and the untrammeled powers given the White House under the bill establishing the new Bicentennial Administration. One congressman asked whether the White House wasn't seeking "absolute and dictatorial powers;" another, Representative Lawrence G. Williams of Pennsylvania, said flatly that "the bill actually establishes a Bicentennial King. . . . It commemorates the revolution to overthrow kings by establishing kings." (Said future king, by the way, was rumored to be one Jeb Stuart Magruder, before that gentleman was sucked under by Watergate.)

For all the thrashing and churning in Washington, what is being done for the states and cities that will bear the brunt of the bicentennial planning and the bicentennial throngs? Damn little, apparently. A flat grant of $40,000 a year is being made to each state out of funds raised by selling commemorative medals (a rather dubious-sounding venture which involves $200,000 in advertising expenditures and the hiring of a Baltimore ad agency). This sum is given whether the recipient state is like, say, Connecticut, neck-deep in Revolutionary history, or like Illinois, which, as Harr says, "was populated almost exclusively by Indians 200 years ago." Worse, the cities such as Boston, New York, and Philadelphia, which must expect staggering onslaughts of visitors, have received zero or negative help from the Commission.

I talked to two senior people in these city programs, most of which are strikingly sensible in scope and far advanced in planning—without a cent of federal aid (with the exception of Philadelphia, whose Mayor Frank Rizzo, a supporter of Nixon before the fall, had been promised a cool $100 million in federal assistance). One administrator said, "The ARBC set up a system of bureaucracy that's not really supportive of the cities and states. It's more of a hindrance than a help. The reputation of the ARBC is so bad that local businesses won't cooperate unless we declare we're a separate organization. So far, everything the ARBC has done has been counterproductive. The one thing they could do is provide money—but there's no provision whatever for impacted cities like ours." The people who are trying to build local dikes to channel the hordes of tourists—and to salvage some works of permanent value for their communities at the same time —are enraged at the ARBC's copious expenditures on a vast national calendar of bicentennial dates and activities and on BINET, a computerized Bicentennial Information Network created, after two years' work, by the ARBC, the National Bureau of Standards, the General Services Administration, and the Computer Science Corporation. "What's happening in Boston on a given day is irrelevant to the planners in Richmond or Washington," one official said. "The whole damn thing's a glorious waste of time and money."

Even the media kits I've mentioned have come under attack. George McDonald, of the Rhode Island Bicentennial Commission, said recently that he'd been trying to build awareness of his own group's work in Rhode Island, and that the ARBC kit simply created confusion among the local media.

Even though the old ARBC is dead and the new ARBA is not yet born, it's amusing, if not very reassuring, to note that the headless bullshit machine grinds on apace. A recent issue of the Bicentennial Newsletter, published by the ARBC and/or its heirs and assigns, calls our attention to a touching recent ceremony in Pittsburgh. On April 26, 1974, just as the Watergate fuse sizzled down to its charge, "Mr. and Mrs. David (Julie Nixon) Eisenhower received these patriotism awards in Pittsburgh on behalf of then President and Mrs. Nixon as part of the Pittsburgh Committee of '76's first Bicentennial Salute program. The Patriot Award . . . which goes to Mrs. Nixon, is inscribed, '. . . who by her outstanding dedication to American ideals exemplifies the true spirit of the early American patriot.' The New Constellation Award . . . is for President Nixon. It cites the President '. . . for his devotion to the ideals of freedom, a dedication that has kept our New Constellation ever new and bright.' "

I can no more. I'm going to finish this column, encarcel my typewriter, get in my car, and drive on down to the town common to see them celebrate the Fourth. I can hear the sirens of the volunteer fire department now. There'll be a parade of fire trucks (and maybe, if that old fool Joe Gargery, the septic-tank man, feels like it and is liquored up enough, a rather grungy septic-tank-pumping truck), a drum-and-bugle corps, a scattering of veterans in costumes of assorted wars, some more illicit cannon crackers and salutes, a League of Women Voters' flea market, and a bright-red hot dog with bright-yellow ball-park mustard for me to eat and a bottle of cheap, but good, Genesee beer to drink.

Best of all, I can promise you that there won't be a single discouraging word about goals or ideals or a new birth of freedom. Just *moyen-apathétique* Americans eating, guzzling, watching, and generally enjoying themselves.

Sick of Dick

Though he may have abdicated his regal seat by the time you read this, the resignation of Richard Nixon will not invalidate the force of this confession—the first, I believe, to be made by a plain citizen who is simply satiated with the continuing bungled nonfeasance of a man who was perfectly clearly not cut out to be president of anything larger than a used-car lot.

But let me enter a few demurrers. First, in spite of my bethedging supra, I don't think it a bit likely that Mr. Nixon will have stepped down by the time this article appears in March, 1974; it's not in character. Second, I'll counter the charge of kicking a man when he's down by reminding you that our President pro tem thrives, by his own admission, on opposition and adversity (see *Six Crises* and his repeated self-assertions of poise, coolness, and toughness during the last year of his presidency). Third, I wish to point out that my pique is prompted not so much by anger at the man himself as by sorrow over his inadequacy to fulfill the obligations of the high offices he has held.

Very well, then. I have had it. After twenty-eight years of following his Checkered career—of being confronted alternately with the Sweet Nixon (almost any formal public appearance or television address) and the Sour, or Real, Nixon (the post-'62-election California press conference, *et seq., et seq.*), I am fed up to *here,* and possibly beyond, with the burden of lugging the continued knowledge (and fear) of his ineptness around at all hours of the day and evening. It is very little consolation to have been vindicated in my early and frequent dislike and suspicion of the man; that's a bit like seeing your prediction of a stock market crash come true while your life's savings go down the drain.

Nonetheless, I am prompted to report at this late hour on my long-running hate affair with Richard Nixon—an affair that began as a cloud no bigger than a congressman's hand in 1946 and has now grown to overspread the earth and cast darkness on all things within my ken.

The feeling is a little like the one I remember having during World War II: of walking a long, weary, frustrating road which had no turning, and over whose length I had no control. Put shortly, then, I am feeling both angered and swindled by having The Ordeal of Richard Nixon visited, willy-nilly, on nearly thirty years of my young life.

The central fault, I think, is not in ourselves but in our stars: Nixon's radical inability to fit and suit his time stems from the fact that he is an anachronism. Consider his advent: into an America that had been awakened to internationalism by its second global war, an America that had voted, under the New Deal, to be permissive to and supportive of its people, stepped a Horatio Alger caricature, a self-made man in the mold of the 1890s, say, big on the Protestant Ethic, self-reliance, and free enterprise, rough on Red Menaces, parlor pinkos, and assorted leftish rats, roughest, of course, on those omnipresent C-c-communists.

From the beginning, Nixon was a flat-earther, a proponent of ideas and interests the nation at large had thought to be outworn. He was a spokesman, in a sense, for the previous generation —or maybe the generation before that. His subsequent career proved, if it proved nothing else, that there were (and are) still large pockets of people who cleave to the old ideas, and whom progress has passed by. Orange County, in short, is reduplicated all over America, but it took Richard Nixon to bring it out in voting force.

Now it is neither shameful nor evil (though it may be misguided) to make a forthright, honorable appeal to the holders of the old values and virtues in this country; Barry Goldwater, who has made a career of such an appeal, has only gained in stature as the years have whitened his amiable brows. But it was the genius of Richard Nixon to wed the conservative appeal to the modern scare techniques of advertising: to entice the insecure into his camp—and thereby ditch his enemies—by a not-so-subtle application of fear.

From the first, he settled on the Red Menace as the principal weapon in his arsenal. Nothing original about that, but there *was* originality (for which, of course, he must share credit with Senator Joseph R. McCarthy) in his inventive extensions of and elaborations on the Red idea.

This strategy first bore fruit in his successful—and infamously memorable—campaigns against Jerry Voorhis and Helen Gahagan Douglas, in both of which he imputed irresponsible leftism to his foes. This strain was continued, though in a muted, legalistic way, in his again successful prosecution of Alger Hiss; it burst out again in its full glory during his 1952 campaign for the vice presidency. But then, for the first time, a discordant note was struck; in a comic prelude to the later dirge of Watergate, Nixon's personal finances came into question, and, for the first of many times, he took to television to vindicate himself with the marvelously mealymouthed Checkers speech. It worked, not least on doubtful Dwight D. Eisenhower, who, seeing public opinion veering back in favor of his running mate, re-embraced Nixon and carried on with his campaign.

During his two terms as Vice President, Nixon was not, presumably by his President's wish, abundantly evident, though the Sweet Nixon made hay in Venezuela, where he contrived to be stoned by reputed Communists, and in Moscow, where he inveigled Khrushchev into the slightly ludicrous, but politically useful, kitchen debate.

The Sour Nixon was not far behind: he resurfaced in his own 1960 presidential campaign, in the course of which he grew increasingly dark, dour, and brusque as it became apparent that his opponent was outpacing him. Sourness shone out again in that famous California press conference, when the defeated candidate turned on his supposed oppressors and enunciated a new issue: the press against Nixon.

Then, eclipse. The Kennedy years and the early Johnson ones

began to move the country forward again along the lines laid down by Roosevelt and Truman; after the pallid quiescence of Eisenhower's two lassitudinous terms, the tempo of social action increased. Under Kennedy it was mostly heat and light; under Johnson, at least before Vietnam became a running sore in the integument of America, there was real power and motion toward the much-mocked Great Society. Nixon almost invisibly moved to New York to practice law; the eyes of the people were elsewhere occupied.

Until. Until the Democratic Party split into bitter factions and emerged from Chicago in disarray, and Nixon saw and secured his chance for the nomination—and the presidency—in 1968. Then was a new, still sweeter Nixon unveiled by Roger Ailes and a corps of packagers: the firm and statesmanlike leader, the courteous answerer—on television, naturally—of seemingly tough questions posed by a seemingly random sample of seemingly ordinary Americans. It was no great trick for this newest of Nixons to nose out the tiredly garrulous Humphrey, who had to suffer silently—and smilingly—the burden of Johnson's Vietnam policies, of which he was all too unarguably the heir apparent.

Nixon in office: a fanfare of pomps, a paradiddle of early executive pretensions, including the Ruritanian uniforms of the White House police. A clear and growing rightward drift on civil rights, on law and order, on Vietnam (*and* Laos, *and* Cambodia). An attitude of laissez-faire toward the economy, corrected, too lightly and too late, by the halfhearted imposition (and early relaxation) of economic controls. A short way with critics, especially the ladies and gentlemen of the press, leading to an ambitious campaign, quarterbacked by the unfortunate and now hoist Spiro Agnew, against the credibility of the media.

And then the PR masterstrokes: the triumphal progresses through China and Russia, the sudden vision of a generation of peaceful coexistence with those erstwhile Commie rats, our giant allies to east and west.

And then the noncampaign of 1972: a silent, monolithic working President, not given to stump speeches, against an outgunned, ill-starred liberal whose humanitarian propositions had not been market-tested. And then victory, the landslide of landslides, conferring, for the first time, a genuine stamp of popularity upon the President.

And then, conveniently after the election but most inconveniently for his place in the presidential pantheon of history, Watergate and all its writhing sequels. Shame! Grief! Mortification! Woe! Embarrassment! Richard M. Nixon, at the very height of his semi-imperial majesty, was struck from the dais at one blow and left struggling on the ground, entangled in the voluminous folds of his cohorts' sly intrigues. And perhaps—but will we ever know?—his own. At any rate, this was the all-newest of the new, new Nixons, and the all-sourest: the quiet, dog-tired, squinting face, alternately growling and whispering out of the television screen, alternately explaining, denying, and pleading for a renewal of our faith. Which was not to be. For the tiny cloud of questions that arose from the burglary of June 17, 1972, had multiplied into an armada of unanswered queries about every aspect of the Nixon presidency.

Soon the cohorts began to fall in droves. Haldeman and Erlichman, followed by a host of lesser fry, retired from office and took up new positions at the bar of justice. Then Agnew, caught in an isolated, prior peculation, took a great fall of his own and left the beleaguered President sidekickless. Nixon was seen to smart and waver under the onslaught of his hostile questioners; the soft answer that turneth away wrath sometimes became a taunt. The newly inoperative Ron Ziegler got pushed by the presidential digit. And an innocent Air Force sergeant got slapped, or patted, depending on which version you read. The fat was in the fire, all right, and nobody knew if the President would still occupy his Oval Office on January 19, 1977.

Finally the whole story degenerated into what would, if the presidency of the United States were not such a gravely consequential office, seem like pure slapstick farce: the disclosure of the existence of the tapes, their withholding, their surrender, and, along the way, the sudden Saturday Night Massacre which plunged Nixon's already stained and tattered credibility into a bath of ink. Then—can there be more, one laughs and cries?— the gallows humor of the eighteen-minute gap in the key tape, and all its public repercussions.

And still they came, the improprieties, the anguished cries of rectitude from the impugned President, the bungled attempts—like Operation Candor—to retrieve the irretrievable, the inept and shifty explanations, the cans of worms opened to clear the air (the income tax returns, for one) that proceeded to darken the air with plagues of worms and questions. The loans, the campaign contributions, the real-estate deals, the state income taxes—

Surcease! I—we—sat for far too long—twenty-eight crisis-packed episodes on the Saturday serial screen—through the comically menacing career of the man who will surely be known to fame as our worst and most inept President. Ladies and gentlemen, I give you Richard M. Nixon. Will you please secrete him in some hidden place? For I am sick of him and all his works.

I-Less in Gaza:
The Greening of
Charles A. Reich

What, to paraphrase the maddeningly pandemic opening lines of that infernal nonsense *Love Story,* do you say about a 395-page book of personal opinion and impassioned argument in which the pronoun "I" never appears? When I first read the carefully edited *New Yorker* condensation of *The Greening of America,* I was so struck by the author's categories of consciousness that I overlooked the missing first-person singular. But when I came to the whole rambling, repetitive, contradictory book, the countless "one's" and "we's" began to wear away *my* consciousness like water dripping on a stone. At first I thought that Mr. Reich, being a lawyer, might be using the juridical, or courtroom, we; later, I toyed with the idea that it might be some sort of editorial we, cloaking its arguments in impersonal credibility; still later, having considered the prophetic nature of his message, I wondered if it might be a divine or royal we; but finally, I hit upon an altogether simpler and more consistent answer, which I'll come to presently.

My original reading of the magazine version prompted the reaction that Mr. Reich was one of us—one of my generation, that is—who had gone on seeing things with the eyes of youth long after I and most of my contemporaries had become rigid and blinkered in our middle-aged perceptions. No one, not even Mr. Reich, seems to remember it now, but the brighter college kids of the classes from, say, 1940 through 1950 felt pretty much as alienated and as disrespectful of the system as bright kids do today. The big difference was that there was not a large enough number of dissidents to form a substantial community, or a single issue outrageous enough to rally around. Nevertheless, as Mr. Reich indirectly concedes, his college generation produced most of the seminal books that have implanted the idea of challenging the system in the minds of young people today. *From Here to Eternity* and *The Naked and the Dead,* both of which he mentions, deal with the depersonalization of men by armies—American armies—in peace and war; *The Catcher in the Rye,* which he also mentions, deals with the alienation of young men from their schools, their cities, and their families; *Catch-22,* which he omits, and the novels of Kurt Vonnegut, Jr., which he includes, are the new generation's basic texts in the mindless metastasizing of our institutions.

In short, though Mr. Reich seems to believe that his new consciousness is a product of the very recent past, I think it can safely be argued that all of its roots, all of its basic thoughts and attitudes, go back to the Second World War generation. On first reading his book, I was inclined to believe that Mr. Reich had at last taken his rightful place among the iconoclastic thinkers and writers of that generation after long and painful meditation. His personal credentials—graduation from Yale Law with one of the highest averages on record, editorship of the *Yale Law Journal,* law clerk to Justice Black, professor of Law and American Studies (whatever that is) at Yale—seemed to suggest that here was a man of the very highest intellect and judgment who had decided to bring his powerful powers of reasoning to bear on the central problems of our time and place.

On second thought and second reading, though, I was frankly appalled by the naïveté and slipshodness of his book, which, by his own admission, was ten years in the writing. There is no doubt that his three categories of consciousness are a genuine contribution to our understanding of America today; but beyond this basic premise, his book is such a tissue of imprecisions, contradictions, and generalizations, not to mention unsubstantiated predictions and prophecies of the most apocalyptic kind, that it is difficult indeed to associate it with an outstanding legal mind.

To cite a few of its idiosyncrasies at random: "Kafka, Dostoevsky, and many Victorians" are insequently lumped together on page 44; one of a number of glaring non sequiturs—"His efforts produce good for the corporation or institution, good for the public interest, good for his fellow man, for the more he helps his institution, the more 'self-sacrificing' he is, the more he helps himself to get ahead"—short-circuits the reader's mind on page 75; such sweeping generalizations as "No person with a strongly developed aesthetic sense, a love of nature, a passion for music, a desire for reflection, or a strongly marked independence, could possibly be happy or contented in a factory or white-collar job" (p. 135) stud the text; such questionable observations as the suggestion that a casual walker in a "nice" "clean" suburb "is watched with suspicion. . . . Police cars cruise by slowly, inspecting him. . . . Housewives look out from their windows, as if spying an unexpected patch of dirt. . . . Storekeepers . . . follow him with their eyes" in "Darien, Bethesda, or Paoli" (pp. 145–146) destroy the credibility of Reich's arguments; such contradictions as that in the passage on Consciousness III clothes (pp. 234–238), in which, after stating that they are "a deliberate rejection of the neon colors and plastic, artificial look of the affluent society," Reich says at one point that they are functional, since—in a phrase from the magazine article which is significantly deleted from the book—"people are not objects to be decorated," and later itemizes the decorations these functional dressers wear, including "a military dress jacket, all buttons and brass . . . a Mexican peasant's blanket-shawl . . . a David Copperfield hat" and "beads, a hand-tooled belt, decorations sewed onto jeans . . . ;" such jaw-loosening pronouncements as "rock music has been able to give critiques of society at a profound level" (p. 247); and such, to me at least, irresponsible positions as the impassioned defense of psychedelic drugs as "one of the most important means for restoring dulled consciousness" on pages 258 to 260. I could go on and on—at one point, for a last example (pp. 346–347), the inextinguishable lines of Wallace Stevens' "Sunday Morning" are printed side by side, without comment on relative merit, with the eminently disposable lines of Bob Mosely of the Moby Grape's "It's a Beautiful Day Today"—but for my sake and yours, I won't.

I will add, though, that the book has been equally strongly challenged on a variety of other grounds by Nathan Glazer, who, in the *New Leader,* questions Reich's picture of the weakening of constitutional safeguards, derides his arrogance in "putting down others for leading lives of inauthenticity," and generally makes sport of his pomposities and solemnities; by Roger Starr, who, in a fine, thoughtful, and unhostile piece in *Commentary,* points out Reich's baffling vaguenesses and unwarrantable assumptions on such subjects as the dating of America's fall from national grace, the conditions of life of eighteenth-century Americans, the unalloyed evil of the "Corporate State," and the unspecified mechanism by which the new consciousness will sweep away the present system; and by a host of other reviewers.

Since I have spent some years in advertising, I was particularly interested to see whether Reich would approach that business in an accurate and unbiased way. He begins by saying (on p. 12 and again on p. 79) that "the media systematically deny any fundamentally different or dissenting point of view a chance to be heard at all . . . the opinion that does get on television is commercially sponsored and thus heavily subsidized by government tax policies," a statement with which viewers of such recent programs as the coverage of the 1968 Chicago convention and riots and *The Selling of the Pentagon* might not agree. On page 80, he adds that "nothing is more subsidized in our society than commercial advertising itself." Surely not more than the Department of Defense? On page 162, he remarks that "failure to safeguard footpaths does sell cars," which suggests that somebody has deliberately placed a low priority on the patrolling of paths so that walkers will become frightened and buy cars, a species of deduction that I can only label academic-paranoid.

But he comes to his real argument about advertising on page 194, where he suggests that because advertising sells commodities "by playing upon a supposed underlying need, such as sex, status, or excitement," it "cannot help but raise the intensity of the needs themselves" and create dissatisfaction, which "is no mere toy; it is the stuff of revolutions." Thus, "when advertising paints a picture of consumer hedonism . . . the machinery of the Corporate State begins to work toward its own destruction."

While advertising that offers to fulfill these underlying needs may only cause "troubled emotions" in the well-to-do, he says, it will keep on trying to subvert the "still somewhat satisfied" middle class and raise a "fury of dissatisfaction" among the poor, for whom TV "might justly be called a riot box." As for young people, "advertising is capable of creating a maximum of dissatisfaction . . . in the volatile 'youth market,' and it has made them promises that the rest of us have not yet heard."

But when Reich attempts to portray advertising as a subversive and revolutionary force that will bring our country to a change of consciousness, he handily forgets a convincing counterargument in an earlier chapter of his own book, a chapter entitled "It's Just Like Living." Here he points out the striking credibility of material goals and their connotative, need-fulfilling, artificial backdrops that suggest "nature, adventure, traditions." He uses Disneyland as an example. After "advertising and promotion . . . work to convince the people that they are really experiencing Main Street, the Wild West, the history and adventure of America" and "the families flock to the clean, sunny, happy enclosure, how many of them realize that something precious has been taken from them, that they are being charged for a substitute that offers only sterile pretense in place of real experience? How many find the chief experience at Disneyland to be a sense of *loss* of all that they are seeing?" Mr. Reich's answer is, obviously, none of them; "the people" have been convinced that they are really experiencing America.

While it is probably true that television has a more inflammatory, more ideological, effect upon the poor, it is worth noting that the item of choice for looters during urban riots is, of course, a television set. And while it may also be correct to say that the disaffected young have received from advertising "promises that the rest of us have not yet heard," the nature of those promises is still, at this early stage, in doubt. While Reich chooses to believe that television has made youth eager to "live *now*" and to reject "the drudgery of life," it seems more reasonable to suppose that today's young people, the first generation to be fed on material promises from infancy, will, when their rebellion against parental authority has passed, fall back into the system and become the greatest consumers in our history, the first generation, in fact, of superconsumers. For evidence, look about you at the new material goals of the young: at burp guns and GI Joes, at chopper bikes and minibikes and trail bikes, at slot racers and Ruppsters and surfboards and dune buggies.

Clearly, something has gone very wrong here. A man of the highest talents and attainments has written an almost laughably slipshod and vulnerable book. Why? Let me float a hypothesis: because, in W. H. Auden's words on the death of W. B. Yeats, "he became his admirers." Perhaps, in a less literal death, a death of the mind, or at least of the higher reasoning powers, the author of *The Greening of America* became *his* admirers, assumed their ideas, their life-style, and their limitations. Who were they? Let me quote from Thomas Meehan's article in *The New York Times Magazine,* from which I've also cribbed Mr. Reich's credentials: "As he spoke, a band of long-haired, hippie-like students drifted quietly into the room and settled about Reich. . . . Known at Yale as Reich's disciples, the students are all residents of Ezra Stiles. . . . He had asked them to come because he says they had helped him to develop the ideas put forth in the book, much of which was in fact written by Reich while seated in the midst of his disciples in the Ezra Stiles dining room." Reich, who "does a good deal of smiling" and "continues to smile even when his book is being attacked," who "had left off his love beads, which are usually strung around his neck wherever he goes," "had had what he calls his vision about the levels of consciousness" in 1967, not long after he began to teach an undergraduate course at Yale, according to Meehan.

All this strongly suggests that Reich, who told Meehan, with a curious insularity, that he had had "a life like everybody else's —New York private school, college, Yale Law School," and that "I did everything right," was well on his way to making it, in the sense made infamous by Norman Podhoretz, making it in the essentially lonely corridors of intellectual power, when he was suddenly arrested—in, I'm afraid, both senses—by a human hand on his arm, the hand of a student who could become an acolyte, and who, conversely, could make Reich an acolyte of youth, but only at the expense of the maturity of his judgment.

Robert Brustein, again in Meehan's article, comments censoriously on this reversible reaction: "There is a strain of sentimentality running through some members of the Yale faculty, a strain of general unworldliness, that takes its form in flattering students by all but becoming one of them. . . . It's okay to hang around all of the time with students, as Charlie does, but this is the first time that anybody has ever tried to base an ideology on it."

So we come, a little sadly, to the significance of the all-pervasive "we" in Reich's book. It is the collective, the communal we of "all the people of the dining hall" whose help Reich acknowledges in a postscript to his book, of all the confused and alienated young admirers Reich has become in his thoughts and his writings, of all, to coin a phrase, the cop-ins upon whom he has conferred the highest distinction within his giving, the style and title of Consciousness III.

High Wind on
Madison Avenue

Don't look now—if you do, you won't see much clear-cut evidence as yet—but the man in the gray-flannel suit is on his way to the showers. A high wind on Madison Avenue is sweeping him out of power; what just blew in to take his place is a gaggle of mod-dressing kids who are changing the rules of American advertising for better and for worse.

Back in the thirties and forties and fifties, the days of *The Hucksters,* certain truths were held to be self-evident about the Ad Game. The men who played it were updates of the Arrow Collar man or the characters in Scott Fitzgerald's "May Day": WASP, handsome, Ivy, ruthless, cynical. They reputedly manipulated colleagues and clients for their own ends; stayed sober and shrewd through three-martini lunches; consumed and discarded women like cigarettes; talked, half-seriously, of running things up flagpoles; lived on the Sound in Cheeverville. All this, of course, was tosh, or nearly all of it. Superficial evidence had led outsiders to build another all-American stereotype.

The truth of the matter was quite different; the signs had been misread. (I speak with some assurance here, since I am a second-generation advertising man and a twenty-year veteran of the business.) The man in the gray-flannel uniform was a victim, not a victor, and his manners and morals, to use a dear old *Time* phrase of the period, were not the earmarks of success but the symptoms of pain, failure, and frustration. Of all American businessmen, his lot was the unhappiest: in a nation celebrated for its anti-intellectualism, he had to sell the productions of men who worked with their heads to men who worked with their hands. No flinty, self-made manufacturer or millowner was about to accept without question the words and ideas of people whom he privately —and sometimes publicly—considered overeducated, effete, overpaid, frivolous, and impractical. Worse, since advertising seemed to him simply a matter of scribbling words and pictures on paper, he often succumbed to the urge to show those city boys how it should be done—or took counsel from such other experts as his wife, his directors, and the fellows at the club. Worse still, his suspicion and hostility toward admen, who, as outside suppliers, were easier to humble with impunity than his own employees, led often to all sorts of sadistic excesses. Whole laboriously conceived campaigns were summarily dismissed; creative people worked night after night to replace them with new ones; account men with years of faithful service were banished for an imagined slight; and agencies were fired at a kingly whim.

All this led, quite predictably, to an endemic neurosis among admen. With their dignity and expertise at a discount and their jobs always in the balance, they did indeed become cynics, though seldom ruthless ones; their greatest ruthlessness was self-preservative. Flattering, entertaining, and placating the client occupied much of their time, and the advertising they produced was almost, in many cases, incidental to the client relationship. Thus it was easy for them to accept another stereotype of the time and look upon the public as the great unwashed, as the twelve-year-old minds (the result of a misreading of the First World War military-classification tests) put on earth to consume, without let or complaint, their clients' products. Secretly hating and looking down on both client and consumer, the trapped, affluent admen became elitists, and their advertising showed it. They condescended shamelessly to the consumer; they played openly upon his fears and confusions, creating new ones (B.O.) where none had existed before; they deluged him with empty, unbelievable claims and promises ("a treat instead of a treatment"); they dinned repetitious nonsense into his ever-suffering ears. And, while they played advertising as a bitter and cynical game, they dreamed of release and rehabilitation for themselves. There was, in truth, many a novel in a bottom drawer.

What we have seen so far is a classic confrontation between what Charles Reich would call Consciousness I—the client as self-made man with primitive-American values—and Consciousness II, as represented by the college-trained, verbal, melioristic ad-man. But in 1949 the signals began to change with the emergence of a new kind of adman—one could call him Consciousness IIA—who was so disenchanted with the situation that he was determined to counterattack, to reverse the roles of adman and client, to bring a new dignity and cachet to his calling. Two assumptions were necessary here: first, that the advertising man is a professional who deserves as much respect as any other well-qualified outside consultant; second, that the consumer is not a boob to be talked down to and patronized, a drone or prole, but a first-class citizen who is equally deserving of respect.

Two men stepped forward to revolutionize the agency-client relationship: William Bernbach, whose new agency, Doyle Dane Bernbach, changed the rules of advertising overnight with ads (Ohrbach's, VW, Levy's Bread) that talked modestly, amusingly, and disarmingly to the consumer in colloquial, everyday language; and David Ogilvy, whose urbane, impeccable copy persuaded the reader, step by logical step, to buy the product, and made him feel at the same time that he was in the presence of a charming, charismatic mentor of whose company he, the consumer, was eminently worthy.

Advertising has never been quite the same since then. The sensation that Ogilvy and Bernbach created on Madison Avenue echoed throughout the country, conferring a new prestige on the advertising agency and its creative people. The polarity began to change, and the client, accustomed to a buyer's market, suddenly and shockingly found himself selling his company to one of the hot new agencies. This dose of crow was highly salutary, and it resulted in almost the first advertising that took full advantage of the consumer's ravenous hunger to be talked to like a grown-up human being. The satisfaction of this hunger made the newly literate, newly affluent postwar citizen, long turned off by the patronizing prattle of ads, a voluntary consumer again. It made the

Volkswagen—a well-finished but cramped, dated, and unstable 1936 design—a best seller for nearly twenty years; it made travel to England almost a necessity instead of a luxury; it put the primitive, unwieldy Polaroid Camera on the map; it made the Rolls-Royce—a sad simulacrum of its prewar self—the hallmark of arrivism once again. In the hands of such new practitioners of the art of talking on the level to consumers—with a modicum of fun at one's own expense thrown in—as Stan Freberg and Howard Gossage, the Chun King line of Chinese foods rose from deserved obscurity to bestsellership, Eagle Shirts became the subject of an audience-participation game involving thousands of readers, and the Rover 2000, according to a *Road & Track* owner survey the most trouble-prone car in import history, became the symbol of safety and security on the road.

(I do not mean to suggest that the new admen callously plugged marginal or defective products with their eyes open; it is simply in the nature of things that an agency man, given a new assignment, will do his often very competent best to look on, and project, the bright side of the product.)

Though—needless to say, if you read any magazines or newspapers or look at any television—the great mass of advertising was terribly slow to follow the lead of these innovators, and is likely to remain so for years to come, it's still a fact that an *apertura a sinistra* was opened in the late forties, and that the whole client attitude toward agencies and their creative function continued to evolve.

By the early sixties, the young copywriters and art directors who had learned their trade under the tutelage of the Bernbachs and Ogilvys began to spread their wings and fly to other places. Some lighted in the bigger, older agencies, where they proceeded to bore from within to change the structure; others banded together to form small, new creative agencies, or boutiques, which often substituted creative brilliance and intuitive judgment for the needed and useful techniques—research, marketing, media selection—of the bigger shops.

Many of these young creative people are radically different in their backgrounds and viewpoints from the older agency men. They are often the sons and daughters of blue-collar New Yorkers, which makes them hungry, upwardly mobile, and ambitious. They are often non-WASP's—many Greek, Italian, and Jewish names now appear on the annual lists of advertising awards. They are often less than traditionally college-educated; many are graduates of art schools or film schools. And they are the first generation of advertising people to have been brought up on movies and TV rather than books and magazines; they are visual thinkers and nonreaders, for the most part.

Because of their extreme mobility (and its accompanying social insecurity), because of their lack of traditional cultural roots, they are exceedingly trend-conscious, exceedingly anxious to be with it. They make (or break) a fad or more a year in art styles, interior decoration, fashions, films, media, restaurants, and resorts. They are largely responsible, in an age of the decline and death of magazines, for the relative success of *Esquire* and *New York*—both of which, be it noted, are art-directed and designed by members of their own circle of commercial artists (it could also be said that the young agency people had a hand in the earlier success of Pop Art, much of it created by advertising artists like Andy Warhol).

How are these talented, self-concerned, hard-charging, young creative people (who might, for the sake of convenience, be dubbed Consciousness III, though their greatest interest in an ad for peace or the environment might often be said to lie in whether it will win an award or not) regarded by their agency principals and their clients? In the larger agencies, the booted, bell-bottomed, bearded creative wizards are sometimes treated like a cross between a profit center and a freak show: they are kept in segregated sections of the agency, shown off on state occasions to the clients as physical evidence of the agency's creativity, and seldom allowed to establish a day-to-day relation with the client's marketing department. (Jerry della Femina, in his laughably inaccurate and execrably worded—even though written with the help of a collaborator—book *From Those Wonderful Folks Who Gave You Pearl Harbor,* does give a revealing picture of a creative man's life inside a big, and ultraconservative, agency.)

In the new boutiques, however, the creative teams—copywriter and art director working together, almost living together, in a state of creative symbiosis—are often not the sideshow but the whole show. They are frequently the agency principals themselves; when they are not, they still exert immense influence on their principals and on their "straight" colleagues—account men, research men, media men—and, inevitably, on their clients. They are, after all, the acknowledged stars of the show, as perhaps they ought to be. Their clients must already be adventurous or they wouldn't have chosen such an agency; those boots and beards are a highly visible caveat. But, once embarked on the agency relationship, the clients find that's where the action is and become irresistibly drawn to the young creative magicians. Often they metamorphose from gray-suited, white-shirted boxes in tables of organization to bearded, booted swingers themselves. And today, even in big agencies and big client companies, there's a creeping trend on the part of chief executive officers to cast themselves in a mod mold.

So where does advertising—increasingly in the hands of Young Turks of no great learning and no great handed-down religious, ethical, or political conviction—go from here? If we were to rely on the pronouncements of Jerry della Femina, whose unsophistica-tion takes the form of Know-Nothingism and makes him sound like an apologist for such Consciousness I values as individualism, free enterprise, and laissez-faire, we might conclude that the new admen, like the old ones, would become simply handmaidens of unbridled corporate condescension and rapacity toward the con-sumer. But there are other forces abroad in the land—intelligent and undoctrinaire consumerism is undoubtedly a needed correc-tive to corporate excesses, in spite of the fulminations of Thomas R. Shepard, Jr., the former publisher of *Look*—and I think that most of the young admen who will make the advertising of to-morrow are both bright and malleable enough to accept a greater degree of regulation of advertising and even to regard it as a cre-ative challenge.

If I had to predict the look of advertising in 1980, I'd suggest that it would largely resemble the best of advertising today, which is the direct descendant of the pioneering efforts of Ogilvy and Bernbach. On television, it will position a product or service in the life of the consumer, simply suggesting, for example, that Monday-morning headaches are endemic and that it might be handy to have some Alka-Seltzer around; the memorability of the commercial will lie in the naturalism and the humor of the Feiffer-like portrayal. In print, it will place its tongue firmly in its cheek and spoof a product or a company in order to make it fallible, un-monolithic—and remembered. Finally, it will seek to establish a *dialogue* with the consumer—a two-way communication that will enable the corporation to hear and deal with consumer complaints and desires on a personal basis.

The high wind on Madison Avenue may thus be the harbinger of a great day for all of us—a day when patronizing, maddening, intrusive advertising, with its burden of inflated claims and exces-sive promises, will at last (and none too soon) perish from the earth.

Gare du Midi

South Station. Late, the N.E. States arrives
With no great hissing, but a Diesel hum
And fume under the train shed. I return
To Boston after absence in New York,
Rearmed by my unanonymity.
Down there, beyond the hotel register,
My name was nominal; my printless hand,
Beyond its signature, could grasp but one
Lever of power: the bullying currency
Cached in my wallet. Three days nameless but
For Sir (and I no knight) or Mister, three
Days impotent, unrecognized, and I
Became a fugitive from my unsought self.
The train was refuge; from the pricking plush
In the stale parlor car I got my first
Reintimation of existence, soon
Confirmed by my sweet seatmate, once a prince
Of bores among time salesmen, now a king
Who called me by my right and simple style,
Told dirty jokes for many a measured mile,
And quite restored me to myself, along
With a drab Radcliffe girl who knew I wrote
And whom I helped into her fur-trimmed coat
At Back Bay Station. Clutching my Peal case,

I disembark now one stop down the line
And walk out through the Terminal, a place
Well named for its impending death, and staffed
By proper supernumeraries—two
Young drunken sailors, one whole porter who
Truckles one bag on his vast trolley, one
Sleep-sweeper, who, somnambulistical,
Cleans creepily down acres of the hall—
To Dewey Square, where I come face to face
With my place and my power where I belong,
Am known, hold down a job, command respect
For unclear reasons, order other lives,
Own action and invest it, shape, decide.
Unmet, unwelcomed, undeterred by pity,
I walk out briskly to infect my city.

iv
Auld
Acquaintance

Made by Hand

I might as well admit it, after forty-five years of grudging silence: my parents gave me something I value very much. What they gave me—more or less inadvertently, I think—was a sense of awe for the productions of the human hand.

It happened like this: back in the thirties, when lack of affluence made most luxury goods a drug upon the market, my parents conceived a passion for antiques. Not the fancy Parke-Bernet kind, for the most part, but the run of the small, starveling antique shops in the Midwestern towns of those days—rudely handsome country furniture, much of it migrated in wagon beds from New England, nineteenth-century glass, both blown and pressed, and an occasional odd lot from overseas.

Thus I found myself, on almost every weekend from the age of ten or so, dawdling impatiently in dusty shops in places like Tiffin, Ohio, and Niles, Michigan, while my parents dickered over a lusterware pitcher or a bird's-eye-maple side chair. I hated it, let me assure you. The awful, musty smells of age and decay, the ever-present dust, the crabbed witches and warlocks who ran the shops all repelled me. Yet, apparently, I was learning something. Like my parents, who were tyros themselves at the beginning, I began to develop an eye for the right and satisfying form of those few items that, under the dust, were genuinely well-wrought. Back at home on weekdays I was having a similar experience: passing the drawing boards where the men in my father's art studio sat, I began to sense a magical connection between the smell of paint and the letters and designs taking shape on the blank sheets of Bristol board. At some point I must have stopped and watched those hands creating form with pencil, pen, brush, crayon, air-brush; soon I became an inveterate watcher of single-minded, single-handed work taking place.

These early impressions went underground in my mind, only to surface many years later when I had a house of my own. After a brief flurry of satisfaction with modern furniture—its function-ality seemed a sterile living companion after a while—my wife and I found ourselves turning to country antiques, about all we could afford at the time. And suddenly, standing in a shabby antique shop haggling over a blanket chest or a Biedermeier secre-tary, I had come full circle. This time, though, driven from the present into the past by the congeries of gumwood junk assembled in the model rooms of furniture stores, I was more grateful for the alternative of the past. Slowly, over a period of a dozen years before even the humblest antiques became as prohibitive as they are today, we managed to furnish our house with an eclectic but livable combination of the old and new.

Of which I am glad, because each time I see one of these pieces anew, the justice and economy of its lines please me—and remind me of the single hand and eye that did the work. No amount of automation, it seems, can produce the satisfying forms that one trained man can execute alone; there is something in the com-mittee nature of large-scale manufacturing that frequently fudges, softens, and spoils even the best-conceived line. But the carpenter or cabinetmaker, working alone and with only a book of classical models to guide him, could (and still can, I'm sure) create ele-gance.

I think this is possible because craftsmanship partakes of the nature of art in that a trained intelligence (even if self-trained) is set against a difficult task that he can master—or even overmaster, in the sense of going beyond the model and creating a new and successful variant. It is in the risk and tension of the *attempt* that the fine cabinetmaker, like the writer or painter, can prove and vindicate himself and his craft. This possibility is not open to a collaboration, especially not to the myriad collaborators of a mass-production plant, unless each one is a craftsman who makes an unmistakable personal contribution.

I think of the antique house I lived in some years ago; when I owned it, I made something of a study of antique houses. Most of them—those that hadn't been hacked around too much by later generations—had fine proportions and pure roof lines that somehow seem impossible today. Those old house carpenters had no more than an inbred sense of proportion to go by, in most cases, yet their houses invariably looked right. The builder of my present house—a colonial reproduction—though he had a fine eye and studied antique houses himself, couldn't quite get the textures and masses right; the house looks less than old to a trained eye.

Ruminating on that, I remember it's time to wind the clock in the living room. It's what's called a lyre clock, made probably around 1820 by a follower of the Willards, the family that designed the banjo clock. This one replaces the harsh brass of the banjo with curves of dark-marbled mahogany; on its glass neck, a primitive artist—perhaps the clockmaker himself—has painted the Indian and seal of the Massachusetts coat of arms. The Indian is too short-legged, but he is not ludicrous, any more than the rendering of the Boston Massacre on the glass lozenge below is ludicrous for its drawing errors. This clock is the proud and successful work of one man or a handful, working together, and its integrity, in both senses, daunts and charms me a hundred and fifty years later.

It is the presence of a personal signature, almost as definitive as the signature on a painting, that is implicit in all fine handwork. When a man works so well at his mystery that he can make each piece somehow distinct from all the others in the world, that is craft—and, just as surely, that is art.

Because of the present organization of our economy, it's getting increasingly difficult for us to surround ourselves with such examples of art. And because of the astounding demand for art our present affluence has created, few of us can afford these artifacts, even the most modest. Instead we must settle for a few treasures, if we're lucky, and furnish the rest of our lives with makeshift, mass-made artifacts.

But wait. It's not that simple. I used to think that my parents' old dictum (another hand-me-down) about buying the best because it lasts longer was a dead letter today. I was surprised to find that it still soldiers on in some categories one would have thought abandoned to mass production. Six years ago, I bought an expensive (but not custom-made) pair of English shoes; I'm wearing them, still sound and shiny, now. This typewriter is a Hermes portable, bought ten years ago; it still works as well as ever after zero maintenance, as do my Nikon cameras and lenses. And last year, in the hope of owning just one more fine car before the NHTSA deluge of pollution and safety regulations, I traded my very capable Japanese sports car for a Porsche 911. A remarkable difference: the Porsche is meticulously built and assembled, like fine cabinetry, and handles like an extension of the driver's will. Here's another semi-mass-produced product that justifies its cost by bearing the invisible signatures of many nameless craftsmen. All of these items are foreign-made—which, sadly, is significant.

But these few pet machines are exceptions. Must we, by and large, be damned to live out our lives in a world of tasteless, odorless, colorless, inhuman plenty? I think the answer is no, but it will take a lot of time and many changes before we return to some uniform standard of craftsmanship. First—short-range—we must rethink the peculiarly American assumption that manual work is dirty work and apply our new thoughts to the manufacturing plants we have now. We've heard already of the experiments at Saab and Volvo, where bolt-tighteners have been replaced by small teams who follow a single component through to its completion. Recently, I read an article by David Jenkins in *The Atlantic* which mentioned a Gaines dog-food plant in Topeka where the small staff of the automated production line has been revivified by retraining. Now any employee can do any job in the plant. Turnover and absenteeism have dropped remarkably. And if this idea of individual competence and responsibility and pride in the finished product can be applied to dog food, it must be equally applicable to all kinds of mass-made goods.

Longer-range, though, I think we must tackle that unfortunate American assumption another way. We must stop our schools from mindlessly training minds and ignoring hands. We must make it equally reputable for a boy or girl to practice carpentry or law. We must start early to teach children the creative joy of working with their hands guided by their minds and not with minds alone. And we must have vocational schools that are not simply second-class alternatives for college-course rejects but places to learn love for craftsmanship. And excellence in it.

This does not mean that I posit a nation of pot-makers squatting at their wheels. The Topeka experiment seems to show that a man or woman can be happy making dog food, as long as his personal contribution is solicited and recognized. Why can't we train a new generation of plumbers, mechanics, and repairmen who take pride in their work and do it well? A few years ago, I would have had enough confidence in this country and its sense of priorities to say that it could be done, and in less than a generation at that. Now I'm not so sure.

But consider our present pass. People who hate their work (because their work is dull and mechanical and they've been educated to despise manual labor) make things that don't work for people who hate their work (because they've been educated for brainwork only and find themselves locked in a competitive rat race with their peers and debarred from the hand-work they might have been most successful at). And let's not even talk about getting things that don't work fixed.

America, there's got to be a better way. Can we return to the sound of one hand working?

Dog's Name in Vain and Other Vulgar Matters

As a self-confessed dog-lover, I've spent the last years—ever since I started writing this column—trying to think of a way to write about dogs that wasn't trite or soft-centered or unbearably sentimental. No way. Everything that has been written about dogs to date—from Senator George Vest's flowery (and apocryphal?) tribute on the Senate floor, to Albert Payson Terhune's collie Eddas, and the annals of Silver Chief, Dog of the North—has presented this fortunate animal as the possessor of all the Boy Scout virtues and the invariable object of the highest human esteem and affection. Since my feelings about dogs coincide—roughly, at least —with those of the above eulogists, I didn't appear to have a point of view to stand on.

Not, that is, until I realized one day that the dog, for all the fulsome lip service we pay him in song, story, and daily discourse, is also the butt of our unconscious; that, for all our vaunted and reciprocal loyalty to the species, we are also sneakingly inclined to do the dog dirt, so to speak, behind his back. And in what way? Not so much by kicking, beating, or starving him, or even by vivisecting him in amoral or downright evil laboratories, but simply by taking his name in vain in our everyday speech.

A little brain-cudgeling will produce a number of prime examples of this. Calling a man a dog means he's a rat; calling a woman a dog means she's a fright. A dog's life is a misery barely to be endured. A dirty dog is a moral leper. A dog's chance is no chance at all. In the doghouse is in disgrace. To go to the dogs is to go to one's ruin.

A glance at that curious and lovable volume, Brewer's *Dictionary of Phrase and Fable,* reveals that our verbal castigation of the dog goes back for centuries, if not millennia. The dog is characterized as a scavenger in *I Kings:* "Him that dieth of Jeroboam in the city shall the dogs eat." Horace considered that the sight of a black dog with its pups was an unlucky omen, and for centuries the Devil has been symbolized by a black dog. The phrase, "A black dog has walked over him," was once used of a sullen person. A dog in the manger is one who will not allow others to enjoy something he does not want for himself (from the fable in which the dog, out of sheer cussedness, kept the hungry ox away from the hay). "A living dog is better than a dead lion" (*Ecclesiastes*) suggests that, in Brewer's words, the meanest thing with life in it is better than the noblest without.

If a gay dog plays fast and loose with the ladies, a surly dog is ill tempered and a dull dog boring. Dogs get it both ways in the expression, "Die like a dog," which connotes a miserable death, and in the superstition that dogs howl at death. Prior to death, one is sick as a dog. A dogsbody is a drudge; if he is not, he would probably respond to a request to do menial work with the biblical phrase, "Is thy servant a dog, that he should do this thing?" And so on and on.

In fact, there are hardly any neutral or favorable expressions about dogs; almost all, with the exception of idioms like "a dog's age" and "putting on the dog," are marginally neutral or openly pejorative. Why is this? Perhaps the answer lies in another phrase from Brewer, "The more I see of men, the more I love dogs." Is it possible that humans, long thought to be the dog's best friends, both perceive and resent the moral perfection of their canine companions? Can it be that we secretly despise the dog for his innate decency, loyalty, and goodness? Do we perhaps despair of equaling his high standards in our squalid and messy lives? Does the dog's obvious trust of us lead us to violate it in a language he does not understand?

If that's the case, my friends, we're all in trouble.

The open admission of my vulgar taste for dogs leads me to further confessions of a vulgar taste in other matters. I've long suspected that many Americans who profess some sort of intellectual primacy are really brothers and sisters under the skin with the American proletariat, at least insofar as those vulgar tastes are concerned. And this is not mere slumming; in my case, at least, these lowbrow tastes are part of my birthright, and they are as seriously held and professed as many of my highbrow likings.

For example, I hereby confess to a partiality for all sorts and conditions of low foods, or eats, as they are more properly termed. From childhood, I have been a devotee of such items as Franco-American Spaghetti, Fig Newtons, canned hash, and canned spinach, even though I know better, in the sense of having sampled—and liked—many varieties of real Italian spaghetti, assorted French and other fancy pastries, the sublime hash of various men's clubs, and, of course, fresh spinach straight from the garden sand. No amount of good eating, however, can condition the boy's taste out of me: I still relish ballpark hot dogs (there's another dialectal ignominy for the poor dog), drive-in hamburgers, drugstore malts, roadside fried clams (getting precious and costly now), and even good old fish and chips, guaranteed to arouse the mother and father of heartburns. Similarly, I dote (as S. J. Perelman characters used to say) allegedly Swedish and Italian meatballs, almost any kind of pizza, most varieties of shopping-plaza Chinese cookery, and even diner chili con carne.

I'm still worse, if anything, in the baked-goods-and-confectionery department. I have been known to eat without visible wincing a ten-day-old Dunkin Donut from the glove compartment, and I regularly consume (or did before a recent diet) the fresher, or counter, variety; likewise, I am an aficionado of store cakes and cookies, including especially such Nabisco productions as Biscos Sugar Wafers (those very crumbly oblongs with sweet white paste inside), Oreo cookies, and Coconut Bars (plain or frosted). Not to mention Drake's coffee cakes and Devil Dogs. (Not Twinkies yet, thank God.)

If my gastronomy is far below reproach, my tastes in reading matter are even more irretrievable and damned. I positively love the daily comics, with an evenhanded devotion to both the satirical strips (Doonesbury, The Wizard of Id, the late lamented Pogo) and the fine old soap (or ink) operas like Steve Canyon, On Stage, Rex Morgan, M.D., and Apartment 3G. I read these and other newspaper features—including Ann Landers and Mirror of Your Mind, for instance—with none of the scorn I bring to certain other reading I am hooked on, reading I masochistically consume for its very inanity. Samples of the latter class of delicious self-chastisement might include *Vogue* (and assorted newspaper fashion ads), which I read for their dogged, dated whimsy and archness (there I go, beating those poor dogs again); almost any Hearst columnist, for an undiluted whiff of the nineteen-thirties in full, decadent bloom; the *National Enquirer* (or England's *News of the World*) for its evergreen evocation of the old *American Weekly;* and *W,* the off-colored (not obscene, just a printing problem) offshoot of *Women's Wear Daily,* for its courageous and intransigent irrelevance and idiocy in a world full of problems too hard to bear.

Besides these publications and *Cosmopolitan,* which I rely on for sardonic little bursts of sugary pleasure much like the ones afforded by the twenty-nine-cent boxes of cheap chocolate-covered cherries that I forgot to mention above, I also dip, from time to time, into the mass of popular fiction which surrounds us. While I have never attempted a Gothic novel, I *have* sampled substantial numbers of detective stories and thrillers, mostly of the California-private-eye or English-urban-murder varieties. Not much to be said for most of these, except as cotton-batting time-fillers; but a few rise to the highest wit of their genre and give us a sip of the elixir of good bad books. (A good bad book, by common consent, is one which transcends the trivial nature of its type by some astonishing adherence to that type; thus, the Sherlock Holmes stories, which virtually created their genre, are the best of good bad books, while *The Ministry of Fear,* say, is merely a bad good book.) Among my favorites in this category, besides the predictable Hammett and Chandler and sometimes Simenon, are Michael Gilbert (for his legalistic detective stories), the late J. J. Marric (a/k/a John Creasey, for his police-procedure novels featuring Gideon of Scotland Yard), and Ed McBain (a/k/a Evan Hunter, for *his* procedural stories of the Eighty-seventh Precinct), not to mention an occasional spy story by the likes of John Le Carré or Adam Hall (a/k/a Elleston Trevor).

To conclude this savage indictment of my reading habits, I'd better add that I also regularly read cereal boxes and the small ads for piles remedies, horse liniment, and dream books tucked away in the back of various lowlife magazines. These ads contain the essence of the Simple American Con, before it got fancied up by four-color magazine spreads and sixty-second television spots, and I rejoice to see them still alive and well in the stormy seventies.

Just to prove that I'm totally unregenerate—the thought police will be coming for my intellectual's ID card any second now—I must add to this confession a list of favorite vulgar smells. Yes, I admit, I love the mingled smells of peanuts roasting and dusty floorboards in an old-fashioned five-and-ten-cent store; the odor of deep-fat-fried egg rolls drifting from a cheesy Chinese restaurant; the whiff of fresh-ground Bokar in a thousand A&P's; the attar of patent and ethical medicines and soda-fountain syrups in any good drugstore; and, horrors, the reek of raw 100-octane gasoline in any service station, a pleasure I may soon be bereft of. In my depravity, I have even been known to savor the smell of beer from a workmen's tavern at eight o'clock in the morning and the smell of a crowded movie house (hot buttered popcorn, mostly) at eight o'clock at night. And I am curiously moved by that old (and doubtless deleterious) city smell of soft-coal smoke bellying upward from apartment buildings on a snowy morning.

So there you have it: for all my fine pretensions, I'm just an ordinary guy, replete to the gunwhales with fierce, ineradicable tastes for the plebeian. Before the constabulary comes, if you don't mind, I'll compose myself in comfort, with battered red carpet slippers on my feet, an old beige cardigan buttoned snugly around my torso, my faithful dog curled like a snail shell at my side, a glass of Old Milwaukee (or any other cut-price, off-brand beer) in my hand, a roaring fire in front of me, a plate of Premium Saltines and Pabst-Ett Cheese Food to eat, and a crisp and virgin copy of *Mechanix Illustrated* to dream on while I wait for the heavy tread of the arresting officer.

What I Gave at the Office

Cleaning out my desk recently before leaving my old job, after nearly sixteen years, for a new one, I was surprised to feel a bit of a twinge, if not a pang, at the change. When I stopped to start to think about it, hefting my shopping bags full of letters, verse worksheets, and old advertising awards down the elevator, I realized that the old job still had some claim on me, if for no other reason than the fact that I still had some claim on it, having given it, on the average, some fifty-five hours a week of working, worrying, and commuting, or about five solid years of my life. While I felt neither outrage nor regret at this state of affairs, it got me to thinking about the nature of life at the office and its inevitable effect on the rest of our lives.

At worst, the office is a place you go to to earn enough to provide the necessities for your family; the necessity for work itself may be loathsome, but it is unquestioned. At best, the office is a place where your training and your ego get at least an intermittent chance to shine; where you work with others who, with luck, may include you in a team of motivated, purposeful people combining forces to achieve a goal; where you work for something more than survival alone. In that kind of office, your time is not wasted, your life is not frittered away in eight-hour segments; however trivial the product may be, you are actively furthering your life while earning a living.

The office is, to begin with, a little, closed, and often inalterable diagram of our society. This microcosm may take two forms: first, what Douglas McGregor (and later Robert Townsend) has called the Theory X organization, run largely on the principle that people are fundamentally lazy and must be coerced, by discipline and punishment, to work; second, the Theory Y company, founded on the idea that work is a natural and normal component of human life, and that most people will work best when provided with rewards, incentives, and esprit de corps. There is a third form, which I'll take the liberty of dubbing Theory Z: a Theory Y enclave within a much larger Theory X organism. This is the kind of firm I worked for, and apart from occasional run-ins with Top Management (fortunately based in another city several hundred miles away), our little local operation rocked along quite satisfactorily on its own initiative, though probably not as successfully as if it had been an autonomous local Theory Y.

Within the little social paradigm of a given office, regardless of the theory its managers subscribe to, there is an almost tribal organization which requires each member to behave according to certain tacitly sanctioned standards, or unwritten laws (the British writer Antony Jay is good on this point in his recent book, *Corporation Man,* though he leans a bit too heavily on a literal analogy with the tribal ten-man group). What makes the result fascinating, and an education in psychology and life for anybody in a company who will unstop his eyes and ears, is the tension between the corporate good and the individual good, particularly in firms which are run by paternalistic tyrants. Here, the employee is brainwashed into believing that what is best for the company will therefore be best for him; if his job-security quotient is high enough or his hostages to fortune numerous enough, he will unfortunately believe it, and believe it the more as he climbs higher in the hierarchy. At its worst, in fact, this kind of company reaches out into the personal lives of its people, vetting their wives (and sometimes husbands) before hiring them, dictating what suburbs men on a certain level shall live in, dictating, too, which employees they may socialize with outside office hours. (For an instant Kafkaesque vision of hell, consider the position of the first black executive in a company like this.) This kind of firm, which very closely resembles the present Soviet government, is really far more concerned with preserving its structure than with changing to meet the times. The hierarchy is all. Though there is some revolutionary sentiment among the lower orders, they must check it at the door to their first junior-executive office if they are to prosper with, and profit from, the company.

The Theory Y outfit, while much more open to change and mutation precisely because it has no vested interest in a hierarchy, still has some immutable laws of its own; again, there is a highly educative conflict between individual and corporate good. The problem is this: if you are Y enough to go out and hire Young Turks and revolutionaries to help you run your business, how can you turn them from lone wolves, out only for themselves, into team players? The answer is, you can't, entirely. A certain percentage of brilliant loners can never reconcile themselves to sharing credit, to throwing in their lot with a group of peers; in their own minds, they *have* no peers. These men and women can't last long, even in an exceedingly permissive firm. If nothing else, they will cross, anger, and neutralize the team workers. Fortunately, though, there are a lot of equally brilliant people who need others enough, perhaps because they feel consciously insecure enough, to play on a team and share the credit for the work.

Out of this symbiosis can develop something most exciting, even if the actual work or its result is, as I've suggested, relatively trivial. What seems to happen is that the pooled egos of the team members create something greater than the sum of its parts—a detailed, foolproof solution to a problem, say, that no one member could think through for himself. A creative problem-solving team on the verge of an answer is a stimulating thing to behold and be part of. Each member subjectively makes a contribution. Every other member instantly reacts to this suggestion, but if the group's working right, not in a selfish or egocentric way. Every other member, in short, adds either his objectivity to an evaluation of the suggestion or his creative subjectivity to an improvement on it. Like ants or a bucket brigade or, at the highest level, an ensemble of actors, the group bands together to find the one most logical and productive answer. At moments like this—moments of breakthrough—every member of the group feels a pride in the emerging solution and an exhilaration that can be described only as being off the ground. The group, severally and together, has stood on a frontier, however modest, of human skill or execution, and has raised, so to speak, the flag at Iwo Jima. It is the flag of the human spirit that is raised, though; there is something ennobling about such at least momentarily selfless teamwork. There's a kind of current of love among the members, too: each takes pride in the other's contribution and loves him better for it.

At this point, even in the dreariest of offices, the members of the group also feel another emotion: the emotion a student of the drama feels at a superb theatrical performance, the emotion the painter or writer, alone in his studio, feels when he has suddenly turned the corner and mastered the problem of the work before him. This emotion is signaled by a sort of prickling behind the eyes, by a chill down the spine (or actual gooseflesh), by the desire to weep, not for sorrow but in exultation at what men can be.

So leaving an office where you have often experienced this emotion, have worked harmoniously (at least at times) with others, have thereby learned to love and value them, can be a bit more of a wrench than I would have suspected. There are other things as well about an office where you spend a large proportion of your waking life: the hold it takes on you as an important part of your known world (early in the morning, before the hall lights are on, you can step off the elevator and find the light switch in total darkness without groping); the sense of proprietorship you feel, even if you're the most junior clerk, when you arrive before anyone else and prowl the empty corridors and typing pools at the start of a new day; the sense of purposeful action, of ongoing enterprise, of the life-force itself that you feel when you look out over a roomful of busy people at the height of a workday; the sense of dedication and discipline and worthiness you feel when it's dark outside, the lights are on, and you're working late alone.

All this is satisfying and fulfilling; even if you live for your family, for an avocation, or for some other goal, a sense of belonging at—and to—the office helps to round and validate your life. But it seems especially important and rewarding if, like me, you also practice a personal art or craft outside office hours. For the last twenty years in business, I have attended a sort of graduate school in human behavior—my own no less than other people's—and have, I think, learned a great deal no amount of reading or study or meditating in the privacy of my workroom could conceivably have taught me. What's more, I earned while I learned: my advanced training in being human was wholly subsidized by a kind management. Whatever I gave at the office, I took far more away.

Auld Acquaintance

A great deal is written today about the inspiriting and sustaining qualities of sex, but nothing about the perhaps equally consoling powers of friendship. In a highly competitive society, friendship is likely to be out of fashion, anyway; concentration on a personal goal, almost by definition, tends to force one to don a mask of secretiveness and to exclude others from one's counsel. Every man is his own internal-security force, his own thought police, and the devil take the open or unguarded. This isolation of ego is often reinforced by an especially American kind of self-imposed rootlessness, a desire to avoid personal or geographical entanglements, an urge to keep moving on. Nearly fifty years ago, D. H. Lawrence hit on this truth in a review of Hemingway's *In Our Time*. "Nothing matters," Lawrence said. "Everything happens. One wants to keep oneself loose. Avoid one thing only: getting connected up. Don't get connected up. If you get held by anything, break it. Don't be held. Break it, and get away. Don't get away with the idea of getting somewhere else. Just get away, for the sake of getting away. Beat it! 'Well, boy, I guess I'll beat it.' Ah, the pleasure in saying that!"

Today we'd call it "keeping one's cool," preserving the freedom of movement and maneuver of a whole pantheon of real and fictive lone hands who have entered the niches of American myth—Bogart/Spade, Marlowe, James Dean, James Bond, Bob Dylan, many more. But for all that, friendship persists—almost underground, as you might say, since it runs counter to the alone-ness of the culture—and even flourishes. Many other relation-ships of blood, love, or marriage are increasingly suspect of the taint of exploitation for personal gain. Mothers imprison their sons in a lifelong cage of guilt and obligation; sons demand financial support from their parents, but deny them emotional support. Men feign love to exploit a woman sexually; after mar-riage, the woman enforces her demands by withholding sex. Em-ployer and employee, proclaiming mutual loyalty, each schemes to advance his own interest at the other's cost: the boss chisels on raises, the salesmen pad their expenses.

But friendship has its own ethical code in which most of these holds are barred, which makes it an almost unique relationship in our society. Needless to say, apparent friendship is often abused for gain—friends are used to obtain an entrée, an introduction, a preferment, or even money. But that's not friendship, only the dissimulation of it, which the dictionary definition of "friend" —"A person whom one knows, likes, and trusts"—specifically excludes. If a friend proves untrustworthy, he is no longer your friend.

This is not, of course, to suggest that friends may never be helpful to each other. It is well within the limits of friendship to give a friend a leg up, as long as it is a spontaneous act of goodwill and not connived at by the recipient. On the other hand, most friendships are, by and large, stamped "not negotiable." The essence of the relationship is that it is something held in com-mon, something apart from the acquisitive side of one's life, something where mutual giving and taking are freely and equally balanced. And surprisingly, considering the vicissitudes of life today, it often remains so for a lifetime.

There is something very subtly pleasing and even exciting about making a friend. In a relationship in which two of the chief goods of our society—money and sex—are off limits, we can relax and, for once in a way, really please ourselves, indulge and gratify our taste. One might choose a wife (cynically, but it happens every day) for money or beauty alone. One might choose an employer for money or rapacity alone. But one chooses a friend for companionship and like-mindedness—and sometimes, too, for differences. The friend so chosen is often an alter ego in many respects, but with one element of character—aggression or submissiveness—omitted or put in. Thus a dominant man might choose a submissive friend who will be a good follower to his leadership; thus a diffident man might choose a dominant friend whom he can look up to and follow. These combinations first show up in school relationships, but they often last for life.

When I first meet a man—this applies, of course, to women, too, but the presence of sexuality makes the reactions a lot harder to sort out—I generally place him quite automatically, and within the first few minutes, in one of three categories: No, Maybe, and Yes. The No's (and the fortunately rather rare God, No's) are people who seem to me boors, bores, or just people I'd have nothing in common with. The Maybe's seem pleasant and ingratiating enough, but a faint alarm bell of some kind is beating away behind my eyes; it's going to take longer before I know whether the alarm will fade out or rise to the deafening clangor of a four-alarm boor. The Yesses are people I take to at once, for the naturally flattering reason that they talk and think like I do about the things I do. I seldom encounter one of these—maybe once every two to five years—but it's always, as I've suggested, a subtly exciting experience. It's as if I'm driving a car down an unknown road and suddenly find that I can guess all the curves and contours in advance. As my new-found acquaintance talks along, I find myself anticipating his ideas, his positions, sometimes even his literary citations or turns of phrase. In many ways, he may be quite different from me, but there is obviously some bond of common consciousness.

From then on, if chance permits—that is, if our ambits overlap with any frequency—I find myself avidly exploring the ground of the new friend's outlook. (I assume this pleasure is mutual, though, oddly, I've never discussed this aspect of friendship with a friend.) What begins to take on a special fascination as the friendship ripens is not the similarity but the *distinction* between us. For all our commonalty of views, the friend is no mirror twin of mine: his looks, his gestures, his mannerisms, his speech, his idiosyncrasies are all at variance with mine, which creates a delightful tension between us and puts his ideas—even those I share completely—in an instructive new light. And then something else begins to happen: I gradually come to look forward to each new meeting with this friend, knowing that the familiarity I have learned to savor and enjoy will also be spiced with something new from the store of infinite variety of a human being. It's like watching a favorite actor in a new play. You know and love his mannerisms, his characteristic mode of attack on a part, yet each new performance is something else again.

I'm talking now about close friends; there are, of course, many more casual ones with whom one shares a degree of trust and liking, but never intimacy. With a close friend, though, there is this ongoing and inexhaustible fascination with the contrast between his growth and his unchanging sameness. When, recently, I remet some old (and very close) friends for the first time since the early fifties, and when we all said, "You look just the same," we didn't mean it literally. We were saying, in code, that the relationship had been so well-founded from the start that it could be continued on the spot. Not, of course, that we did not bring each other up to date, both consciously and unconsciously, but that we felt completely free to do so. It's as if a conversation truncated by a curtain fall denoting the lapse of twenty years had been resumed, at rise, without missing a beat. Once, apparently, we possess the key to another person's mind and manner, we never let it go. On occasion, I have sat for several hours with my friends in a reunion where little was spelled out but everything was revealed. The talk was casual, offhand, sometimes disjointed or fragmentary. But no nuance went unnoticed, no implication was missed. And there was, for all the apparent desultoriness of the talk, an underlying impulsion forward, like the slow, deep movement of a ship, long docked, resuming way. Or, to use another analogue, the Old Firm had Reopened Under the Same Management, and we were all glad to be rejoined again in a common emprise.

In order for this to happen, it goes without saying that the ethical writ that underlies friendship—the writ of mutual trust and mutual injunction against manipulation—had to run as deeply and immutably as it had two decades before, that the Decalogue of Amicable Relations remained fully in force. This set of un-written sanctions, commanding honor, respect, civility, and shar-ing among friends, might seem impossibly simplistic, idealistic, and sentimental today. Yet it survives as a reality in a world of short sales and curt expediencies, perhaps precisely because that world demands a leaven for its selfishness and a haven from its storms. In 1973, death and taxes are as calculably certain as in Franklin's time; vicissitudes, comeuppances, bouleverse-ments, transgressions, and betrayals are more likely than they ever were in the past. Under pressures of the age, promising careers tail off into backwaters; challenging jobs dissolve into rote repetitiveness; lovers move on and marriages crack; adults lose control of their lives and their selves; children vanish into the Woodstock limbo, from which no traveler returns.

Where, then, are we to turn but to friends (and, in enduring marriages, to husbands or wives, who become friends by a long mutual process of tempering) for an unchanging validation of ourselves? Who but a friend has the time, the kindredness, the disinterest to take us up again, time after time, and make us whole again by steadfastly refusing to believe we have ever been less than whole? And who but a friend revivifies our own powers by depending on us for the same kind of recertification?

Making a new friend can certainly be as exciting at fifty as at twenty. But in the realm of friendship—a kingdom run on the old-fashioned lines of golden-rule morality—it follows that tradition and continuity must possess some special value, and that the hackneyed truism, old friends are best, is literally true. Some mysterious kind of compound interest is at work in long-standing friendships, enriching each new meeting with a set of unheard—but deeply felt—harmonic echoes of the past. Per-haps, again, because this world is so sheerly motile and rootless, a common touchstone ten or twenty years back becomes a pre-cious stone, the foundation stone of a personal mythology both opposed and allied to the public myth of the lone hero. What we did with Y in the Village in the summer of '48, how we invaded X's birthday party dressed as spacemen in the fall of '51, why Y married Z so unexpectedly in Cambridge in '53—these palpable trivia, forgotten to all but us, become the stations of a crossing of paths, a pooling of interests, which sustain us in our self-belief today. Nostalgia—seeing and recognizing oneself in an antique setting—gives life a shape and point, and the real or possible presence of friends, then and now, reassures us of some stability in a waste of shifting sands of time.

My wife and I don't generally go out on New Year's Eve; we live too far out in the country, and the thought of a long, late drive over icy roads shared by other partygoers is a daunting one. But at New Year's and through the gelid, isolated month of January, I often think, with an involuntary smile, of friends. Some live fairly nearby; others are a continent or more away. Some I've seen fairly frequently and recently; others, not for many years. But all, if they were here with me, would immediately, without hesitation or embarrassment, proceed to open the richly wrapped gift of times we've shared, and, in cutting up old touches, advance the state of our relationship. Even in their absence, I can see and hear them now.

I'll Never Go There Anymore

When I was a small boy going on a big man, I used to admire people—in literature, anyway; I'm not sure I ever met any in life—who refused to suffer fools gladly, or at all. Likewise, I stood in awe of the motto ascribed to Evelyn Waugh: "Never apologize, never explain." Though I've gone through most of my life so far suffering fools, apologizing, and explaining, I've never ceased to envy those slightly supernal beings who could hew to such tenets.

But now that I've turned forty-five, I think I've discovered their secret: age. If age is enfeebling (and it is), it's also liberating in a curiously parallel way. Age frees you to contemn, to cut, to ignore, precisely because it deprives you of tolerance, stamina, bonhomie. At forty-five, one is no longer constrained to stand for hours at a party in the company of a notorious gasbag; even if one's reserves of reverence were unimpaired, one's leg muscles would be unequal to the task. And a rising flush of irritation over the imposition will generally assure a satisfactorily rude termination of the interview.

Now I see how all the stylish terrors and curmudgeons, from Dr. Johnson to Edmund Wilson, did it: they simply let their infirmities take the upper hand. No blooming, bouncy young man, however artful, could ever equal the fatal acerbity of their wit and malice, for the simple reason that no young man hurts as much as an older one. Now, I'm hardly decrebid (as I think the great dialect humorist Richard Bissell once had one of his Iowan characters say), but I do have enough aches, agues, scars, and wound stripes to let them take command in social situations when, formerly, I would have suffered in pasted-on smiling silence, or with placatingly murmured "um"'s. So, as a set of easy-to-observe resolutions for this and future declining years, I have decided to adopt the following code of curmudgeonly behavior. I've been to the place where sympathetic, ingratiating young men subject themselves to all kinds of needless trials and torments in the name of politesse; having served too long an apprenticeship, I'll never go there anymore.

First of all, I'll never again walk across the street (literally or figuratively) to meet some literary Great Man. When I've walked that way in the past, I've invariably found that (1) however gracious and human the G.M. might be, we had nothing whatever to say to each other, or (2) the G.M., undoubtedly exercising his own curmudgeonly prerogatives, refused to recognize my (or anybody else's) existence. An extreme example: not long ago, a famous literary man attended one of my poetry readings. At a small party afterward, he had not one word to say about the reading; according to a mutual friend, he never comments on other people's work. Well, bully for him; but, equally, bully for me for not sitting at the feet of his ilk in future.

Then there's the Young Suppliant, who stands in somewhat the same relation to me as the one in which I used to stand to the Great Man. He's always sending me an unsolicited sample of his work (sometimes the sample is so generous as to constitute a lifetime supply) or calling to see if I can spare him "just an hour or two" or asking me to send his unpublished works to some editor I know. Well, from now on, with certain unavoidable exceptions fomented by friendship, the answer is going to be No. And, if the Y.S. doesn't bother to include a stamped, self-addressed return envelope with his samples, the answer is going to be Nil. There.

Another class of parasite who never will be missed by me in future is the representative of some church, school, or good cause who wants to wangle a free poetry reading. Since poets are hardly supported by the state—or by any of the aforementioned institutions—it is not incumbent on the poet to support them by giving away what he normally sells. I'll take increasing pleasure in saying No to this bunch, as I will to their relatives, the chintzy school and college English teachers who exploit a poet by asking him to give a reading, attend a vapid party, *and* address six English classes for his usual fee. Ditto the *conférenciers* who think I'll be so smitten with a couple of big names that I'll attend their boring, pointless, three-day workshop/gabfest/seminars for next to nothing.

Now that I'm warming to my work, I should say that the scope for my new crustiness is by no means wholly literary. There are all sorts of people I've been dying to cut all my life, and now, by God, I will. At parties (I've already tried this, and it works) I'm going to drift slowly but resolutely away from bores of all ages and sexes, leaving them, preferably, in mid-sentence, without a word of explanation. In stores I'm going to ask for service in no uncertain terms. In restaurants I'm going to put aside my diffidence and raise some hell when the food is cold or bad or I'm made to wait unconscionably. And when a store really fouls up my order, I'm going to call the president at once (this, too, I've already tried; it, too, works fine).

In fact, now I think of it, it's not just people that I want to cut out of my life. There are lots of *things* that I've been a fall guy for, whether because they were fashionable and "in" or because I've just never thought them through enough to realize that I don't need them. Booze, for one. It used to be thought fashionable to drink, sometimes to excess, and maybe it still is in certain circles. While I haven't driven home from a party on the wrong side of the road or vomited all over somebody else's bathroom for at least fifteen years (well, I can think of one later incident), how many times have I had a drink or two or three more than I really wanted, just because it was hard to say No? And cigarettes. I quit for three years once, but naturally went back. What's natural about that? I wasn't born a smoker, and I didn't smoke for my first fifteen years on earth. So to hell with cigarettes. And to hell with boozy lunches. (I'll keep you posted on my progress in both areas. If I backslide, you'll hear it first from me.)

And to hell with wasting time. I hereby solemnly swear to can, avoid, and eschew all those time-burning occasions that wanting to seem a good fellow has led me into in the past. No more stultifying lunches-cum-speeches, hearing some benighted, outdated past master extolling his pastmastery. No more noisy, kitschy gallery openings, with their poison sherry and poisonous people. No more big fund-raising galas of any description; to give both money and one's presence seems to me double jeopardy. No more gossipy cocktail parties full of people so far in they're out, or at least as few as I can possibly manage.

No more creaky, mildewed Broadway plays. No more overblown memoirs by prominent nobodies. No more top-rated comedy sensations on TV—the plastic kind that come apart in your head after the first half hour.

No more. No more fudging around with my own imprimatur. Either it has some modest value, or it doesn't. So no reviews—never, ever again—of my friends' books. No endorsements or recommendations of books or people I can't wholeheartedly recommend. No going along with a claque because it's for a buddy. And no attacking the cult object of another claque on anything but objective grounds (and I know that's a tall order).

And, to replace those No's and put all that time to gainful use, what then? Well, work. What else? All kinds of work that cries out to be done. Answering my mail, to take a humble instance (I'm a pretty reliable correspondent, but apologies herewith to kind readers who have written and had to wait for answers). Reading enough books to spot the worthwhile ones and then finding time to call them to public attention. Thinking about writing this column and writing it better and more interestingly. Thinking about writing verse and writing it to the limit of my ability. Thinking about other kinds of writing I've wanted to do and doing them.

And, more than all that, enjoying life. My generation got itself herded, or maybe stampeded, in the general direction of the future, without much time for reflection. Its values, like its clothes, were more or less foisted on it by forefathers, who knew best. But now many of us have seen our goal close up and perceived it to be a windmill—a beat-up old simulacrum of inflated self that doesn't grind any more grain and isn't even worth a lance. So we are now free. Free to turn away from the old minuet of manners and respect and precedence, free to give less of a damn about our teeth, our visage, our image, the state of our armor (decrebid). Free to let values readjust themselves on those big old ponderous scales. Free, specifically, to look down at the ground again after forty years of looking straight ahead— or up, excelsior!—and renew our acquaintance with our own feet, those flat, ignoble paddles that have carried us so far, and with the insignificant, hitherto dismissible violets in the turf around them. (There is something touching, maybe heartbreaking, about the idea of man not as master but as part of a landscape; one of the most affecting photographs I've ever taken shows a small section of spring meadow, about two feet by three, with some healthy, springing grass, three blooms of bluets, and, in the middle, a battered, red-and-blue-striped pint thermos bottle, put out to pasture and taking its ease long after some farmer's nooning.)

I expect that what I'm saying is that I've suddenly, with a touch of the shock of recognition and a demiflourish of one trumpet, found myself back where I started from in relation to the real world, regarding its things and creatures with at least an imitation of my earliest wonder. I've been more than a casual looker at meadows, voles, and sunsets for some years now, and I've become increasingly aware of the real value of my friends, my wife, my home, but all of it, till now, has been in glimpses and glances snatched from other concerns, like intercut bits in a movie. I've always been tearing myself away from some ongoing concern—success, money, the next boring hurdle to clear —to notice momentarily, and then forget, the things that give my life whatever meaning it may have.

Now that is finally, blessedly changing, for reasons I'm not fully aware of, though I suspect that age, with its intimations of mortality, may have helped most to bring me back to my senses, as I've written before this. The transformation—phony prince into earthly frog—is slow and unsure, but every month I seem to become a little better able to shake off my comet's tail of inconsequentialities, gathered over the years—meaningless obligations, courteous artificialities, trivial fears—and stand up on my own, for once, and look down at those lonely, ugly feet and the springing turf around them.

That being so, you will find a wodge of once-treasured values and illusions filling the trash barrel in the back of my car on the way to the dump. In their place I hope you will also find one new-minted curmudgeon, older, sadder, slightly wiser, and with, on the whole, a hell of a lot better idea of what to do with the rest of his life than he ever had before.

A Pledge of Allegiance

For the first time in eleven years, I am not ashamed of my citizenship.

From the day of John Kennedy's assassination, in 1963, through the slow, painful escalation of the Vietnam War and the grudging, snail-like revelations of Watergate, hardly a week has passed that I haven't felt slightly sick over the course—and the presumed destination—of our country. On trips abroad in 1966, 1971, and 1974, I've winced a little at each glimpse of my fat, pea-green, Great-Sealed American passport, a document that seemed to shout my identity as another brash and callous American to my righteous enemies. At home, I've braced myself almost daily before settling down with the morning paper, forewarned and all too sure of the official hypocrisies I'd be reading under unending Washington datelines.

Now it is suddenly different. In the silence of a late-summer Saturday after the change of Presidents, I feel myself suffused with a new, unfamiliar circulation of hope. And pride, after all these barren years, pride in a country I'd given up for lost. Not that I think our national warts will fade and clarify over the months to come. Not that I think a new President will routinely face and dispatch all the hydra-headed problems of late capitalism. Not that I think we'll all be marching forward, two years hence, into a roseate aura of peace, prosperity, and full dinner pails at pre-inflation prices.

No. Simply that I can believe again in the essential goodness and fellow-feeling of this people, and in its capacity to shape its future in a human image. This radical change of heart was brought about not by the slow and evenhanded grinding of Constitutional machinery—though that was deeply reassuring, too—but by a totally unexpected three-day revelation of the people and its will: the opening sessions of the House Judiciary Committee's debate on Articles of Impeachment.

That I was moved, shaken—converted, even—by the appearance of these thirty-eight grave and troubled faces on my television screen was due, at least in part, to the shattering of several misconceptions that had been growing in my mind. First, like many American dissidents in the past decade, I had made up my mind that most politicians spoke and acted—for publication, anyway—from behind a mask of image, that their every expression, word, and gesture was cynically calculated for electoral effect. The account of the erection of Richard Nixon's own image in *The Selling of the President* was a formative influence on my prejudice, but my conviction of guile had been bolstered by many more commercials, press conferences, and public appearances by a host of other aspirants to office.

Second, I had begun to lose faith in the capacity of spoken language to carry sincerity, truth, or even meaning. Partly because of the assaults of politicians and their spokesmen on the language (in, for example, their increasing use of painful euphemisms like "incursion" for "invasion" and "inoperative" for "untrue"), partly because of the growing practice of all sorts of experts, specialists, and power-hoarders to cloak their trade in pseudo-technicalities like "on stream" and "interface," and partly because of the vain (both senses) tendency of a writer to discount the efficacy of ordinary speech as opposed to extraordinary writing, I'd more or less rejected the possibility of being reached and touched by spoken words.

I should have known that this was not the case; indeed, my enthusiasm, several years ago, for the truth and rhythm of the recorded reminiscences of Studs Terkel's *Hard Times* should have reminded me that there are those worth hearing when they speak.

At any rate, I was wholly unprepared for the consciousness-raising I experienced when I flipped my television set on to the first day of debate. Here was a panel of Representatives—that lower order of legislative life—well and truly empaneled in paneling, prepared to persuade me with their ceaseless droning of platitudes—as if I needed persuading—that their wits were dull, their ambits earthbound, their language trite and hackneyed, their chief desire to win the acquiescence of their equally dullard constituents in bars and living rooms back home.

Not so, to say the least. From the first of their opening statements, I was jerked awake and slapped into eye-rubbing incredulity by the spectacle of real people—palpable characters, distinct and individual—saying real, not manufactured, words in the service of a real conviction. At what amounted to a distance of three or four feet from my face, these dusty, rostered names sprang one by one to life, assumed differentiated features, spoke to me openly and emotionally of their struggles to decide. An hour or two into the debate, someone nearby said scornfully, "It's a bore," and to my surprise, I found myself hotly defending the interest of the proceedings. More, I was defending the integrity of the men and women who were speaking and the honor of their seriousness.

For the great triumph of the debate, it seems to me, was not in the Constitutional achievements of the committee in the face of each member's political partisanship—great as those achievements were—but in the ability of each member to voice, both honestly and humanly, the choices he was torn between. There was little or no attempt to hide behind the cloak of image, to equivocate in fatuous, orotund language; on the contrary, nearly all the members spoke a soliloquy in which they painfully traced their personal and Constitutional options for all to see and hear. These three dozen Hamlets spoke, appropriately, of regicide with all the anguish of the original Prince. And if their language did not soar like Shakespeare's, neither did it limp along in Federalese. The statements, written for the most part in plain English, came alive because they were thought through, not simply read through. Beyond that, there was the diversity of a dozen ethnic and regional accents and styles, a cross section, as Anthony Lewis called it, of America.

Throughout the debate, those who held the greatest interest for me, perhaps naturally, were those who felt constrained to vote against their conservative constituencies. Of these, I felt that Walter Flowers led all the rest. The dapper, slight, soft-spoken Alabamian, willing himself to the logical conclusion of his argument against the almost palpable wills of the voters who had sent him to Washington, held me breathless in the inevitability—and the daring—of his choice. Step by step, he worried his way to a proof of his contentions before the people of his district—and the nation. (I was heartened later to know that this was not simply the stance of a moment in the heat of impeachment; in a *Times* story filed from Alabama the following week, Flowers was discovered still brooding manfully about his constituents' willingness to accept his decision. According to a sampling taken by the reporter, most of them thought better of him for it.)

Railsback, the Illinois Republican, had perhaps even more to lose in impeaching a President of his own party, but his defense of his vote was both dogged and impassioned. Like so many members of the committee, he appeared to have an eye on history as well as on the fall elections: ". . . if the young people in this country think we are going to not handle this thing fairly, if we're not going to really try to get to the truth . . . it's going to make the period of LBJ in 1968, 1967—it's going to make it look tame."

Mann, the quiet South Carolinian, lamented the circumstantiality of the case ("How much I would have liked to have had all of the evidence . . .") but pressed on for impeachment ("The President has the evidence. . . . I am starving for it, but I will do the best I can with what I have got"). Ray Thornton of Arkansas spoke softly in the tones of a scholarly small-town lawyer about the role of the House in bringing abuses to justice. Hogan of Maryland, whom some accused of turning against the President to improve his chances for the governorship of Maryland, seemed to rise above that charge in the intensity of his outrage over the perversions of power. Fish of New York coolly represented an old Eastern Establishment view of political rectitude; Cohen of Maine brought a fresh-faced questioning to the givens of executive prerogative as practiced by Richard Nixon; McClory of Illinois embodied the troubled, godly businessman whose auditor brings news of peculation in the works.

And the defenders, what of them? Though I could not take their part, neither could I impute mere political hackery to most of them. Wiggins, the leader of the defense, seemed at the least a fine lawyer with a poor case and at best a brilliant Constitutional parliamentarian; one ached for his bone-weariness toward the end of the debate, but his rebuttals never flagged. Dennis, the saw-voiced Indianian, buzzed like an angry country lawyer defending a once-prominent client in disgrace, but came down solidly and with impeccable legal propriety on the need for what he called "hard proof." Sandman—whom many have accused of unfair partisanship—seemed to me simply a hard-swinging trial lawyer of the old style, whose thunders and gestures before the jury (whose size he misquoted as 202 million) struck me as funny and admirable in equal measure.

Finally, the arch-impeachers, the majority Democrats. These, too, surprised me by, for the most part, their soft-spoken mien. Even the most hawkish of Nixon-haters like Conyers and Drinan appeared subdued, while a number of the lesser-known members —to me, at least—were both thoughtful and moving far beyond the call of mere political partisanship.

Edward Mezvinsky, of Iowa, spoke feelingly as the son of immigrants of his reverence for the presidency. Barbara Jordan, of Texas, moved forward through her paean to the Constitution with a majestic, almost evangelical, beat. Jack Brooks, also of Texas, rapped out a terse and well-constructed catalogue of crimes. And Peter Rodino, the chairman—plainly exhausted by his long and largely nonpartisan leadership of the committee's hearings— husked his way through a movingly humble statement in which he said, with utter believability, that he would urge impeachment with a heavy heart.

I have always sneered at what I thought a glib phrase of the young John Kennedy: "Profiles in Courage." Media hype though that phrase may have been and may still be, it is a sufficient description of many of the members of the committee during their debate before the nation. These ordinary men and women, most of them, had the courage of their convictions, the courage the framers of the Constitution must have wished for their successors. It showed. And it shone at what may be the end of an eleven-year-long night.

Belatedly, sheepishly, I pledge allegiance—not to a flag but to a committee. And to the people for whom they stand.

Presenting the Next
Great Western
Movie

The people who have written and directed some of our more critically and commercially successful movies of the Western genre in recent years have played fairly fast and loose with the ascertainable facts (for example, the lavishly embroidered *Butch Cassidy*), with the maximum plausible death toll (for example, *The Wild Bunch*), and with the palpable imbecility of their protagonists (for example, Bonnie's Clyde, who was transformed, at the stroke of a Royal, from a murderous dim bumpkin to a classic urban case of impotence according to Jules Feiffer). That understood, I hope nobody will take umbrage at my audacity if I present an idea for a new Western epic that features, among other things, two lone men of intelligence and principle pitted against an unscrupulous industrial empire; one small massacre; five dazzlingly successful train robberies; five full-scale shoot-outs; one foiled prison break and one successful one; one eighteen-month manhunt with odds of 1500 to one against the hunted; one touching love affair cut short by death; one casualty list of fourteen dead and twenty-four wounded; one fugitive dying with more lead on his person than the physician had ever seen before; one savagely ironic ending in which the wife and child of one of the outlaws go on stage in a melodrama based on his life in order to raise money for his legal fees; and, from start to finish, a strict adherence to historical fact.

I'm talking, of course, about the strange and eminently cinematic case of John Sontag and Christopher Evans, two now-for-gotten popular heroes who allegedly, though never provably, carried on an inspired guerrilla war against the Southern Pacific Railroad during the early 1890s. Sontag, a Minnesotan and former brakeman for the SP, blamed the railroad when he was injured on the job and made permanently lame in one of the sketchy company hospitals; Evans, a Canada-born Vermonter and former Indian scout who was also a serious reader (of Darwin, Huxley, and Shakespeare) and writer (of *Eurasia,* a utopian novel published in San Francisco), could never forgive the SP for having unconscionably multiplied the price of land to San Joaquin Valley settlers beyond the announced $2.50 an acre, thus causing many farmers (including relatives of Evans' wife and, some sources say, Evans himself) to lose their holdings and to be forced out completely. The bad feeling between the farmers and the railroad had first come to a head in May of 1880, when, at Mussel Slough, an SP agent and a U.S. Marshal escalated a dispossession proceeding into a gun battle which left five farmers and two officers dead; seventeen farmers were tried and jailed for their part in an affray in which they had fired only in self-defense.

Evans' general dislike of the Southern Pacific was probably reinforced throughout the eighties as he met the harassed local farmers in the course of his duties as the manager of three Bank of California granaries; his own uncertain fortunes took a turn for the worse when a livery stable he had just opened at Modesto burnt to the ground, killing all his livestock. In any case, the first of the mysterious series of train robberies occurred in February, 1889; two masked men stopped an SP train, dynamited the express car, shot a trainman fatally, and made off with about $5000 from the express-car safe. No clue to the robbers was found, nor did the police and SP agents have better luck when the crime was repeated, this time with a take of $20,000 and no deaths, a year later. Early in 1891, a third robbery led the police to some false arrests, before a fourth holdup, at Modesto, proved that the bandits were still at large and resulted in the serious wounding of an SP detective. Finally, in August, 1892, the robbers struck for the fifth and last time, dynamiting an express car and making off with 125 pounds of silver coin.

Now, at last—and largely because a young man named George Sontag, John's brother, had spoken indiscreetly about being a passenger on the held-up train—detectives were led to suspect Evans and Sontag of the crimes. Two of them went to Evans' home in Visalia to question him. As they entered, they saw John Sontag coming into the house at the rear. Without knocking, they walked into the living room, asked Chris Evans' pretty sixteen-year-old daughter, Eva, for Sontag's whereabouts, and when she told them he wasn't there (for she had no way of knowing he'd just come in), called her "a damned little liar."

Eva ran to the barn and told her father two strangers had accosted and insulted her; Christopher Evans picked up a gun, and a shoot-out ensued in which both detectives were wounded, and Sontag and Evans fled in the detectives' wagon.

This was the start of what one informal historian calls "the greatest manhunt California had known." Against a force of three thousand men all told, Evans and Sontag had only their superior tactical sense and the fact that the country was on their side and up in arms against the excesses of the railroad, which Frank Norris had dubbed "The Octopus." Their clever tactics began to pay dividends at once. After eluding a posse on the night of their escape, they returned to Evans' house, dined, provisioned their wagon, and killed another inquisitive officer, who had staked out the house.

While Evans and Sontag roamed the Sierra, George Sontag had gone to jail for his almost certainly imaginary role in the train robbery. Eva Evans and some other friends arranged to smuggle guns in to George and his fellow prisoners, but the attempted breakout was a failure in which three convicts were killed and six injured, including George himself, who was crippled for life.

Meanwhile, the railroad bent every effort toward the capture, dead or alive, of the two presumed train robbers. A $10,000 reward was announced, dozens of special agents and police were deputized, packs of hounds and pairs of Indian trackers were put on the scent, and the hills became so congested with armed men that no fewer than eleven deputies managed to shoot each other. All this activity, though, began to produce a predictable result: Evans and Sontag were slowly brought to bay. After eluding a gunfight at Young's Cabin, the two fugitives were ambushed by a U.S. Marshal and his posse at Stone Corral. Firing back from the inadequate cover of a manure pile, both men were grievously wounded in the course of the night: Evans' left arm was nearly severed, his right was immobilized by a shoulder wound, and his right eye was destroyed by a charge of buckshot; Sontag was shot repeatedly in the right arm, side, and chest—not to mention numerous flesh wounds.

During the small hours, Evans somehow managed to make his escape, but Sontag, weak from loss of blood, tried ineffectually to kill himself with two disfiguring but superficial shots to the face. Next morning, he awoke to find himself ringed by deputies. He was taken to Visalia jail, where he died, and where the physician volunteered the statement that he'd never seen so much lead in one body before.

Evans, astonishingly, survived to give himself up, on condition that the reward money should go to his wife. In jail, after the amputation of one arm, he lost none of his utopian dreamer's cunning: with the connivance of Ed Morrell, a waiter at a Fresno restaurant, who included two revolvers in his jail-delivered blue-plate special, he freed himself and headed, one weary time more and now eyeless, or at least monocular, for the hills. The police, also sadder and wiser, attempted no shoot-out; instead, they lured the serious paterfamilias Evans home, where he was quietly subdued with the message that one of his children was sick and asking for him. He was captured by a heavy posse and remanded for trial.

Before his last excursion at large, Evans had been the subject of a bitter, touching, and unparalleled public enterprise. One R. C. White, a San Francisco melodramatist, had written a play called, appropriately, *Evans & Sontag.*

To insure its success, he offered a quarter of the net profits to Mrs. Evans and Eva if they would play themselves in the performance. To pay Chris Evans' lawyers, they agreed; while Mrs. Evans shrank diffidently into the background, the handsome Eva —who had been engaged to Sontag at the time of his death—galloped onstage on a black charger and won a bold headline from

the San Francisco *Examiner:* "Eva Evans Given a Genuinely Enthusiastic Reception and Proves to Be an Actress." In 1894, despite all the efforts of his family and friends, her father was sen-
tenced to life in Folsom; in 1911, through the intervention of
the late Governor Hiram Johnson, an ancient foe of the Southern
Pacific, he was paroled, and moved to Portland with his family
for the last six years of his life. According to Stewart Holbrook
—who, along with Alvin F. Harlow and C. G. Glasscock, is
Evans' principal modern biographer—Frank Coulter, a violin-
maker who had known Evans in Modesto in the early nineties
and had become reacquainted with him in Portland, found it hard
to believe that this "soft-spoken and genial sort of man had successfully defied the Southern Pacific and the State of California—
at that time almost the same thing—for so many years."

Clearly, Evans and Sontag were brave, resourceful, and, in
their own quite countercultural way, principled far beyond most
of the childish and cretinous sadists—from Billy the Kid and the
Daltons to Bonnie and Clyde—whose thoughtless, bloody deeds
are so frequently celebrated on film today. Evans and Sontag were
men who lived and died for something real, and in doing so,
wrote a curious and imperishable footnote to our history; a film
about them, with all its implications for today, might carry the
Western to new and higher ground.

The Tree Warden

I. A FAREWELL TO ELMS

In late July, now, leaves begin to fall:
A wintry skittering on the summer road,
Beside which grass, still needing to be mowed,
Gives rise to Turk's-caps, whose green tapering ball-
Point pens all suddenly write red. Last year,
The oriole swung his nest from the high fan
Vault of our tallest elm. Now a tree man
Tacks quarantine upon its trunk. I hear

An orange note a long way off, and thin
On our hill rain the ochre leaves. The white
Age of a weathered shingle stripes the bark.
Now surgeons sweat in many a paling park
And bone saws stammer blue smoke as they bite
Into the height of summer. Fall, begin.

II. THE SECOND EQUINOX

Perambulating his green wards, the tree
Warden sees summer's ashes turn to fall:
The topmost reaches first, then more, then all
The twigs take umbrage, publishing a sea

Of yellow leaflets as they go to ground.
Upon their pyres, the maples set red stars,
The seal of sickness unto death that bars
The door of summer. Bare above its mound

Of leaves, each tree makes a memorial
To its quick season and its sudden dead;
With a whole gale of sighs and heaving head,
Each ash attends its annual burial.

The warden, under a boreal blue sky,
Reminds himself that ashes never die.

III.   DECEMBER THIRTY-FIRST

The days drew in this fall with infinite art,
Making minutely earlier the stroke
Of night each evening, muting what awoke
Us later every morning: the red heart

Of sun. December's miniature day
Is borne out on its stretcher to be hung,
Dim, minor, and derivative, among
Great august canvases now locked away.

Opposed to dated day, the modern moon
Comes up to demonstrate its graphic skill:
Laying its white on white on with a will,
Its backward prism makes a monotone.

In the New Year, night after night will wane;
Color will conquer; art will be long again.

IV.   MAY DAY

Help me. I cannot apprehend the green
Haze that lights really upon the young
Aspens in our small swamp, but not for long.
Soon round leaves, as a matter of routine,

Will make their spheric music; and too soon
The stunning green will be a common place.
Sensational today runs in our race
To flee the might of May for willing June.

To reach a bunch of rusty maple keys,
Undoing a world of constants, more or less,
I tread on innocence. The warden sees
In May Day the historical success
Of labor; a safe date for planting trees;
A universal signal of distress.

V
Assignations

The City Shepherd's Calendar

When my wife and I abandoned the city for the country, some twelve-odd (some of them exceedingly odd) years ago, we didn't, of course, know what in the world we were getting into.

Our shoebox-shaped house—not old enough to be old, not new enough to be modern—was 35 miles from the city and 18 feet from the road (not, luckily, the main one); it had eight midget rooms, a splendid view, abundant argyrol-colored wallpaper, some of it six layers thick, a nonfunctioning parlor organ, a fireplace, a condemnable barn, and no heat. After a summer of steaming and scraping wallpaper while subsisting on chocolate doughnuts, after a fall of throwing good money after bad into new heat, new plumbing, and new floors, we moved in in mid-October and became instant countrymen.

That is, of course, to laugh. No confirmed city person ever becomes a genuine rustic no matter how hard he tries (he is prevented, for one thing, by his unshakable, if unconscious, belief in the natural superiority of the urban breed), and in my case I was further disqualified by my ill-disguised ignorance of and loathing for hard manual labor of any kind, overlaid by an equal ignorance (though not an equal intolerance) in such matters as birds, trees, flowers, crops, wild and domestic fauna, and the astronomical and meteorological course of the country year. I was a quick study, though, and between swotting up the six-point type in back issues of the *Old Farmer's Almanac* and listening, nestling-mouthed, to the obiter dicta of post-office sages with *Biglow Papers* accents, I soon found myself at least bearably equipped to be on terms with woodcock, Baldwins, Brown Swiss, British Soldiers, cinquefoil, hawthorn, nighthawks, blue flags, silver freezes, popples, loom (a dialectal soil type), meadow voles, the Pleiades, mare's-tails, sap flush, hames, chain saws, power takeoffs, brown-tail moths, swale, saw-whet owls, abutters, and the Cruel Sisters (three mid-February days reputed to be the coldest of the year).

To this vainglorious glossary was added, when we sold our shoebox and bought an antique Colonial seven years later, a rich, exclusive argot of old-house words: summer beam, keeping room, gunstock posts, chimney well, sills, plates, king- and queenposts, courses (of brickwork), cellar hole, bulkhead, captain's stairway, tree nails. My wife truly understood the principles of post-and-beam construction and could converse, in fluent Colonial, with workmen. To me, they were mainly added party patter; I still wouldn't know what a post should do to a beam.

Nevertheless, twelve years out into the country, I feel I've gained something from the expensive, frightening, and somehow ennobling experience. If I were, ungratefully, to be merely wry about it, I could easily compile a calendar of terrifying home truths that seasonally assail the displaced city man. Bills and ice backup, ruining all the shed-dormer wallpaper, in January; snowblower failure, compounded by inscrutable and incapable country servicemen, in February; whole pampas of lawn gone to glutinous mud, of quicksand tenacity, in March; bulb failure in April, with entire plantations of costly Holland tulip, daffodil, hyacinth, anemone declining to bear; a plague of starlings and a total absence of bluebirds, swallows, or anything else avian and gracile in May; cruel heat in June; thunderstorms, bearing fruit-bruising hail, in July; deeply depressive heat and humidity immobilized in August; equinoctial gales—hurricanoes, even—in September; snap frosts and heavy rains, downing the turning leaves and interdicting foliage displays, in October; unseasonable cold and oil bills, compounded by an early assault of Christmas décor in shopping centers, in bleakest November; Christmas ad nauseam through flat-cold, wither-wringing, and bleaker still December, except for the dark and fatal final week.

But I'd like to suggest that even the city man's invincible ignorance is unwittingly, and happily, infected by the country ambience, and that even he is capable of extracting from the rich pie of nature set before him an occasional and redeeming plum. These plums are almost certainly scorned as intolerably commonplace by the real rustics, but they are new and magical to the city man, and he secretly revels in them and in his latent and only lately discovered capability of taking part, if only as an innocent bystander, in real life. Therefore I present without apology, four hundred years after Edmund Spenser, my own homemade City Shepherd's Calendar. The chief virtue, as I now see it, of moving from one's expertise and competence in the city to abject ignorance and helplessness in the country is that it stimulates a faculty not often present in the blasé adult, a faculty associated, indeed, with innocent childhood: the faculty of wonder. Here, then, are the occasions of wonder I've discovered in each twelve months on my six acres.

JANUARY. Snowdrifts are perfect aerodynamic shapes, mimicking the natural forms designed for flying in a fluid: swallows, gulls, seals, dolphins; since they're shaped directly by the wind, that stands to reason. The shadows in deep snow hollows are never black or gray, but always some shade of blue; on a bright, sunny day, they're a voluptuous light ultramarine. Tree shadows cast on snow are also blue on bright days, but their texture varies with the texture of the snow (and the cirrus, if any, over the sun) from a solid, hard-edged pen stroke to the softest, haziest charcoal.

FEBRUARY. Great horned owls begin their mating season. You can hear their very deep—almost felt rather than heard—hoots, sometimes from a great distance, in the small hours of the morning. They sound delightfully (and scarily) as you expected owls to sound. If you're lucky, if they're near enough, and if there's any moon, you can see them perched in the upper crotches of tall elms, vertical bumps on upright logs. Very occasionally, you'll see their diurnal opposite numbers, the snowy owls, swoop down like ski troops to catch field mice in the snow.

MARCH. Spring has many forerunners. Maples turn redder and

willows yellower toward the tips of their branches; this is known as sap flush. Redwing blackbirds and their allies arrive, filling the treetops, the second week in March in our neck of the woods. Their call is unmelodious and welcome. Ice thins on ponds. Some early mornings you can see muskrats swimming purposefully under a thin skim of ice. The sun develops real heat at midday—equal to that of September—and the snow melts down to slush and grass-laced mud out of which squills and crocuses rise marvelously overnight. The squills, with their native Siberian courage, bloom the truest of blues in the teeth of murderous March winds.

APRIL. Under the impact of a very serious sun, the grass quite suddenly flushes green, especially on south-facing slopes, about the tenth. That green is unreal, almost a Day-Glo-poster color; if it lasted, it would make summer intolerably virid. But it is happily accepted as an outrider, as the first summer replacement for dead hay and grizzled mud. Birds now arrive in almost daily groups, all of a kind, like tourists on a chartered flight. The last fire of the winter—applewood, for preference—simmers and stews, unpoked, in the fireplace, and overheats the room. The air is full of promise and ozone.

MAY. All flower names: iris, including the incomparably haughty blue flags in the stream bed; lilac, sweet white, not quite cloying lavender, grape purple; tulips, all looking forbiddingly manmade; dandelions, tough, independent, beautiful; last daffodils; first buttercups. The sound of cows; the smell, cutting across the lilacs, of fields freshly fertilized. At night, the largest and pearliest of possible moons.

JUNE. First heat, hitting the earth like a cloudburst. Roses and dust. The immemorial hum of lawnmowers.

JULY. Haying: more fragrant than any flower, the smell of acres of grass and clover cut, baled, and wired. In the mornings, you sniff the early, watery scent of coming heat. In the afternoons, grass browns on the front lawn. At night, fireworks burst like strings of lady crackers at some distant amusement park hull down on the horizon. Night bugs begin to sing in earnest. Thunderstorms turn on fluorescent lights and throw trunks downstairs in the dusk and dawn hours.

AUGUST. A vision of heaven and hell. Heaven comes on those

clear, dry days that predict fall and question the very existence of summer in the North. Hell comes in dull flares of sun and yellow-greenish haze, into which brownish-green trees bleed and fuzz. Grass dies; flowers droop; Vivaldi's summer, creeping languidly to a crippled obbligato, seems the truest of his Seasons.

SEPTEMBER. Summer meets fall in the classic annual contest and loses, 3 to 2. Sixty percent of September is crisp and purposeful; 40 percent is becalmed in the backwaters of summer. Trees decline imperceptibly, insects play an octave higher and several decibels louder, new flowers spring up in summer's dry-grass waste, chipmunks and squirrels thriftily provide, wasps reach the peak of their activity before winter thickens the glycol in their veins.

OCTOBER. More color that would strike us as indecent in art museums or on movie screens. Ashes gone perfect, blinding ochre. Hickories a thinner, lighter, purer yellow. Maples mixed Kelly green and hemoglobin scarlet. Oaks red, rust, russet, forest green. Woodbine vermilion; blueberry red-violet. Grass now greener again to heighten the early-Technicolor contrast. Sky bluer, too. Somehow we take all this excess in stride.

NOVEMBER. Soft, soft: hoarfrost on dying coverts of lank grass; bushes now hushed in the quietest tones of brown; swamp maples antiqued silver; lawns dying back to shades of bone. A day or two of Indian summer clarifies the round shape of the year and the long night we're headed into, a prelude to a longer night.

DECEMBER. Away from the cities and their parroted chatter of Christmas, which would fail to fool any self-regarding child, the world rolls to the brink of the solstice, where life lives banked in burrows and the earth is a surface of storm tracks: wide miss, near miss, direct hit, and snowbound. We burn our cordwood, make cocoa, walk out in waders, smile smugly in our highly temporary isolation. Not a bad way to greet a new year.

JANUARY. Another round of the carrousel begins with a sense of circus music. I'm glad to have found the funds to buy another ticket.

A Little Night Music:
The Curvature of
the Earth

Throughout our lives, far more efficiently than responsibility or taxes, we evade the idea of death. This is no mean feat: in a world of massacre and genocide, of widely reported individual deaths in Belfast, in Vietnam, and in our own backyard, we keep our blinders firmly on. Even the deaths of our friends and relatives do not persuade us fully of our own mortality; it's always somebody else that death happens to. In adolescence we are reckless with our lives, as if there were more than one life to a customer; in middle age, we are cautious and husbanding of them, but as an affirmation, not an admission; in old age we fight tooth and nail—or toothless and horny-nailed—to keep our licenses to live, as if they could never be revoked by the Registry of Spiritual Vehicles. We are all of us always, in the words of the noble old cliché, living a lie.

Or almost always. Sometimes there comes to some of us, at ages when the knowledge would ordinarily be immaterial, a stinging vision of the inevitability of our own death. It is like, I should imagine, being the first man to see for himself—was he Major General Orvil Anderson, the USAAF balloonist, or one of those RAF fighter pilots who flew special high-altitude reconnaissance missions in supercharged, camera-bearing Spitfire MK IX's toward the end of World War II?—the proof of the theory of the curvature of the earth. At any rate, I felt just like an explorer of the bourns of our existence when, in the fall of 1965, a doctor told me (with considerable embarrassment, as if he had somehow been responsible for the dreadful foul-up) that I was the newest case of Hodgkin's disease.

Hodgkin's—which has had a good press lately but was obscure, almost reclusive, in those days—is a kind of cancer of the lymph nodes which used to be routinely fatal, and was still thought to be so in 1965. (A brave young woman I knew slightly in the forties and fifties had died of it, after an eighteen-month siege, in 1956.) So, although the skillful and kindly doctor did everything he could to pillow the blow, I soon became aware, after a little blunt-phrased digging, that I was in for it myself in a year or two or—possibly—ten. There would, of course, be radiation treatment—the doctors had great hopes for some new techniques of cobalt therapy—but no guarantees were given or received.

When my wife suddenly put her arm around me in the corridor leading to the garage from the medical building, a gesture both generous and possessive, I realized that both of us were about to lose me, a fact that I was, to draw it mild, quite unprepared to face. Apart from the beastly injustice of the whole idea—and beastly, bestial, is exactly how it seemed, like the wanton killing of a child, for who isn't, all his life, as innocent and vulnerable as a child in matters of life and death?—it struck me as a double injustice to my wife, who would go on suffering, mentally and materially, long after I had broken ground for my new venture. Equally, it was a serious—indeed, fatal—hardship for my old venture, a belated resumption of a career as a poet that I had just succeeded in relighting two years before. Finally, I realized that I was going to have the greatest difficulty in renouncing, however involuntarily, my wife, my house, my friends, my work, my dog, and certain ash and maple trees, not to mention various winsome bit players in my life so far.

My first reaction, an almost entirely unconscious one, was to clamp a tight lid of security down on overt expressions of these feelings. It seemed that the only way to deal with this crisis—different in degree but perhaps not, after all, in kind from others I had had to deal with—was to negate it, to pretend to myself and everybody else that, though it *had* happened to me, it couldn't happen to me. This ersatz stoicism, grafted on from the outside after the fact, worked fine. It took my wife and friends in, not to mention me. I soon convinced myself that *che serà, serà,* and to hell with it. My wife found me an uncomfortably uncomplaining monolith. The doctors took me for some unheard-of man of steel. And all the time I was simply denying the enormous, realistic likelihood of an untimely (whatever that means) death.

This high-flown irrefragability did not, however, extend itself into the area of physical discomfort. Always a sissy about pain, I moaned and writhed unconscionably during the various surgical and diagnostic procedures, especially a new one called lymphan-giography, which, by pumping a dark dye into the lymph vessels in the insteps, permits a fluoroscopic detection and examination of the infected and enlarged lymph nodes. The dye needles were bad enough, but their predecessors, a series of Novocain injections to deaden the skinny, bony insteps, were worse; between the two, I had soon put down the copy of R. P. Blackmur's *Form and Value in Modern Poetry* I was rereading the same page of and started wincing and groaning in earnest long before the hour-and-a-half procedure was over. This was characteristically ironic, too, because it was probably the newly invented lymphangiogram that saved my life; a year or two earlier, nobody would have known how to locate the affected nodes in order to treat the area with a bearable dose of radiation.

From diagnosis, I crept on to treatment: a character in a 1935 movie of a 1905 H. G. Wells novel, I lay on a table, pinioned by lead bars, while a huge, rocket-shaped GE radiation machine circled a circular room and drew a bead on me, day after day. Ports clanked open; light leaped out in the darkened room; a buzzing X ray zapped me in the offending abdomen; the monster rang down its metal shutters and wheeled away. Soon I got sick from this: diarrhea, weight loss, constant nausea, wooziness.

But it was nothing to the sickness of the cancerous recidivists, two- and three-time losers to the disease, who sat beside me in the radiation waiting room. These frail, brittle, sallow people, decently, patiently awaiting the next failure of treatment and loss of hope, are probably the most courageous men and women I've known, and it still pains and frightens me to think of them.

From inpatient I went to outpatient, creeping out of the office at four each afternoon to my rendezevous with the cyclotron, creeping home afterward, feeling very much an old man at thirty-eight, to inspect my burns, getting serious by now, and to slough the burnt skin off my belly like a snake. In the midst of all this dubious progress toward a cure, or at least a remission, a bizarre and unexpected thing occurred: my boss precipitately left the company, and I was promoted overnight in his place, the youngest and sickest vice president they had. The money was more than welcome, in view of the backlogging medical bills; the responsibility was not, at least at first, though I now suspect that it helped keep my mind off illness and on recovery. When my treatment at last ended, and further fluoroscopy showed that my lymph nodes had shriveled back to normal size, I was pronounced remitted—a kind of temporarily burnt-out case, like a dormant volcano. Again, no guarantees were given, though, and I was made aware that my next attack, should it ever come, might be my last. Nobody said this in so many words, of course, but the aura of irrational malice that hangs over a hitherto fatal disease made it clearly understood.

I was still in a state of *rigor mentis* after all this uproar of diagnosis and therapy and putative cure, still less than willing to admit to myself that, from the moment the painless, seemingly innocent lump on my thigh was biopsied and found malign, I had been in view of the curvature of the earth, of the whole trajectory of my life, and had seen the black and negative jackpot at the rainbow's end. Yet, in this state of inadmission of the evidence, I was still able to make certain basic decisions about the future course of my affairs, if any. First, my wife and I decided to sell a handsome 1743 house we had bought barely a year before, on the substantial grounds that I didn't want to burden both of us, if I survived, or her, if I didn't, with the constant, costly care and feeding of a delightful relic. We were lucky enough to find a buyer at a profit, and to build a brand-new colonial, not too badly reproduced, on some other land we owned. Next, and still on the serious side, I determined to step up the pace of my verse writing to complete a first book of poems before any further fatal hands were laid upon my throat. Fortunately, the onset of my illness had found me full of plans for poems, and even more fortunately, I was able to pick up where I had left off and spend 1966 writing them; by the end of the year, I had a manuscript which was soon after accepted as my first book.

Meanwhile, I also reacted frivolously to my experience. Moving my personal timetable a couple of years forward, I bought an expensive sports car (a Jaguar roadster) for the first time since I'd been a spendthrift kid, and took a five-week trip to England and Scotland with my wife. The motivation here was plain: though I might not have admitted it, I was damned if I'd die without having driven very fast and seen London at least once. (We saw a great deal more than London, driving at what now seems an exhausting pace, at least in a Mini—the Jaguar remained at home—over 2700 miles of Chilterns, Wenlocks, Cotswolds, Highlands and moors.) In pretty much the same way, I threw myself into my work, both at the office and at home, as if I were making up for lost—or borrowed—time. While I still officially dismissed the suggestion that my illness had had any very deep or lasting effect on my life, I was busy proving with my almost every action that I valued that life far more comprehensively than I ever had before.

This was not all demonstrated, of course, in sound and fury. A lot of it came out in the increased sensitivity of my personal emulsion to the otherwise quite ordinary things in life. I could be startled, for almost purely asexual reasons, by the great spectacle of a young girl smiling; I could be transported by the odor (for example) of thyme crushed underfoot; I could be moved, almost embarrassingly, by the sound of a friend's voice over the telephone; I could be stunned by the taste of the first Macoun apple of the fall. Though, as a writer, I had always been aware of the analogy between our life and the seasons, I now began to invest those seasons with an almost tactile significance and power. Spring, in its universal renovation, rejected my irradiated body, but summer, brandishing umbels, accepted it; I saw my decline summed up in fall, my death in winter, my revivification in the following spring, the first in which I had truly taken part since a childhood April on a farm. Somehow, my personal home demonstration of the fleetingness of life redoubled my perception and enjoyment of its mutant shapes and shadows. Instead of a curtain falling, a curtain rose. And stayed up, revealing a stage decked in defining light, until Doctor Hodgkin's second call—which I'll tell about in a future article.

M'aidez

May comes and stands in my window in a blur, a jiggle, a dazzle of dappled green and yellow light, and I get weak in the knees with the annual visitation of paradise and my increasing distance from it. "M'aidez," or "Mayday," is the modern SOS that pilots use, and I'm increasingly moved to say it silently when May Day comes.

Probably only a child is perfectly gaited to the lenitive blandishments of May, its intimations of perfectibility, its grasshopper suggestion that winter can never come. An adult is too damaged, too knowing, to eat of the forbidden fruit of its insinuations: he has seen too many Decembers. This doesn't prevent him, though, from greeting May each spring with a cautious renewal of hope and an increasing degree of objective observation.

And, even if we beat back our ancient instinctual impulse to go a-Maying, there is much to observe in the perfection of the month, as there is in any natural creation at the height of its sway. After the slow, erratic recession of the winter, the fits and starts of warmth and cold of early spring, May represents a unified, concerted movement toward a goal in view, like the last movement of a symphony.

Consider how May begins. First, there is the light: the clear, strong light of a rejuvenated sun, striking down powerfully even in the early hours, irradiating the new grass with its diamond yellow-white, paling the blue sky, turning white house sides to solid glare, falling into the cups of daffodils to recharge and re-double their goldenness, casting sharp-edged shadows, seemingly enlarging textures—of tree trunks, roadsides, stone walls—as it illuminates them in a brightness that compels our attention.

Next, there is the sound: at sunup on an early-May morning, the almost alarming sound of hundreds of newly returned birds in atonal chorus, shattering sleep and scaring the waker, momentarily, into believing the animals have usurped the world. There is joy in all those unorchestrated calls, but also fierceness; the birds, the gay but somehow menacing sound says, will brook no interference with their plans to nest and mate and guard their territories. But that noisy, archaic carol, almost as old as the world, is also a not so subtle call to us to be up and Maying: to accede to the animal in our natures, to sport and mate, to set rationality and routine aside. Later in the day, when the chorus has subsided to impromptu solos, there are other sounds of May: a tiny, quiet crackle as the old grass dries and curls still further under the unremitting sun, a whispering hint of wind through still bare branches, the sounds—bicycle chains, axes, footsteps, voices—of men venturing out in shirt sleeves to repossess the world they forsook last autumn.

Finally, there is the color. A whole second fall takes place in reverse in the treetops. Leaf buds and flower buds, tinted to match their parent trees, transform the uppermost twigs to a fine haze of green, red, russet, saffron. In the slant sun late in the afternoon, these treetops glow like growth, the opposite of fire, prefiguring the gravid foliage of summer. On the ground, in the new grass, flowers answer with a flash of color: paper narcissi, as delicate as antique valentines, tough tulips, butter-colored daffodils, and the small, wild bluets, springing in violet-edged white nosegays from the tussocks of a stony field. Redwing blackbirds sport vermilion epaulets; tree swallows perch in an aura of iridescent greeny blue; bluebirds, rare and transient, flaunt azure backs at us. Color is ruler for a day.

As May goes on, unfurling leaves, springing new grasses, loosing bees to worry the glistening flowers, the human incumbents begin to feel both upstaged by all this primal action and invited to partake. We develop that slightly woozy defense mech-

anism called spring fever, walking hatless and unsteadily under
the gentle weight of all that sun, grinning idiotically, fantasizing
about everything coming right again, conjuring youth and love
out of the hummingbird-wing of breeze, feeling our age and no
age at all. The month wears on, grows serious. Now the lawn
settles down into a tall and ragged chore, needing to be mowed
each week; leaves come out in earnest, providing shade from
coming summer; the first hot day in the dried and cloddy garden
sends us, weak and sweating, back indoors for a cold glass of
water. We are rescued from the impertinence of spring—the rising
pulse, the flush upon the cheeks, the dizzy onset of desire—by the
assurance of predictable, sometimes unpleasant summer drawing
near.

We were not, either by temperament or experience, meant to
live in paradise. A little Eden goes a year-long way. May is welcome to come, more welcome to be gone. Unlike children, who
can make Edens out of the unlikely raw materials of any season,
we are rather resentful of a month that seduces us away from
our pursuits and troubles and back into our childish selves.

Yet May—the singular spell in the annual round that really
gets through to us with a different and disturbing message—deserves, somehow, to be commemorated, just as our childhood
deserves to be commemorated. I, for one, can't let a May go by
without an itch to write a poem, just as, I suspect, others feel the
need to seize a camera (which I've done, too) or a paint box or
maybe simply play a pickup game of sandlot ball. In my case, the
poem-writing urge is usually prompted by a single observation
of some detail of May. This goes into some back corner of the
mind where it gestates quietly for hours or days. Then it springs
back to consciousness, quite unexpectedly and forcibly, prompt-
ing a frisson at the back of the neck and a prickle behind the eyes,
and I know there is nothing for it but to sit down with a piece of
paper and a clipboard and four long, sharp No. 2 pencils and try
to put it down on paper.

It is different, though, from writing poems at other times of
year. The swaddling haze of May warms the bones (and, sometimes in a perverse way, the heart), but it also, as I've suggested,
addles the brain into a state unlike any other state of conscious-

ness. Now, seated with clipboard and yellow pad in, and in- spired by, May, I don't think or write as I usually do. I'm a bit drugged, a bit under the influence of the tides, the moon, and the coming solstice. Instead of the usual, literally formal, beginning of the poem, wherein I quite coldly conceive the opening lines and then wait for a wave from the unconscious to lift me up and sweep me into the body of the poem, in spring I am carried irre- sistibly from the start into a kind of rhythmic equating of writing with feeling. There is no calculating pump-priming; instead, I am caught up from word one on paper in the movement of the earth—and the answering tremor of the heart. The poem is so internal to me, so rooted in obscure, instinctive ritual origins, that I'm not even fully conscious of my role as transmitter of sentience into language. The poem rolls on and over me, the twelfth wave that comes just once a year, leaving a residue of pencil tracks on the lined paper. A residue for me to puzzle over afterward, won- dering if it's any good or not, this *donnée* from the season, won- dering if my usual standards of content, form, and diction can or should apply.

Sometimes this business of taking dictation from my ur-self works, at least by those usual standards; sometimes it doesn't. Some years, I wake up in June to reread the May poem and find that it's banal or platitudinous or, on the other hand, arcane gib- berish; some years, though, it all seems to come right, and I hold in my hand, that day in June, one of the rare magic poems, com- posed of earth, air, and fire, that poets are very occasionally blessed with. Sometimes they take the form of dreams, real dreams set down on paper, a form that somehow seems to suit the shifting evanescence of the time of year. And sometimes they are simple, straight, and literal, merely (but more than merely, when they work) the recording of an observation of color, light, or sound. It's not a way I'd like to write all year—too uncontrolled, too chancy—but it is a surprise, sometimes a revelation, on the fifth page of the calendar.

Another May will soon be upon us. The tentative begin- nings of growth and greening, leafing and nesting, will rise to a climax in the later weeks, and summer, in green bunting, christened by thundershowers, will slip ponderously down the ways. In between those seasons, one year in three, there comes another, miniature season: the perfect week of spring. Usually it is the last week in May if it comes at all, and, when it happens, it is the apotheosis of perfection in the world. Nights go cool and dry and starry; dawns come up in a fire storm of antique gold and pale, celestial blue; days burn softly, like a twelve-hour taper of white-gold light; sunsets layer the sky into a softly graded pousse-café, reading upward, of yellow, orange, red, aquamarine, pale blue, mid-blue, dark blue, indigo, midnight. And the May moon, when it is waning into newness in that last week, casts the subtlest of silver lights on lawn and garden, deckling the edges with marine fluorescence, coloring the intervening stretches the faintest, blackest shade of forest green. The days are warm with fair-weather cumulus and a mild breeze; hazes on distant mountains dissipate, leaving a clear view of their green tree lines all day long till afternoon, when clear ink-blue creeps up their slopes. It is a week, when it comes, to make the rest of the year and the rest of life seem dingy, trivial, unfulfilled. It is also, of course, a fitting finale to May.

What will I do, this week or next or the one after, when wild violets bloom half-hidden in the grass and wrens build their scraggly nests with maximum ferocity and noise, like jabbering straw bosses? Well, I'll walk around in a pleasant daze, gathering, like the wrens, odd bits of scrap for a poem. Then, *un bel di di maggio,* I'll sit down and write it, giving myself up to the primal scream like a surfer borne on a monstrous wave. Then, and last, I'll look out on that perfect week (if it comes) and think ruefully of the chances missed, the failed attempts, the throat of the human thirst for perfection forever destined to be dry. And forever destined to be soothed and exacerbated at once by the merry, scary month of May.

M'aidez!

A Little Night Music:
A Tangential Line

In the winter of 1966, while I was still undergoing radiation therapy for my first attack of Hodgkin's disease, I wrote, very secretly and shamefully, a poem about the experience. It was called "Dying: An Introduction;" when I had finished it, I carefully filed it away—perhaps forever—because it seemed at the time a shockingly self-pitying, self-indulgent view of the illness. In all my other relations with myself and the world, I had adopted a stoical mask; in this poem alone, I had admitted my fear and panic. The poem sat in my desk for a year. At the end of that time, I had reached an uneasy accommodation with the likelihood that the disease would recur—a sort of low-grade, back-of-the-mind queasiness not unlike the muted, manageable horror most of us felt about atomic warfare three or four years after Hiroshima—and I felt composed enough to take "Dying: An Introduction" out of its hiding place and read it again. This time, though it still seemed to embody an unwarranted admission of weakness, I felt that it belonged to an already distant period in my life and could therefore be permitted to exist. So I sent it to a magazine, saw it published, and made it the title poem of my first collection of verse, all without more than a minimal twinge of guilt at having spread this confessional *cri de coeur* upon the public record.

At the time, and as more months passed by without a recurrence of the disease, I found myself indulging in a kind of balanced doublethink, holding two contradictory propositions to be self-evident. First, I believed, more strongly with each passing month, that I would beat the system and get off scot-free without a second illness; second, I simultaneously harbored a gloomy conviction that, in accordance with the statistics, I would sooner or later fall victim, this time fatally, to the disease. I somehow managed to feel guilty about both ideas: guilty if I frivolously indulged myself, grasshopperlike, on the grounds that I would live out my normal span; guilty if I planned every action and expense, antlike and frugally, on the premise that I would soon be swept away. Actually, though, these countervailing anxieties were nowhere near as obsessive as I might have supposed; I was so busy with work and writing that they stayed, mercifully, in the back of my consciousness most of the time. In an idle moment once or twice a day, the conflicting scenarios might flash into my conscious mind, but not for long and never very painfully. I was still, of course, perfecting my stoic act, and by then I'd gotten pretty good at it, aided by the odd cachet—the fund of moral capital—which a successful brush with death provides among one's friends, or among those very few friends I'd breached security to tell about it.

So I bowled along pretty easily over the surface of life until the late summer of 1969, nearly four years after my first illness. I knew that, actuarially speaking (and according to a doctor whom I had finally pinned down on the subject), I was good for five to ten years at the outside from the date of my first attack; but, with four years safely crossed off on the jail-cell wall, I had begun to have serious hopes of beating the odds. Then, at a party, I noticed that my first sip of my first drink gave me an odd, sharp pain in the pit of the stomach; each time I drank again, the experience was repeated. After a month or two of this, I reported the pain to my doctors in the course of a routine checkup. They nodded gravely. It turned out that the pain had recently been discovered to be diagnostic of Hodgkin's in the lymph nodes of the diaphragm, near the stomach wall; the alcohol, swiftly passing through the wall, apparently enters and irritates the enlarged nodes nearby.

This time, the doctors were far more sanguine than before;

they talked of "staging" the disease, of "new treatment," of the increasing likelihood that they had removed Hodgkin's from the list of invariably fatal illnesses. But now I was even less convinced; I felt that I was being blandished, that time had run out, that I simply wouldn't make it the second time around. I entered the hospital in outwardly good spirits but with an inward and unshakable belief that this was it.

The doctors—eleven of them, all told—marshaled their forces for a truly impressive attack on the disease. Everything, I felt, was meticulously planned in some War Room in the depths of the hospital: the battery of tests in just such a sequence; the alternative battle plans contingent on the outcome of the tests; the choice of weapons—radiation or chemotherapy—for the mopping-up afterward. I was impressed with their intelligence, their high degree of organization, their dedication to duty, their esprit; but none of it rubbed off on me this early in the game. I went about my business between tests, reading, writing a book review on the hospital tray table, greeting my wife and friends who loyally showed up every day (it was now January of a cold, snowy, iron-hard winter, and it took real fortitude for them to visit me); but I never believed that the doctor's big medicine would work.

The tests themselves were a grisly diversion that confirmed my fatalism: another lymphangiogram, far quicker and less painful than the last (the technique had improved in four years), to dye-mark the infected nodes; a fiendish-looking method of withdrawing a liver sample at the end of a long needle; a similar technique for securing a smitch of bone marrow for testing; and assorted other triangulations of the disease. These were all hors d'oeuvres; the entrée—and I use the word advisedly—came when my spleen, which was presumed to be loaded with the disease, came out on an absurdly narrow operating table from which I joked with the doctors, being lightheaded from the preliminary sedation, until I went under the main anesthetic. There followed a nightmare night under the eye of two cheerful, watchful nurses in the recovery room, and a groggy day in which I clung pitifully to my wife's hand when she bravely came to see me. When the sedation had cleared the following morning, I was given to understand that the spleen had been rightly judged the villain—"I held it in my hand," the doctor said, shaking his head at the extent of its corruption—but the great question now was whether a biopsy would show that the disease had spread to the liver. If it had, I would be out of luck, since the liver, unlike the spleen, is, of course, not expendable.

After another day of local and general discomfort and abundant gas pains, I got the good news that the liver was OK. However, there were a lot of nasty lymph nodes that could not be removed by surgery; these would have to be dealt with either by radiation or by chemotherapy. If they were confined to an area not previously treated by radiation, the X ray could be used again; if the two areas overlapped, I would have to resort to a grueling, eighteen-month course of chemical treatment which would leave me sick and debilitated throughout the period of therapy. Again, I was lucky; radiation was chosen, and the young and ebullient radiotherapist got busy drawing a map of the area to be treated and directing the building of shields to protect my vital organs. (One Saturday morning, he came bounding into my room to show me the master diagram he'd just completed, to him a work of art, to me Greek, but nonetheless a heartening evidence of his consuming interest in the case.)

Finally, in February, I left the hospital, weaker, thinner, and unconvinced that I could be cured, to convalesce at home. For the next two weeks, in the guttering dead of winter, I lay under blankets that seemed insupportably heavy, dozing, listening to classical music and reruns of Spike Milligan's *Goon Show,* and being waited on with unremitting devotion by my wife. It was then, I think, that I made up my mind that I would never make it back. I fell into the equivalent of a postpartum depression, feeling myself a dry husk already harvested to wither quietly away. This time I felt vulnerable, not stoical; for the first time in a relatively happy, relatively untroubled life, I realized that I was not stronger than dirt—or dust—and the realization robbed me of élan.

My gloom was compounded two weeks later when I rose from my bed to resume radiation treatments at the hospital. In the place of the old missile silo with its giant cyclotron, there was now a brand-new radiation clinic with pastel walls, colorful hangings, Naugahyde sling chairs, and accursed Muzak. In these painfully breezy surroundings, the other patients seemed not only fated but somehow sinister; their patent weakness, their paper-white and yellow faces, their halting voices, their ominous limps seemed almost an affront to the impersonal cheeriness of the waiting room. The radiation machine itself was new, an apple-green monster built around a swinging, tilting table for the patient. Overall there was a faint, sickly, sickening smell: part electrical, part mechanical, part photographic (acetic acid for X-ray developing), part failing human being. Nothing else has ever depressed me (or literally sickened me: entering the waiting room invariably made me nauseated, which had nothing to do with the effects of the treatment) to a like extent, and I hope nothing ever will.

On April 17, 1970, I had my final treatment. That clear, brisk early-spring weekend, with my wife and a couple we knew, I went to revisit the world. We stayed at a seaside resort just open for the season; walked by the icy sea in a stiff wind; went to a cocktail party for the guests where we met nobody; tramped through an Audubon bird sanctuary; and came home. I still felt dreadfully weak. I walked and talked little. I did not take part in many conversations. I was, if anything, more depressed than ever. And without reason, for my doctors had told me that the therapy had really worked this time. With far greater conviction than they had ever displayed in the past, they predicted that I stood an excellent chance of being completely and permanently cured; it seemed as if Hodgkin's was finally being conquered, and that I might be one of the first beneficiaries. If I could go three years without a recurrence, I was home free.

As close to a clean bill of health as I could have hoped for. But the depression persisted, and I found it a genuine effort to deal effectively with routine things, with daily decisions at home and work. All through the late spring and summer, I seemed to be trundling a snowballing stone uphill; not until six months after the last of the treatments did I begin to feel that I had become fully functional again. During this period, I put together a third volume of poems with an odd mixture of fear and detestation, as if publishing another book were an act of supererogation ill-suited to my reduced emotional and physical circumstances; even my editors' enthusiasm failed to raise my spirits.

All this changed again—thankfully, for the better—over the following winter and spring. The depression occasioned by the illness melted gradually away; the vacuum it left was filled by new plans and new interests and by resumption of my older ones. I began, after a lapse of nearly a year, to write poetry seriously again, and to take something like my old interest in the world around me. This time, though, the stoic mask had gone, to be replaced by a shaken realization of mortality, a new, more realistic sizing and distancing of myself in time.

Time. It is now two years since my last illness. The latest X rays and blood tests are perfectly normal. I'm doing fine, the doctors say. I have a year to go. Early in 1973, if all continues well, I'll almost certainly be absolved of the disease. These are strange days and not unhappy ones. I'm building up my gambler's stack of one-month chips in front of me; when I have thirty-six, I will have won the game. Meanwhile, not knowing yet quite what literary use (if any) I will make of it, I have been looking down at the curvature of the earth, at the trajectory of my life and death, from a new perspective: from the perspective of a tangential line lifting, straight as a contrail, away from the earth and myself and all the other things and people. It is, and has been, a lonely journey. But so, if we only knew it, is every life.

A Novembrist Manifesto

November is the unsung month. October has, by courtesy of Helen Hunt Jackson, otherwise the author of *Ramona,* its "bright blue weather;" December has its tiny, weary army of worn-out Christmas carols, suitable for rasping reproduction on shopping-mall speaker systems. But nobody has a good word, verbal or vocal, for November, that uneasy interregnum, at least in allegedly temperate areas, between fire and ice.

Nobody but me, apparently. I hereby confess to a sneaking liking for the eleventh month, as Walt Whitman would call it, though its name means "ninth." November is, in the best sense, a natural month. For nature, it is a time of necessary death and burial. For men, it is a time for return to roots, if rooms are roots, from the temporary playground of summer's outdoors. It is a month without the pressures of anticipation of, say, March, when spring becomes unbearably promising because withheld. It is a month without the recirculated tedium of holidays—except Thanksgiving, a sad and modest feast—to be got through. Best of all, it is a month worse than its precursors, better than its successors, a month that breeds resignation, evaluation, and acceptance.

In the northern latitudes, it divides itself, if unpredictably, into three segments. The first begins on All Saints' Day and All Souls' Day—a twenty-four-hour transit from the sublime to the subterrene—when the debris of Hallowe'en, shattered front-porch pumpkins and toilet-paper streamers, nests on the leaf-covered, frost-whitened stubble of the still green but dying lawn. The night-time frosts rise into mists under the sun, warming to the watery, chill haze of a late Indian-summer day, falling and cooling again to ice at night. This cycle runs a week or so, when it mutates over-night into the first real long-range forecast of a long, hard winter: those days of boundless, pewter-colored stratus cloud that lay lead darkness on the land and shut out the sun except at rise and set. In the dank chill of those ten days or more at the heart of most Novembers, the bone first feels its fallibility, cold's intimation of mortality, absent all summer long. But, at the same time, the eye sees, and delights in, the subtle colors of another mortality on the face of the earth. There, underfoot and all around, are the pal-ing greens of dying leaves, the whited ochres and umbers of dead ones, the sturdy yellows and russets of weed stems and umbels long past seed-bearing, the silvering boles of maples and ashes, and the barely pink-tinged tips of apple shoots. Under the snow cloud too thin to give snow, everything is subdued, diminished, re-duced to Dürer colors, given pause until spring. And people, also given pause, imbued with fear by the hostility of the cutting cold and the death color in the air, are driven indoors to their artificial summer by the fire, driven in upon themselves. Though Novem-ber's final days will bring another change—this time to a small-eyed, distant sun in a faded sky from which fierce winds and an unanticipated snow squall or two may blow—we stay indoors now to confront ourselves.

In the dark day of November, it is often three o'clock in the morning. We sit alone, freshly reminded of our mortal state, in in-consolable judgment on the waning sources of our unfounded pride. Our achievements wither and dry and shrivel to insignifi-cance until they'd fit the head of a pin; our ego, a summer roarer, now sits, a bad boy, in the dunce's corner; our petty crimes against ourselves and others now pass in review at regimental strength before our routed-marshal's eyes.

It is the Phoenix all over again, of course. Out of our chastened ashes, out of our misspent summer's dust, rises a puny, unfledged chick, a blue and bony shadow of our potential to renew ourselves and redeem ourselves by humble, dogged application to our last— and to our next, since every métier constantly dies to be reborn.

In his essay on Arthur Koestler, George Orwell compares Koestler's *The Gladiators* unfavorably with Flaubert's *Salammbô;* in seeking an explanation for the superiority of the nineteenth-century novel, he ventures the suggestion that "Flaubert could think himself into the stony cruelty of antiquity, because in the mid-nineteenth century one still had peace of mind. One had time to travel in the past. Nowadays the present and the future are too terrifying to be escaped from, and if one bothers with history it is in order to find modern meanings there."

How true: the present and the future are not only too terrifying but also too insistent, too mind-and-body consuming, to be escaped from into meditation, consideration, and remembrance. Except, I think, in such a pause as November, a limbo in nature which induces an answering limbo—a break with the immediate past that confers perspective on the more distant past and hence on the present and future—in our minds.

The ice-gray light falls levelly in the study windows, forbidding us from the outdoors for the duration of a winter. It chisels the outlines of books, pictures, furniture. It provides deep shadows for the fire to prosper in. It creates an utter calm that is diametrically opposed to the furor of the world, a calm that is at first mistaken for despair and then seen clearly as a hope of hope. To buoy ourselves up and carry our frail selves through the rising insupportability of life, we take on, through the year, a thick, false costume of defenses crowned with a raffish, reckless, smiling social mask and founded on false pride and false belief in our immortal *Geist*. In November, all that falls away, and we sit alone with the knowledge of a failing body and a failed mind that has hardly begun to attack its objectives.

Then, of course—the larder bare, the slate wiped clean—the hope is free to start. Once our attention has been distracted from the screaming, constant claims of self, we can begin again from square one of our humble, real, deflated self. We suddenly have time—for the first time in a year—for pity that is not co-extensive with ourselves. We have time to stop taking others for granted or for pawns in our personal politics and to see them, objectively and shamingly, as more steadfast and less self-blandished than we are. We have time to pay our respects, our too-long-deferred tributes, to the people who have sheltered and nurtured us in spite of our pretensions. We have time to read books and judge them with impartiality and a sense of wonder and to pay homage to the writers who must, against all odds, have snatched success from the jaws of failure to create them. We have time, in a time when the garden is a scurf of blackened, white-rimed leaves, to cultivate our own neglected garden, ignored all blazing summer long, and to plant the first seeds of a project, an idea, a far-off achievement that could conceivably redeem us from that most sterile and barren of all moonscapes, the waste of time.

Another November comes. Whether it proceeds through its three traditional segments or throws the book away, I welcome it because it will restore me to the company of a friend and companion of my youth who is a virtual stranger now. I mean, of course, myself. And, when I sit down at the end of the long, gray month with that old self and my rediscovered friends and intimates to eat turkey and cornbread stuffing and squash and pumpkin pie, I will offer mentally a kind of left-handed thanks: not the "I'm all right, Jack" thanks for abundance, but the tentative, self-doubting thanks for the return to normal size and sanity that November brings.

Summersend

Among English railwaymen, "Summersend" used to be an imaginary, but usefully generic, place-name; at the other end of its primitive single track, "Summersend" connected with an equally hypothetical village called "Winterstoke." To avoid collisions, trains were only allowed to proceed in either direction when the engine-driver was in personal possession of a large staff like a shepherd's crook (of which there was only one, of course), bearing a substantial tag marked, naturally, "Summersend to Winterstoke."

In spite of this provenance, though, I'm sometimes inclined, when this time of year arrives again, to think that "Summersend" is a real place, or at any rate, a real state of mind. There is no place in the Julian Calendar quite like our own late August, with its electrically charged deadweight of muggy heat and heavy cloud, implying its own end in heavy, thunderous rain, quick clearing, and a cool and crystal dawn of palest peacock blue.

But it is under the steaming fog of August mornings—soon burning off to a universal heat haze with the mean, piggy red eye of the sun shining implacably through—that we suffer and triumph more, perhaps, than at any other time of year. January is wicked and wither-wringing, but warm clothes, warm cars, and warm houses force it to keep its pretty distance: there is a picture postcard in every window even when the biggest blizzard of the season does its worst outside. At the end of summer, there is less escape: we feel burdened by the weight of heat and moisture, and we sag as the trees do (as they do almost palpably in the "Summer" movement of Vivaldi's *Seasons*). If you suffer from the heat, like me, you rise in the mist of morning to the certain knowledge of another scorcher just ahead, and you wait fearfully for the first drops of sweat to break out on your brow. If this happens on the way to work, you know it will be a fierce one, and you slump in your air-conditioned office for half an hour before getting seriously to work, letting the chilled and filtered fake-fall air soothe you back into a semblance of crisp and able humanity.

Twenty years ago, I had the extreme displeasure of working for two summers in an office devoid of air-conditioning. Moreover, it was located on the second floor over a filthy, garbage-reeking alley; to make the world more manifest, my desk was just above the exhaust fan of a cheap restaurant that specialized in fried foods. On the sidewalk below the fan was a large and ineradicable pool of smelly dark-brown grease. Fortunately, my employer was an easygoing fellow who, though he would not allow us the luxury of an air-conditioner—he alone had one—looked the other way when we spent two or three hours for lunch in any of a number of low bars, all with boreal iced air, in the near neighborhood.

It's eleven-thirty. I glance out my office window at the square outside. All hard edges are dissolved in heat. The big granite public building opposite seems to be bathed in a pinkish, prismatic light that softens its bulky outline. The sixty-story building one block over never reaches its apex; its steep sides tumble home more steeply than at other seasons, and it tapers to a vanishing point somewhere around the forty-seventh floor. The walkers on the street plod laboriously, as if through Gobi sands. I ask myself if it is really worth going out to lunch. At this point, one of three things happens: either I have brought a sandwich in a brown bag, in which case I stay inside and eat with the other brown-baggers at a conference-room table; or I whisk mouse-like round the corner to a sandwich shop and bring back an unsatisfactory replica of the corned-beef sandwiches of yesteryear (a yesteryear like, say, 1972) for a thoroughly modern price (like, say, $2.00); or I make a date and step out with a friend to while away a longer lunch hour at some more distant eating place.

For a heat-sufferer, this walk to lunch is an odyssey, or at least an anabasis. Each sticky step in molten tar under the uncompromising sun is a step down into the inferno; I wait again for sweat to start, for the wall of humid, superheated air to overwhelm my personal thermostat. After three blocks on a ninety-five-degree day, I know I'll begin to fume, wilt, and go delicately purple; and cabs are no help in my town, since none of them are air-conditioned.

At last the restaurant, a cool cave of dim white napery and faintly throbbing refrigeration plants, which almost makes it all worth while. The friendly waiter—and why not, since he's been taking his ease in this cool air all morning?—hurries back with our drinks, and we lose our tetchy irritability in the glacial, chinking depths of a martini, or, more temperately, a frosted goblet of Johannisberger Riesling. Now the real work of the day often begins, assuming my companion is also a colleague. Away from the urgencies of the office, we erect and study long-range schemes, some plausible, some not. Great summer trees of consequences ramify, and maybe for the first time all week or all month, we understand the implications of the day-to-day chores we've been grinding out, willy-nilly, against our deadlines. Finally, as the second drink seeps in and exalts us slightly and alas, temporarily, we move to some astral plane where our chatter seems inspired and our comfort seems only a meet reward for having braved the tortures of the August morning. Then we order lunch—with, perhaps, more wine—and the two deep-green salads come, earnest of summer, the only native produce of the year. We can taste the earth—though not the dirt, since this restaurant purges its vegetables efficiently of sand—in every crackling lettuce leaf, and the real olive oil and wine vinegar suggest some sort of Italian holiday, perhaps on a terrace on Anacapri, with Vesuvius poking an ignorably monitory finger of smoke into the azure sky.

Back to work. The return march, gravid with drinks and lunch in the height of the torpor. I swim like a turtle through the brackish water of the glaring afternoon. Again, the rest cure—over a bitter, black iced coffee—at the office. Half an hour later, I am restored and typing some not-too-trying little copy job. By four, the second wind arrives, and I tackle some more demanding project. A little after five, I flick off the IBM electric and compose myself for the third encounter with the heat.

As I walk out of the building on my way to the bus, great cumulonimbi have at last moved up to overawe the sun; I walk slowly in a black shade no less sticky and humid than the preceding sunshine. The bus is crowded, packed with sweating people and their raveling bundles homeward bound. I get a too-small seat and hope the air-conditioning will function when the engine is started. At five-thirty, the driver kicks the starter; the tepid coolness begins to trickle out of the window vents, no match for the Quonset-hut-like heat that has built up inside the alloy shell. I am doomed to sweat miserably throughout the forty-minute ride to where my car is parked.

Through hissing, lowing traffic, the big bus makes its way to the outer suburbs. Right on time, partly because the traffic, without winter's tens of thousands of student cars, moves more quickly in the summer. At Howard Johnson's, where the bus stops, I retrieve my car from under a tree that does not shade it very well. Having forgone air-conditioning for assorted reasons, including the ridiculous expense of cooling a Porsche, I strip off my tie and jacket, open the sunroof and the rear quarter windows, and take off in a blast of moving, if not cooling, air. Five miles down the road, the blast has equalized my temperature, and with drying forehead, I am free to survey Vivaldi's drooping trees. The country is locked in summer. The dog days rage and bite. Relief is seasons, even years, away.

At home, my wife, who does not sanction air-conditioning, though she indulges me, ushers me into my air-conditioned workroom and supplies me with a sizable iced coffee. I sip and read *Newsweek*. Soon dinner is ready, and we sit down to another salad: this time, unconscionably costly crabmeat, but what the hell, it's August. Melon for dessert. And more iced coffee. This being Thursday night—I don't work Fridays so that I can attend to my own writing at home—I leisurely perambulate the browning lawns and flowerless gardens and settle down to read a book for possible review or just for pleasure. Tonight it is a rereading of *A Coffin for Dimitrios*. The air-conditioner drones; I glance occasionally out the window at the building thunderheads and the yellow cracks of heat lightning between the hills on the horizon and the occluded sky; I return to my iced coffee and the exigencies of Ambler's evil men, as typical of the thirties as Auden's scouts and spies among the pylons of the new forbidden country.

The storm breaks. Against the total dark of nine o'clock, chain lightning and all its variegated brethren; a gusty roll-cloud wind; then steady rain, pouring and beating as if to penetrate our house (which it sometimes does, to the disgust of our insurance agent). More reading as the storm slackens sail and regresses to a solid drum of rain; then news, mostly trivial and local; then to bed. I sleep, at the end of the week, with unusual panache. Dreams, which often surface memorably on other nights, remain submerged. I lie unclaimed by wakefulness until, at four o'clock, my over-forty-year-old bladder sounds the charge, and I totter to the toilet.

Morning. I awaken at eight, a late hour for me, and look out the window at the mountains (mountains here, foothills in other, more precipitous parts). Surprisingly, they are there, some thirty miles away, against a backdrop of blue, chilled, cloudless sky. The storm has passed; August has, only temporarily, passed; the dog days have been replaced by the first morning like real fall.

I shiver, characteristically—unhappy at change, for all my glee at summer's end—at the first chill. The temperature must surely be—what? fifty-five? I place my bets. I'll say, experienced countryman, fifty-one. I go downstairs and look at the thermometer outside the dining-room window, already beaded with condensation, a forerunner of frost: fifty-two. Close enough: I have again accredited myself as a supreme weather prophet. I walk out, conscious of my flapping bathrobe over my summer shortie pajamas, to get the paper. When I return, the coffee's on the boil. I am delighted with the prospect of a hot drink: how fast the summer flies. I look out the window at the woodpile. Two cords ready for the burning, and this would not be an unthinkably warm day to start.

I retire to my workroom (or study or library—what is a sufficiently unpompous term?) to write a poem. The cool airs spur the juices. I find myself writing a fall poem, complete with all the requisite stigmata, including the felled leaves and the first killing frost. I finish it and walk outside, lost in a comically tolerant philosophic mood. I address the ash leaves, the marigolds, and the budded asters, asking them, without actually speaking (I'm not that far gone yet), whether they're ready to meet their maker, whether extreme unction is their wish. They don't respond. Neither do the worm-worrying robins, dotting the lawn, or the thrush that still sings in the woods. No matter; I have done my bit. I am at one with the changing world.

Friday morning metamorphoses into Friday night. There is a faint aurora, the autumn's first. Lavish draperies bar the vexed way to the north, impeded by high clouds. What's this? Another low?

Of course. Morning dawns foggy and dripping. Saturday is summer's end resumed: the weeping trees, the coruscating air, the hills locked in a vaporous sunrise, the temperature and humidity both streaking toward the hundred mark. Cicadas tune their resined strings for many more bars of their arched song—a song that returns to chained earth after its highest flights.

Summersend is not yet. But now I welcome summer's continuance—heat, sweat, and all—in view of the alternative.

The Crystal Year

The twenty-seventh of this November—almost certainly, like so many of its predecessors, a chill and pewter day with a crack in the west to let the coming winter in—is my wedding anniversary. My fifteenth, to be exact. The sign in a gift shop I sometimes go to says that the fifteenth is the crystal year; if I get diligent and order the monograms in time, I may surprise my wife with some Orrefors or Waterford.

But that's hardly the point or purpose of the occasion. If there is anything in fifteen years of cumulative marriage to mark them besides an arbitrary milepost on the calendar, it's, well, a kind of crystallinity. Five thousand days of union, if not unity, lend a certain distance and clarity to one's view of oneself and one's marriage. And, doubtless, of one's wife. (I realize it is not lately fashionable to stay married, and faithful, for so long; nonetheless we, in all our unconscious gaucherie, have done it, and I think we have little to repent.)

My wife. I have learned a lot about her. She must be among the last of those perfectionistic creatures who itch to pat, fold, and tuck the world into order like a bed, and, though I am not of that vanishing kind, I find myself increasingly in admiration of her gift. To see her asserting herself over matter—the fork pricking the ideal number of steam vents in the top pie crust, the knife slicing its hoop of excess off the pie's circumference with micrometric exactitude—is to see a very grave and honorable human candle lit.

To see her, conversely, lose a long-fought battle over garden weeds or bagworms in the saplings is to see that noble candle snuffed, to be relit again elsewhere. To know mechanisms and to try conclusions is my wife's lesson; though it will never apply to me, I've studied it long and carefully.

Myself. I've learned—by contrast with my wife over these married years—that I will always be a Sunday plumber, a slapdash, intuitive paperer-over of projects and problems. Not for me the unrelenting penetration of the malfunction to its source and the ensuing rebuilding, step by step, of the delicate tissue of structure; instead, I'll coin a phrase or make a law (on no known precedent) to cover it. Patience makes me impatient; I am too slack for rigor; I'm witlessly willing to live by my wits.

My marriage. Surely such opposites disagree? Surely they do. But, just as surely, they don't sunder. There is some cement in oppositeness, some saving grace and glue in being different. My wife regards me as a friendly curiosity, I'm sure, but one well worth respecting; I think and hope I do the same. Where is there any novel or tetralogy one-half so gripping as the ongoing saga of another person coping with all the vicissitudes of everyday? Where is the bombshell film that captures all the panoply and nuance, all the shadings of face and speech, of a whole life lived in front of one?

But to retrace my steps to the beginning. We entered on this marriage—this frail skiff which has become a stout ship through time and use—in thunder, lightning, and storm at sea. It was the disaffected dead end of the fifties, when so many of us who had started out with bright, simpleminded hopes after the war found we had to take our first tuck of compromise. My wife and I had both been married before; the age of anxiety and a wealth of small, repeated nags like poverty had laid waste both our marriages; now we joined up together in uncertainty, hoping not for radiant new horizons but for a small, plain, homely fresh start, surrounded not by glamorous vistas but by the humble, light-washed things—a crook-legged nightstand, a rusting pair of scissors, a bloomless, pot-bound Christmas cactus, a dog-raveled afghan somebody's mother made—of ordinary life.

It was immediately apparent that our earlier experiences had almost disqualified us for family life. Both of us were proud and touchy, both afraid and ashamed to play the roles we had played and lost at in our former marriages. There was formality and constraint; there were long silences. If we had been living in our former haunt, the city, I think we would have given it up as a bad job, shaken hands, and made off somewhere else. But we had had the good sense or good fortune to pick up our traps and move to the country, where the strangeness of the scene, the days, the seasons was a constant challenge to our senses.

One can't stay rigid and inhibited very long in the face of a new world. Paradoxically, the experience of being caught in an old-fashioned blizzard, with six-foot drifts, a seventy-five-mile-an-hour gale, and a frozen soil pipe thawed us and brought us closer together. In the spring, the assault of growth and greenness from all quarters—the peepers' wall of sound, the first-quarter moon sliding down a dim-lit sky between new leaves, the first tough, tiny crocuses levering themselves up through frozen earth with the muscular power of a Charles Atlas—warmed us and made us, in both senses, sensible. Suddenly we were free of the past, even of our past feckless selves, and free to partake of these un-manmade happenings around us.

My wife's hands took up trowels, almost unconsciously, and began to shape and mold a garden out of dead, clayey soil; my hands picked up a camera and began to record the close-up images of flowers and grasses. I admired her garden; she, my pictures. Accord began to take turns with disharmony; I began to look on her face, in all its changefulness, with a proprietary smile, and she, I think, on mine. We were still different as noon and night and always would be, but our common wonder at the blackbirds, the sound of partridge drumming, the pink puff blossoms of rabbit's-foot clover gave us a single ground to stand on gladly. It was the earth, a place elusive to city people in these times.

We were also drawn together—how simple, how sentimental it now seems—by the dogs we owned. A pair of beagles, purebred but paperless, bought for ten dollars each from a kind farmer who had raised the litter in his cow-fragrant barn, never far from the lows and stomps of the horned cattle. We took our puppies home —already named, Fanny and Daisy, for two of their forebears, since simple names ran amply in that family—and learned all over again the responsible joy of having helpless dependents. It's all been written about dogs, and I don't want to plow that furrowed ground again, but the simple decency and happiness of the two puppies touched us more than we thought possible. Their adventures were our adventures; when they made a discovery, we made it too; and we ran the fields behind them as young as they were—and as innocently reliant on the endlessness of life. That innocence was cured: Daisy was killed by a car when she was just over a year old; Fanny, after a short life plagued by respiratory illnesses, was killed by a car at five. But my wife and I found ourselves united even by that small—by human standards—but incredibly persistent sadness (to this day, we find it difficult to think of Fanny's death).

And there were the houses—not sleek, functional machines for living, but tumbledown engines of survival. I see my wife on a ladder, cigarette in mouth, paint roller in hand, hair in a bandanna, attacking a bare wall we'd scraped eight layers of old paper off; I see her refinishing an eight-dollar junk-shop table—mission oak, a ton of it—for us to dine on; I see her helping me put up the huge, shuddering porch screens, clumsy and flimsy as dobsonfly wings, at the onset of summer; I see her in the chiaroscuro of our low-ceilinged kitchen, baking the first flat biscuits of the strawberry-shortcake season; I see her in a kind of mind's-eye book of hours, tracing the seasons with her pertinacious housework. (I see myself, not incidentally, mostly helping at the fringes, or standing by and getting out of it; I am incorrigibly of the observing kind, not one to see a job of manual work through on my own.)

All these occasions of striving and unity have been ameliorated now, of course. Our present house is relatively new and relatively trouble-free. We can afford to save our labor with more machines than we once possessed. Our dog—a second Fanny from a later litter—is growing old fatly and docilely, kept alive and well because we will not let her run.

Our pleasures are more sere and settled, seen through our fifteen years of crystal light, of testing and discarding and going on from there. But those fields out there still get a rise out of us, and it is touching to see a pine and a blue spruce, tiny when we arrived, now growing to tower over our declining years. Each spring and fall, we make a certain old, fixed pilgrimage over meadows and through orchards in the manner of some mystic praising God. Bluet and violet in spring, woodbine and aster in the fall: these are resurgent evidences of our imbrication, together, as a couple, in the nature of things.

Is this all too high-flown for the flatness of our ordinary days, when we communicate at cross-purposes or maybe, tired out, not at all? I don't think so, for the point of marriage—and perhaps its hope of surviving in a world of such staccato change—is to create a kind of gestalt, a whole greater than the sum of its parts, from just such orts of ordinariness.

We are born alone. We live and die mainly alone. It is not given to us to share wholly the consciousness of another person. But in the long loom of marriage, an intimacy and interpenetration that have little to do with sexuality per se begin to operate. Long-married people are said to come to look alike; even if not, their extended proximity must make them more deeply aware of every changing nuance of each other. Marriage must then be the state closest to true understanding of another, if not as well the state in which real love is nearest to realization.

In any case, I treasure—as you must surely know by now—the years of my marriage and the knowledge they have brought me. I can't begin to tell you what a rare and remarkable person my wife is, any more than I can tell her—in either case I would founder in unbelievability and mawkishness—but I can perhaps convey some of the sense of privilege in pursuing any decent marriage over the years, over the hills, as John Gay wrote, and far away. To come to understand another over time must be among the highest and most difficult of human aspirations.

Mere token as it is and as such gifts must always be, I *will* proceed forthwith to order that monogrammed Waterford. For one who's grown accustomed to my face.

Dying: An Introduction

Always too eager for future, we
Pick up bad habits of expectancy.
—PHILIP LARKIN

I.   RING AND WALK IN

Summer still plays across the street,
An ad-hoc band
In red, white, blue, and green
Old uniforms
And borrowed instruments;
Fall fills the street
From shore to shore with leaves,
A jaundiced mass
Movement against the cold;
I slip on ice
Slicks under powder snow and stamp my feet
Upon the doctor's rubber mat,
Ring and Walk In
To Dr. Sharon's waiting room,
For once with an appointment,
To nonplus
Ugly Miss Erberus.
Across from other candidates—

A blue-rinsed dam
In Davidows, a husk
Of an old man,
A one-eyed boy—I sit
And share their pervigilium.
One *Punch* and two
Times later comes the call.

II.   PROBABLY NOTHING

Head cocked like Art, the *Crimson* linotype
Operator, Dr. Sharon plays
Taps on my game leg, spelling out the name,
With his palpating fingers, of my pain.
The letters he types are not visible
To him or me; back up the melting pot
Of the machine, the matrix dents the hot
Lead with a letter and another: soon a word,
Tinkling and cooling, silver, will descend
To be imposed upon my record in
Black-looking ink. "My boy, I think," he says,
In the most masterly of schoolish ways,
In the most quiet of all trumps in A
Flat, "this lump is probably nothing, but"—
A but, a buzz of omen resonates—
"I'd check it anyway. Let's see when I
Can take a specimen." Quiet business
With the black phone's bright buttons. St, ssst, sst:
An inside call. In coded whispers. Over. Out.
"Can you come Friday noon? We'll do it then."
I nod I can and pass the world of men
In waiting, one *Life* farther on.

III.   O.P.O.R.

Undressing in the locker room
Like any high school's, full of shades

In jockstraps and the smell of steam,
Which comes, I guess, from autoclaves,
And not from showers, I am struck
By the immutability,
The long, unchanging, childish look
Of my pale legs propped under me,
Which, nonetheless, now harbor my
Nemesis, or, conceivably,
Do not. My narcissistic eye
Is intercepted deftly by
A square nurse in a gas-green gown
And aqua mask—a dodo's beak—
Who hands me a suit to put on
In matching green, and for my feet
Two paper slippers, mantis green:
My invitation to the dance.
I shuffle to the table, where
A shining bank of instruments—
Service for twelve—awaits my flesh
To dine. Two nurses pull my pants
Down and start shaving. With a splash,
The Doctor stops his scrubbing-up
And walks in with a quiet "Hi."
Like hummingbirds, syringes tap
The Novocain and sting my thigh
To sleep, and the swordplay begins.
The stainless-modern knife digs in—
Meticulous trencherman—and twangs
A tendon faintly. Coward, I groan.
Soon he says "Sutures," and explains
To me he has his specimen
And will stitch up, with boundless pains,
Each severed layer, till again
He surfaces and sews with steel
Wire. "Stainless." Look how thin it is,
Held in his forceps. "It should heal
Without a mark." These verities
Escort me to the tiring room,

Where, as I dress, the Doctor says,
"We'll have an answer Monday noon."
I leave to live out my three days,
Reprieved from findings and their pain.

IV. PATH. REPORT

Bruisingly cradled in a Harvard chair
Whose orange arms cramp my pink ones, and whose black
Back stamps my back with splat marks, I receive
The brunt of the pathology report,
Bitingly couched in critical terms of my
Tissue of fabrications, which is bad.
That Tyrian specimen on the limelit stage
Surveyed by Dr. Cyclops, magnified
Countless diameters on its thick slide,
Turns out to end in -oma. "But be glad
These things are treatable today," I'm told.
"Why, fifteen years ago—" a dark and grave-
Shaped pause. "But now, a course of radiation, and—"
Sun rays break through. "And if you want X ray,
You've come to the right place." A history,
A half-life of the hospital. Marie
Curie must have endowed it. Cyclotrons,
Like missile silos, lurk within its walls.
It's reassuring, anyway. But bland
And middle-classic as these environs are,
And sanguine as his measured words may be,
And soft his handshake, the webbed, inky hand
Locked on the sill, and the unshaven face
Biding outside the window still appall
Me as I leave the assignation place.

V. OUTBOUND

Outside, although November by the clock,
Has a thick smell of spring,

And everything—
The low clouds lit
Fluorescent green by city lights;
The molten, hissing stream
Of white car lights, cooling
To red and vanishing;
The leaves,
Still running from last summer, chattering
Across the pocked concrete;
The wind in trees;
The ones and twos,
The twos and threes
Of college girls,
Each shining in the dark,
Each carrying
A book or books,
Each laughing to her friend
At such a night in fall;
The two-and-twos
Of boys and girls who lean
Together in an A and softly walk
Slowly from lamp to lamp,
Alternatively lit
And nighted; Autumn Street,
Astonishingly named, a rivulet
Of asphalt twisting up and back
To some spring out of sight—and everything
Recalls one fall
Twenty-one years ago, when I,
A freshman, opening
A green door just across the river,
Found the source
Of spring in that warm night,
Surprised the force
That sent me on my way
And set me down
Today. Tonight. Through my
Invisible new veil

Of finity, I see
November's world—
Low scud, slick street, three giggling girls—
As, oddly, not as sombre
As December,
But as green
As anything:
As spring.